Vignettes
of
Legal History

by Julius J. Marke

with an introduction

by Bernard Schwartz

FRED B. ROTHMAN & CO.
South Hackensack, N. J.
1965

To
Sylvia
and
Lisie

Table of Contents

LIST OF ILLUSTRATIONS

PREFACE

THAT ASTUTE AND WISE JUDGE, Benjamin Cardozo, once wrote "It is a false and cramping notion that cases are made great solely by reason of something intrinsic in themselves. They are great by what we make of them. McCulloch v. Maryland—to choose almost at random—is one of the famous cases of our history. I wonder, would it not be forgotten, and even perhaps its doctrine overruled, if Marshall had not put upon it the imprint of his genius."

I wrote the *Vignettes* to illustrate the point made by the eminent judge. My purpose was to recreate not only the drama, excitement and emotionalism of those passionate and extraordinary conflicts in Anglo-American legal history which brought forth our great landmark decisions, but also to relate them to the bold and profound personalities who wrought them into epoch making issues.

I had the added purpose of going beyond the lawyer and the legal historian. In a sense, the term "*legal* history" is misleading. The legal effect of statutes and momentous decisions may long since have been changed or completely lost. Statutes are repealed and courts change their viewpoint. The historical and practical impact may long endure. In many instances, it may be difficult to trace the effect back to the cause.

The cases, the trials and the books which are the bone and sinew of the law are more than words and events of legal import. They were not heard or read in a vacuum. Involved were men and women, statesmen and politicians, businessmen and smugglers, editors and privateers, imbued with the ideals and the weaknesses to be found whether it be the seventeenth or the twentieth century.

Sir John Macdonnel, with penetrating insight, said: "A trial is in its substance a struggle, a battle in a closed arena. It is a shock of contending forces, a contest which may arouse the fiercest passions . . . Often a trial is the one luminous point in darkness, the one opening in an otherwise blank wall between us and the past. It takes one outside the formulae of the textbooks. Faithfully reported a trial is a living picture; it brings us nearer to life than the best literature; you hear the voices, it is life itself."

Then too, the manner in which the circumstances occurred leading up to these cases of great historical interest, the conflicting policies and strategies of the contending parties, the remarkable forensic efforts made by counsel, the melodramatic sidelights, the often theatrical dénouements, add significantly to an appreciation of the decision reached by the Court. They are more than a revelation of why the cases are considered so important. They actually are the matrix from which an understanding of their implications may be derived.

The *Vignettes* consist of reportorial presentations of historic trials and historic men and books in the field of law. What I have attempted to do is to present an enriched version, albeit an accurate one, of these memorable events, introducing anecdotal and biographical background, heretofore buried in contemporary newspaper reports, memoirs and diaries. I have also taken advantage of court reports, commentaries, biographies and texts. The main difficulty I encountered arose in piecing together from these diverse and sometimes incurious sources, a free flowing story reflecting its excitement and glory, as well as the striking personalities of the leading actors, in the enfolding drama.

These *Vignettes* for the most part, were originally published in the Law Center Bulletin of New York University. They were so well received, that I was encouraged to add, revise and enlarge and present them in book form. In revision, I have attempted to trace the legal effects of early cases so as to reflect the momentous changes in constitutional law wrought by the Warren Court. It is my thought that these *Vignettes* should be of interest not only to lawyers and law students, but also to those concerned with an understanding of and thus a clearer perception of our present governmental structure. In other words, it was written for those interested in knowing the why and how of our present situation.

I would like to acknowledge my deep appreciation to Professor Bernard Schwartz for his generous and highly perceptive Introduction. As always, it reflects his mastery of the broad sweep of our legal system, and profound scholarly attainments.

It is a pleasure also to acknowledge my indebtedness to my good friend, Professor Sylvestro Petro, Faculty Editor, of the Law Center Bulletin of New York University. His editorial advice in the writing of these *Vignettes,* indeed served me in good stead.

Finally, I would indeed be derelict in my duty not to acknowledge as well the valuable contribution of the publisher, Fred B. Rothman, and his assistant, Eugene M. Wypyski, in preparing my manuscript for publication.

"The main part of intellectual education", wrote Mr. Justice Holmes, "is not the acquisition of facts, but learning how to make facts live." Certainly, the same may be said for legal history.

JULIUS J. MARKE

New York University
School of Law
April, 1965

INTRODUCTION

ONE INTERESTED IN LEGAL HISTORY is sorely tempted to paraphrase a famous passage from Macaulay: "There were gentlemen and there were seamen in the navy of Charles II. But the seamen were not gentlemen, and the gentlemen were not seamen." There are historians and writers in the field of legal history; but, all too often, the writers are not historians and the historians are not writers.

It is, therefore, a particular pleasure to be accorded the honor of introducing the reader to a work that is both a real contribution to legal history and is, at the same time, well written. Professor Marke's book is composed of the very "stuff" of legal history. From Bracton to the *Five Knights' Case*, to *Marbury v. Madison*, to our own day—the great names and great landmarks of the law are all here—and written in a way to give learning and delight to lawyers and laymen alike. To them, the interest and felicitous style will be among the cardinal virtues of this book, for its pages literally breathe the life of the epochal cases and controversies which form the basis of our Anglo-American legal heritage.

And what cases and controversies they were!

From the beginning, Anglo-American law has been but a reflection of the society it was destined to serve. In this sense, our law has been the juristic mirror of the different stages through which Anglo-American history has passed. "Our jurisprudence is distinctive," said Justice Jackson on the 150th anniversary of the United States Supreme Court, "in that every great movement in American history has produced a leading case in this Court." Yet the same has been true of all the great developments in Anglo-American history. They all have left their juristic imprint in cases that are now rightly considered landmarks of the law.

As already stated, all of these great landmarks are in this

book. From Bracton—"the crown and flower of English medieval jurisprudence"—down to Fortescue, Professor Marke shows us the early development of the common law. Then, in his discussion of *Cowell's Interpreter*, he shows us the start of the struggle between the common law and Stuart pretensions to absolute prerogative—a struggle that was to come to a legal head in the *Five Knights' Case*. All too few people today realize the extent to which our modern liberties are based upon the crucial battles waged against seventeenth-century Stuart tyranny.

But the men who secured the independence of the American nation were fully aware of the vital importance of the Parliamentary victory over the Crown. They considered themselves the direct heirs of those Englishmen who had met and mastered the Stuart efforts at absolutism. This was especially true of James Otis, whose impassioned argument against general writs of assistance is brought to life in Professor Marke's pages. The Otis oration, said John Adams, "breathed into this nation the breath of life," and "Then and there the child Independence was born." What followed in the next twenty years was, in many ways, a gloss on the Otis argument, just as his eloquence was but the restatement in his day of the seventeenth-century opposition to the claims of the Stuarts.

With the new nation established, the great movement in our legal history was that to establish federal power upon a workable basis. In the law, such movement produced the great cases of *Marbury v. Madison* and *McCulloch v. Maryland*. In them, John Marshall and his colleagues established both federal supremacy and the vital constitutional role of the Supreme Court. Professor Marke shows clearly how this was done and how the Marshall Court built so firm a constitutional foundation that it could not be shaken either by the *Dred Scott* case (that grievous self-inflicted wound of the highest Court) or the constitutional crucible of the Civil War. Of particular interest, too, is the treatment of the post-Civil War *McCardle* and *Slaughterhouse* cases.

Two things are particularly noteworthy in the Marke treatment of the cases dealt with by him. In the first place, he constantly realizes what all too many legal writers for-get—that cases are instituted by individuals, whose person-alities and idiosyncracies are of interest and importance to the cases themselves and their outcomes. In these pages, we meet the key figures in the landmarks of our law, both as human beings and as actors in crucial legal dramas.

In the second place, what makes the Marke treatment of such value is the manner in which he constantly relates the historical episodes he describes to the problems of our own day. The result is not only historical exposition, but also comparative analysis in the best sense—comparative in point of time, rather than in the more usual connotation of the term, i.e., comparative in space. The reader is never left in doubt of the revelance of the different vignettes to his own experience.

The temptation is strong to comment in more detail upon the pages that follow; but it would be unfair to both the author and the reader for me to do so.

BERNARD SCHWARTZ

New York University
School of Law
April 1965

Marbury
v.
Madison

A Political Dilemma
and
Judicial Review

JOHN MARSHALL SERVED as Chief Justice of the United
States from 1801 to 1835, longer than any other Chief
Justice. It was a crucial and formative period. The 62
decisions on issues of constitutional law delivered by the
Supreme Court, of which Marshall wrote 36, have been
appraised by Justice Burton as "the firm foundation on
which the loose stones provided for the nation's structure
were built." That Marshall was one of the really great men
of our country has rarely been disputed. Yet he had an
idiosyncrasy which curiously set the stage for one of the
most dramatic political confrontations in American history
and which culminated in a landmark case of such unusual
significance that it permanently placed its imprint on the
American form of government. For Marshall, on occasion,
was prone to negligence, especially when involved with
details — and his failure to perform an ordinary ministerial
duty was the cause of it all!

John Adams, second President of the United States,
was exceedingly distressed after the November, 1800,
election. Severely beaten by Thomas Jefferson and the
Republicans, he realized that his Federalist Party and the

principles for which it stood were doomed to extinction unless preserved by other means. Thomas Jefferson was preparing to assume the Presidency on March 4, 1801. The decisive election victory had also returned a Republican-dominated Congress which was more than ready to effectuate his program. The Federalists favored a strong national government, and as property owners were reluctant to allow the electorate to control its policies. The Republicans preferred to depend on the judgment of the American people and by the same token looked with suspicion on the centralization of authority in the national government. There was only one recourse left to Adams and he decided to pursue it; by all legal means the control of the judiciary had to be retained by the Federalists. The government could survive only if the Federalist influence in national affairs could be continued by the politically inspired leanings of the Federalists on the bench.

Adams first turned his attention to the Supreme Court. Late in 1800 the Court consisted of six judges, all of whom were Federalists. Chief Justice Ellsworth was in poor health, however, and actually was in France at the time acting as Minister to France.

Ellsworth was persuaded to resign, rather than present Jefferson with the opportunity to appoint a Republican to the Supreme Court in the event his health later required his resignation. Adams offered the position to former Chief Justice Jay. Jay declined. Although many Federalist leaders recommended Associate Justice Paterson for the vacancy, Adams decided to elevate his Secretary of State, John Marshall, to the high office. Marshall was confirmed by the Federalist Senate on January 27, 1801, and was installed as the new Chief Justice on February 4, at the age of 45. Important as this event appears to us today, it attracted very little attention at the time, going practically unnoticed in the press.

ADAMS WAS AVERSE to appointing a new Secretary of State for the few remaining days of his Presidency. Marshall, therefore, remained in office as Secretary, doubling as

Chief Justice, "on the same day issuing reports in one capacity and delivering judgments in the other."

Now that provision had been made for Federalist interests in the Supreme Court, Adams and his Congressional leaders looked to other influential judicial positions to entrench Federalists. The Judiciary Act of 1789, which had established the Circuit Court System, provided for Supreme Court Justices to sit on the Circuit Courts. This system had been bitterly criticized by the Justices, as "riding the circuit" entailed great physical hardship, much loss of time, both to them and to litigants, and added the difficulty and embarrassment of hearing a case on appeal after having decided it below. Here was an opportunity under the pretense of reform to accomplish an important political coup and the Federalists eagerly seized it.

On February 13, 1801, just 19 days before the change of administrations, the lame duck Federalist Congress enacted a new Circuit Court law which relieved the Supreme Court Justices of circuit duties and authorized the appointment of 16 new Federal judges, with life tenure, to sit in the Circuit Courts. To add to the discomfort of the Jeffersonians, the act also reduced the number of Supreme Court Justices from six to five, in anticipation of the retirement of sick, old Justice Cushing. By this means the new administration would be deprived of the opportunity to fill the next vacancy on the Court. Shortly thereafter, on February 27, Congress enacted an Organic Act for the District of Columbia, creating 42 new positions of Justices of the Peace for five-year terms.

Adams took advantage of these laws with alacrity. Selecting the names for the new Circuit Judges from the Federalist ranks, he filled every one of them. They were confirmed by the Senate on March 2. On March 3, Adams signed their commissions. John Marshall, as his Secretary of State, then affixed the Great Seal of the United States to each commission and delivered them to each new judge, thus officially establishing the legality of his office. On March 2, Adams also nominated 42 Justices of the Peace, who were quickly confirmed the following day by the

Senate. Their commissions were similarly executed by Adams and Marshall.

The haste and expedition with which these appointments were made aroused intense indignation and protest amongst the Anti-Federalists. They derisively called the new appointees "Midnight Judges" and vowed to attack this "piece of political jobbery" when the new Administration assumed office. "Mr. Adams is laying the foundation of future factions and his own shame" commented one Republican paper expressing the thoughts of many Republicans. Jefferson expressed his own disgust with these shenanigans: "The Federalists have retired into the judiciary as a stronghold and from that battery all the works of Republicanism are to be beaten down." He later wrote to Mrs. John Adams, "I can say with truth that one act of Mr. Adams' life, and one only, ever gave me a moment's personal displeasure. I did consider his last appointments to office as personally unkind. They were from my most ardent political enemies . . . . It seemed but common justice to leave a successor free to act by instruments of his own choice."

JEFFERSON WAS NOT A MAN to accept defeat lightly. It must have been indeed a grim situation when Chief Justice Marshall administered the oath of office to President Jefferson the following day, on March 4, 1801. The struggle was joined between these arch-enemies from that moment on, and it ushered in a period as exciting as any in American political history.

Jefferson did not have to wait long to press his attack. The occasion for it arose ironically out of the characteristic negligence of Marshall himself. Marshall, as Secretary of State, in the press of last minute business, had inadvertently failed to deliver the commissions of the 42 persons appointed by President Adams to become Justices of the Peace. Without actual delivery of the commissions they could not legally assume their seats on the bench. After his inauguration, an embittered Jefferson directed his Secretary of State, James Madison, to withhold the delivery of the commissions of 17 of the persons appointed by Adams and to deliver the other 25. "The nominations crowded in by Mr. Adams after he knew he was not appointing for himself, I treat as mere nullities," he explained. "This outrage on decency should not have its effect, except on the life appointments which are irrevocable."

William Marbury, Denis Ramsey, Robert Townsend Hoee and William Harper were four of the 17 nominees whose commissions were not issued and they brought suit in December, 1801, in the Supreme Court for a rule to show cause why a writ of mandamus should not be issued to compel James Madison, as Secretary of State, to deliver their commissions. The office of Justice of the Peace was considered to be so insignificant by the other 13 that they did not even deem it worthy of the cost of litigation. On its face, this was just an ordinary case involving neither great principles nor important rights, but the circumstances were such that *Marbury v. Madison,* in the words of Professor Edmond Cahn, "proved to be one of those very special occurrences that mark an epoch in the life of the republic."

The Washington correspondent of the *Aurora,* a Republican paper, reported the hearing that took place in the Supreme Court on December 21, 1801. The nominees were represented by the former Attorney General under Adams, Charles Lee—the government by Jefferson's Attorney General, Levi Lincoln. "Mr. Lee," the reporter wrote, "entered very largely into a definition of the powers of the Court, and of the nature of mandamus. . . . The Chief Justice (J. Marshall, the *cidevant* XYZ ambassador) asked if the Attorney General was in Court, and had anything to offer. Mr. Lincoln replied that he had no instructions on the subject. The Secretary of State had received notice on the preceeding day, but he could not in the interval have turned his attention effectually to the subject. He would leave the proceedings under the discretion of the court. . . . Some conversation took place on the etiquette of sealing and recording commissions. . . . The Court did not give any opinion . . . . The Tories talk of dragging the President before the Court and impeaching him and a wonderful deal of similar nothingness. But it is easy to perceive that it is all fume which can excite not more than a judicious irritation." The next day the Court granted the preliminary motion for a rule to show cause and fixed the fourth day of the ensuing term for argument on the question whether the petitioners were entitled to a writ of mandamus. The next term, under the Circuit Court Act of 1801, was scheduled to be held in June, 1802.

JEFFERSON CONSIDERED the Supreme Court's action in *Marbury v. Madison* as not only politically inspired, but also as a personal attack on his position as the Chief Executive of the nation. The Jeffersonians had always feared the Supreme Court Justices, believing that they were determined to promote Federalist policies to the detriment of Republicanism. They still remembered the vigor with which the hateful Sedition Act had been enforced by them on circuit. They had fought back by adopting the Virginia and Kentucky Revolutions of 1798 declaring the Alien and Sedition Laws unconstitutional. They agreed with William Giles of Virginia that "the revolution [of 1800] is incomplete so long as that strong fortress is in possession of the enemy. . . . The absolute repeal of the whole judiciary system [was necessary]." The Court would have to be curbed and soon. The time to attack was now, to prevent the Federalist Justices from interfering with the prerogatives of the Executive. Senator John Breckenridge, who later became Jefferson's Attorney General, indignantly wrote to James Monroe. "What think you of the rule entered upon the Federal Court last week against the Secretary of State to show cause? . . . I think it the most daring attack which the annals of Federalism have yet exhibited. I wish the subject of the courts to be brought forward in the Senate next week." On January 6, 1802, he moved in the Senate to repeal the Judiciary Act of 1801, thus abolishing the new Circuit Courts and turning out of office the 16 recently appointed Federalist Circuit Judges.

Then ensued one of the most prolonged and explosive

constitutional debates ever to take place in Congress. Two important political questions were argued—the necessity of an independent judiciary and the power of the courts with reference to judicial review. When asked by Gouverneur Morris whether repeal of the law would not be tantamount to "a declaration to the remaining judges that they hold their offices subject to the will and pleasure of the Senate," Senator Jackson of Georgia replied: "I am more afraid of an army of judges. . . than an army of soldiers. . . . Have we not seen Sedition Laws?" Judges should be independent, maintained Senator Mason of Virginia, but not "independent of the nation itself. . . . Much less have I believed it proper or that our Constitution authorizes our Courts of Justice, to control the other departments of the government." Then with an obvious reference to the pending case of *Marbury v. Madison,* he continued, "Have we not heard this doctrine supported in the memorable case of the Mandamus lately before the Supreme Court?"

The Republicans concentrated their attack on the temerity of the Supreme Court in *Marbury v. Madison* to assume jurisdiction over a cabinet officer. Senator Jackson called it an "attack of the judges on the Secretary of State." In defense of the Court, Federalist leader James Bayard of Delaware retorted: "The Judges did their duty. They gave an honorable proof of their independence. They listened to the complaint of an individual against your President, and have shown themselves disposed to grant redress against the greatest man in the government. If a wrong has been committed and the constitution authorizes interference, will gentlemen say that the Secretary of State, or even the President, is not subject to law? And if they violate the law, where can we apply for redress but to our Courts of Justice?" The power of the Courts to declare laws of Congress unconstitutional was hotly debated. The Anti-Federalists denied this right to the Courts. The Federalists insisted that judicial review could be implied from the Constitution and the American form of government.

THUS, THE STAGE WAS SET for the momentous decision of *Marbury v. Madison*. The challenge thrown at the Federalists by the Jeffersonians had to be resolved and it was only in their last stronghold, in the Supreme Court, that the Federalists could give battle. For when the debate was over, the bill was passed by Congress on strictly party lines and it became a law on March 31, 1802. As a result, the 16 new Circuit Judges lost their positions, and a new Circuit Court System was established in which Supreme Court Justices sat with District Judges to constitute the Circuit Court. The Federalist reaction was one of dire prophesy: "By this vote the constitution has received a wound it cannot long survive. . . ." Even of more concern was the fate of the Supreme Court Justices. The independence of the Judiciary had to be preserved. Alexander Hamilton's reaction to Charles Pinckney epitomized the sense of Federalist thinking. The repeal of the Judiciary law was "a vital blow to the Constitution. In my opinion it demands a systematic and persevering effort by all constitutional means to produce a revocation of the precedent and to restore the Constitution." Chief Justice Marshall resolved to make the effort. But how to do it? With his analytical, albeit political, approach to problems, he determined that the salvation of the Federalists lay in the trivial and inconsequential issue presented in *Marbury v. Madison*. Marshall grasped at the opportunity!

But first, he had to bide his time, for the Republicans had enacted a second law to prevent the Supreme Court from interfering with the repeal of the Judiciary Law of 1801. It abolished the new June and December terms of the Court and reestablished the old February term, but not the old August term. Consequently the Court did not sit for 14 months and it was not until the February, 1803, term that it could once again consider the case of *Marbury v. Madison*.

When the Court convened for the February, 1803, term, the Anti-Federalists confidently believed that the Justices had been taught a lesson they would not forget. The threat of impeachment was uppermost in everyone's mind and it was well understood that if the Justices stepped out of line the Administration would react violently. Representative Caesar Rodney reflected the Republican attitude towards the Court when he warned the Justices just a week before *Marbury v. Madison* was to be heard: "Judicial supremacy may be made to bow before the strong arm of legislative authority. We shall discover who is master of the ship." Already there were rumors of the impending impeachment of their colleague, Justice Chase. If successful, it was known that Marshall was being marked as the next victim. Certainly impeachment was inevitable if they were to gainsay the Republicans in the *Marbury Case*.

Marshall was sufficiently sophisticated as a politician and aware of Republican motives to realize the significance of these partisan attacks. He had followed the debate in Congress over the repeal of the Circuit Court Act of 1801 and he was disturbed that the constitutional status of judicial review had been treated as suspect by so many Republican Congressmen. Ringing in his ears still was Senator Breckenridge's angry question. "Where [the courts] got the power [of judicial review], and who checks the courts when they violate the Constitution?" "Is it not extraordinary" he had thundered," "that if this high power was intended it should nowhere appear? Is it not truly astonishing that the Constitution in its abundant care to define the powers of each department, should have omitted so important a power as that of the Courts to *nullify* all the Acts of Congress, which, *in their opinion* were contrary to the Constitution?" Only Congress had the "exclusive right to interpret the Constitution," he had vigorously concluded, "in what regards the law-making power, and the Judges are bound to execute the laws they make."

"Only partly true," mused Marshall for he was well aware of the history of judicial review. The colonists had practiced it when their courts had passed on acts of their assemblies and the jurisdiction of the Privy Council to invalidate colonial laws had been generally accepted.

Portrait by St. Mémin.   Copyright, 1901, by Thomas Marshall Smith.

Chief Justice Marshall at the age of 53.
From the crayon by St. Mémin, made in 1808.

Judicial review had been favored by many of the delegates to the Constitutional Convention, as a necessary and self-evident part of a constitution, although no official position was taken on it during the proceedings and the Constitution failed to grant it expressly. After the Convention, some of the Framers of the Constitution, had recorded their approval of it. Alexander Hamilton for example, wrote in the Federalist, No. 78:

"The interpretation of the laws is the proper and peculiar province of the courts. A constitution is, in fact, and must be regarded by the Judges as a fundamental law. It therefore belongs to them to ascertain its meaning, as well as the meaning of any particular act proceeding from the legislative body. If there should happen to be an irreconcilable variance between the two, that which has the superior obligation and validity ought of course, to be preferred, or in other words, the constitution ought to be preferred to the statute, the intention of the people to the intention of their agents. . . . Accordingly, whenever a particular statue contravenes the constitution, it will be the duty of the judicial tribunals to adhere to the latter and disregard the former."

JUDICIAL REVIEW HAD ALSO been applied by the state courts in cases in which they had invalidated state laws violating state constitutions, although not explicitly granted in their constitutions. Even the Supreme Court had reviewed the constitutionality of state laws as respects Federal laws and treaties, without criticism. Then again, although the Supreme Court before Marshall had never exercised its authority to declare federal laws unconstitutional, it had actually assumed it had such a right in *Hayburn's Case, Van Horne's Lessee v. Dorrance,* and *Hylton v. U. S.* Marshall too must have been aware of *U.S. v. Yale Todd,* a 1794 case, unreported until 1851 in a note to *U. S. v. Ferreira,* which could possibly have set a precedent for the Court's authority to declare a law of Congress unconstitutional.

The rule to show cause in *Marbury v. Madison* came on for hearing on February 9, 1803. The courtroom was not particularly crowded as people were more concerned with the international crisis existing between France and Spain and the pending negotiations for the Louisiana Purchase. Madison and his assistants refused to cooperate with the Court. When called upon to give information pertaining to the commissions, Madison refused to indicate whether the commissions were signed and sealed or even what had happened to them. Attorney General Lincoln was called as a witness but he objected to tesitfying, insisting that the questions be committed to writing. He explained he felt deeply his duty not only to the Court but to the Executive Department as well. The next day he testified that he could not tell what had happened to the commissions. Apparently they lay on the table when the new Secretary of State took office and were destroyed along with other waste paper found in the room. This must have been a peculiar situation for Marshall as he had personally attended to the execution of the commissions as Secretary of State and was well aware of their existence. Lee, at last, managed to find some clerks in the State Department who proved the existence of the commissions, to the relief of all concerned. Lee summed up at great length, but the Attorney General did not respond, as he had not been instructed to appear. Marshall then announced that the Court would hear anyone prepared to argue the case.

No one volunteered, and Marshall summarily reserved decision. It was obvious to all that Jefferson had deliberately intended to insult Marshall and his Court by cavalierly ignoring their authority. In a sense, it was another warning to Marshall that if he ordered the Executive to deliver the commissions the order would be ignored, and the prestige of the Court greatly affected. Actually, Jefferson expected the mandamus order would be issued by the Court, and he was not only fully prepared to disregard it, but also to impeach Marshall for such impertinence and Federalist partisanship.

MARSHALL KNEW ALL THIS as he fearlessly developed his strategy. Yet he refused to be deterred from his own bold course. He wanted very much to remain as Chief Justice so that he could embody the point of view of the Federalists in American constitutional law. He was even more concerned that there was open talk of his being replaced by Spencer Roane of Virginia, who was diametrically opposed in principle to Marshall's creed.

By the time *Marbury v. Madison* could be decided the issue in it had practically become moot for the term of office for which Marbury had been appointed was more than half over. Furthermore, the position offered little in income and actually was of minor importance. But Marshall realized that if he decided in favor of Madison, it would be an admission of the Court's weakness. This then was Marshall's dilemma! At the same time, he had to indict the President for refusing to deliver the commission, uphold Marbury, but still gently discard him, and above all, establish the Supreme Court's right of judicial review! How he extricated himself from it has been aptly described by Senator Beveridge as "a judicial coup d'état."

On February 24, 1803, Chief Justice Marshall, speaking for a unanimous Court, delivered his celebrated opinion in *Marbury v. Madison.* Marshall's ingenuity became apparent immediately. It consisted of attacking the constitutionality of Section 13 of the *Judiciary Act of 1789,* under which Marbury had sought the mandamus. By this tactic he could establish the Supreme Court's authority to review the constitutionality of laws enacted by Congress, drop Marbury diplomatically, and censure Jefferson. To do this, however, he had to reverse the order in which he considered the issues. Instead of deciding the question of jurisdiction first, which would have defeated his purpose, for it would have meant the dismissal of the case without need for further comment, he considered the merits of Marbury's case instead. He propounded three questions in the following order:

1st: Has the applicant a right to the commission he demands?

2nd: If he had a right, and that right has been violated, do the laws of this country afford him a remedy?

3rd: If they do afford him a remedy, is it a mandamus issuing from this court? . . .

After noting "the peculiar delicacy" of the case, "the novelty of some of its circumstances, and the real difficulty attending the points which occur in it," Marshall answered the first and second questions in the affirmative, thus giving him the opportunity to support Marbury's legal right to the office and publicly rebuke Jefferson for withholding his commission. Marbury had a vested right to the office, his appointment was not revocable and was protected by the laws of his country. "To withhold his commission, therefore is an act deemed by the Court not warranted by law, but violative of a vested legal right." Marbury had a remedy to right this wrong. "The very essence of civil liberty certainly consists in the right of every individual to claim the protection of the laws, whenever he receives an injury. . . . The government of the United States has been emphatically termed a government of laws, and not of men. It will certainly cease to deserve this high appellation, if the laws furnish no remedy for the violation of a vested legal right." When the President exercises political powers, respecting the nation, not individual rights, his decision is conclusive and can "never be examinable by the courts. But when the legislature proceeds to impose on that officer other duties; when he is directed peremptorily to perform certain acts; when the rights of individuals are dependent on the performance of those acts; he . . . is amenable to the laws for his conduct; and cannot, at his discretion, sport away the vested rights of others."

Marshall then turned to his third and most important point—that the Court lacked jurisdiction. Here—he had to tread very dangerous water. Section 13 of the *Judiciary Act of 1789* specifically granted the Court authority to issue writs of mandamus in a case such as the one before it. No one had ever questioned its validity and the Act had been drafted by two outstanding constitutional authorities, Oliver Ellsworth and William Paterson. Both of them had been members of the Constitutional Convention, and later, Justices of the Supreme Court. Even the Supreme Court had held the law valid in several cases it had considered before *Marbury v. Madison.* Marshall, however had to establish that it was unconstitutional, for otherwise he could not execute his grand design. The manner in which he did this was superb. The Constitution of the United States, he reasoned, conferred original and appellate jurisdiction on the Supreme Court. Its original jurisdiction extended only to ambassadors, other public ministers and consuls, and those in which a state was a party. Congress, by law, could only grant appellate jurisdiction to the Court. The issuance of a writ of mandamus to an officer, however, for the delivery of a paper, "is in effect the same as to sustain an original action for that paper, and therefore seems not to belong to the appellate, but to original jurisdiction." Hence, Section 13 was not "warranted by the Constitution."

By this maneuver, Marshall could then proceed to develop his main point that the Supreme Court had the authority to declare laws of Congress invalid when in violation of the United States Constitution. Writing with "magesterial" force and in "the grand style," he imperatively expounded the doctrine of judicial review:

"It is, emphatically, the province and duty of the judicial department, to say what the law is. Those who apply the rule to particular cases, must of necessity expound and interpret the rule. If two laws conflict with each other, the courts must decide on the operation of each. So, if a law be in opposition to the Constitution; if both the law and the Constitution apply to a particular case, so that the Court must decide that case conformably to the law, disregarding the Constitution; or conformably to the Constitution, disregarding the law; the Court must determine which of these conflicting rules governs the case. This is of the very essence of judicial duty." Marshall then discharged the rule.

"THUS BY A COUP AS BOLD in design and as daring in execution as that by which the Constitution had been

framed," wrote Beveridge, "John Marshall set up a landmark in American history so high that all the future could
take bearings from it, so enduring that all the shocks the
nation was to endure could not overturn it."

Although Marshall drew largely from the writings of
Hamilton, especially the Federalist No. 78, in developing
the American doctrine of judicial review, he is to be credited for the manner in which he established its judicial
sanction. Having technically decided the case in Jefferson's favor — what could the Anti-Federalists do?

John Randolph of Roanoke expressed their frustration when he voiced his own perplexity: "All wrong, all
wrong, but no man in the United States can tell why or
wherein." It is interesting to note that contemporary criticism of the opinion concentrated more on Marshall's
attack on the President than on his upholding of the
Court's power of judicial review. Jefferson was furious
and insisted that not only was the case moot, but also, that
Marshall's opinion was "an *obiter* dissertation." The "Court
determined at once, that being an original process, they
had no cognizance of it and therefore the question before
them was ended. But the Chief Justice went on to lay
down what the Law would be, had they jurisdiction of the
case."

The Supreme Court did not find a law of Congress
unconstitutional again until 54 years later in the *Dred Scott
Case*. The power of judicial review was revived after the
Civil War on the precedent of *Marbury v. Madison*, although the Supreme Court self-imposed many limitations
on its application.

A REMARKABLE ASPECT of the Supreme Court's claim to
declare a law enacted by Congress unconstitutional, by
reason of the precedent established in *Marbury v. Madison*, is the fact that it has no means of physically enforcing
its decrees. Congress controls the purse strings, and only
the President can call out the nation's armed forces. In
essence, therefore, if either the Congress or the President
decided to contest the decision, the Court would be help-

less. As a matter of fact, Marshall became so involved, when many years later, President Andrew Jackson, angered by Marshall's decision in a controversy over the Indians of Georgia, is alleged to have burst out: "John Marshall has made his decision, now let him enforce it." A similar situation confronted Chief Justice Taney, sitting on circuit, when President Lincoln ignored his decree in the famous case of *Ex Parte Merryman* during the Civil War. Today the stature of the Court is such that it is doubtful whether the Chief Executive would risk a defiance of it. This was dramatically brought out in 1952, when President Truman seized the steel mills of the nation to settle a strike which was affecting the country's war effort in the Korean Crisis. President Truman unquestionably accepted the Court's decision *(in Youngstown v. Sawyer)* that his act was unconstitutional in that Congress had not authorized it. As President, he could only execute the laws enacted by Congress. Incidentally, this case also illustrates the principle that the power of the Court to declare a law unconstitutional, also applies to Executive action.

It should also be recognized, as Professor Charles Black has so well expressed it, that an important fact about judicial review is a corollary of its basic theory — and that is, it is only exercised by the courts when a concrete case is presented to it. "Now this fact implies a very important limitation. Courts do not decide questions of constitutionality except where these actually arise in real legal controversies . . . what it means in effect is that the political branches have pretty complete leeway until the rights of real people get involved. . . . One aspect of this corollary of the basic scheme of judicial review is that huge areas of governmental action remain wholly outside its reach. There are a vast number of things done by government which do not affect any identifiable person in a manner sufficiently direct to form the subject matter of a legal claim." Government spending, and governmental services are in this category. In this sense too, political questions are non-justiciable as was brought out in *Luther vs. Borden.*

SCHOLARS HAVE WONDERED whether Marshall should not have disqualified himself in *Marbury v. Madison* as it was his own failure to deliver the papers in question as Secretary of State that caused it to arise. If a similar issue were presented to the Supreme Court today, how sensitive would the Justices be to their eligibility, despite the precedent established by Marshall? Only recently, a Supreme Court Justice disqualified himself in an expatriation case, *(Marks v. Esperdy)* because his son had been one of the attorneys representing the government, before it had been appealed to the Supreme Court. Inasmuch as the Court was divided four to four, his participation would have been very important either way.

The reasoning of Marshall in *Marbury v. Madison* has been repudiated by many constitutional commentators, yet the case is still cited as authority for the Court's power of judicial review. Professor J. A. C. Grant has concluded that "nothing remains of *Marbury v. Madison* except its influence." Max Lerner has adroitly added: "Everything else has been whittled away. But its influence continues to grin at us from the Cimmerian darkness like the disembodied smile of the Cheshire cat."

Saga
of
Gideon Olmsted

*A Privateer
and Supremacy of
the Federal Juciciary*

C APTAIN GIDEON OLMSTED WAS TOUGH, tenacious and
resolute. His exploits during the early years of the
Republic not only played a part in American history but
were also instrumental in establishing the supremacy of
the federal judiciary. His saga is one of the most exciting in
the annals of American jurisprudence.

In July, 1778, Captain Olmsted was 29 years old.
Standing five feet, ten inches tall, with gray eyes and light
hair, he was already known and feared by the British as
an adventurous American privateer. Cruising in West
India waters in command of the French privateer *Polly*,
Captain Olmsted was cornered by two British men of war.
A long and deadly battle ensued, in which 55 of the 110
men aboard the *Polly* were killed by the superior British
guns. Olmsted was finally forced to surrender. He and the
remaining survivors were sent to Jamaica as prisoners of
war.

During this period, the British were desperately in
need of experienced navigators. Olmsted was therefore
impressed into service aboard the British sloop *Active*.
The *Active* had been commissioned to run military sup-

plies from Jamaica to the British troops in New York City. Its crew consisted of fourteen Englishmen under Captain Underwood, Olmsted as second mate and three other impressed American sailors.

One night, Olmsted and his compatriots daringly captured the ship by locking Captain Underwood and his men in the hold. Whenever the British became obstreperous and attempted to break out he calmed them by firing a four-pounder into their cabin.

Captain Underwood refused to accept defeat. With marvelous ingenuity, he and his men melted pewter spoons into bullets and fired their pistols at the Americans through the chinks in the cabin. Olmsted responded with his four-pounder, racking the cabin with shot. Underwood then threatened to blow up the ship by firing his pistol into a keg of powder. Undaunted, Olmsted replied "Go ahead and be d-----d!" Despite the restraining pleas of his men, Underwood shot his pistol at the keg, but somehow the explosion failed to occur. Olmsted then fired a swivel gun loaded with thirty musket balls into the cabin. This did the trick, and Underwood capitulated. Master of the ship, Olmsted steered towards Egg Harbor, New Jersey.

Early the next morning, as the *Active* approached Cape May, it was pursued and captured by Captain Houston of the armed brig *Convention*, of the State of Pennsylvania. Captain Houston then convoyed it in as a prize to Philadelphia.

ALTHOUGH OLMSTED IS CREDITED with what appears to be one of the most gallant and daring exploits of the Revolutionary War, it was his misfortune to become the pawn in a most unsavory affair. For the State of Pennsylvania, under the unjustified claim of Captain Houston, argued that Olmsted had never been in complete control of the *Active*. It was impossible, the State contended, for four men to master a crew of fourteen under the conditions involved.

As co-libellant the State of Pennsylvania pursued the case in the Pennsylvania Admiralty Court which had been established for such purposes. The cargo alone was sold in

September 1778 for $98,000, a rather handsome sum for those days! The State of Pennsylvania appropriated all the proceeds from the sale save several thousand dollars which were granted to Olmsted and his men as their share of the prize money. All this was done with the sanction of the Pennsylvania Admiralty Court.

The state authorities of Pennsylvania, however, completely underestimated Captain Olmsted. Their cavalier manner of settling his claim quickened all the more his resolve that justice be done. Thirty years of great hardship elapsed before Olmsted was vindicated. Before the final dénouement, the case became known throughout the United States as its most celebrated legal battle. The greatest men in the Republic became involved. A listing of the *dramatis personae* would read like a who's who of the American revolution and early years of the Republic. Politically, it was of the greatest import for it almost ended in war between the United States and Pennsylvania. Legally, its effect is felt to this very day in federal-state relations.

Olmsted was without friends, a stranger from Connecticut, but having determined to continue the fight, he borrowed money and filed a formal claim to the sloop *Active* and her cargo as his own prize. This time a jury was impanelled by the Admiralty Court, and even though Captain Underwood and his crew testified on Olmsted's behalf, the jury returned a verdict sustaining the claim of the State of Pennsylvania.

The Continental Congress had arranged for appeals to be taken from the state admiralty courts to the Court of Commissioners of Appeals of Congress. Olmsted had been advised to take such an appeal, but security was required by the Court. Lacking funds for this purpose, Olmsted turned in desperation to General Benedict Arnold. Arnold in 1778 was military commander of Philadelphia, and was known to Olmsted as a native of Connecticut. Arnold recognized the validity of Olmsted's claim and not only promised to help him before the appeals court but even purchased a share in the claim. It is not without interest to

Captain Gideon Olmsted

note that one of the charges later brought against General Arnold by the Supreme Executive Council of Pennsylvania pertained to his maintenance of the Olmsted claim. Arnold was later exonerated by an investigating committee of Congress.

THE DAY FOLLOWING THE ADVERSE verdict in the Admiralty Court, Olmsted appealed to the Court of Commissioners of Appeals. Although advised of the appeal, Judge Ross of the Admiralty Court ordered the proceeds of the sale of the *Active's* cargo to be invested by the marshal of his court in Loan Office Certificates of the United States. This strengthened the hold of the State of Pennsylvania on the funds.

On December 15, 1778, the Commissioner of Appeals decreed that Olmsted was entitled to all the proceeds of the sale of the *Active* and directed the Admiralty Court of Pennsylvania to turn the certificates over to Olmsted. One of the four commissioners of this court was Oliver Ellsworth, who later became the draftsman of the law which established the present system of federal courts and still later Chief Justice of the United States.

Judge Ross decided to ignore the court's decree and instead directed his marshal to deposit the certificates in his court. He then turned the certificates over to the Treasurer of Pennsylvania, first taking the precaution, however, of indemnifying himself by bond. The Treasurer was David Rittenhouse, a prominent astronomer.

Thus the battle was joined! The State controlled the money through its treasurer, although he held it in a private capacity as stakeholder. The United States rested on the decree of the Appeals Court. Judge Ross died in July, 1779. The bond of indemnity thus became part of his estate. And — what about Olmsted? He was the pawn. He waited for the certificates to be delivered to him by the State of Pennsylvania. This was not done. He waited for the Appeals Court to enforce its decree — the times were such, however, that this, too, was not done.

Olmsted realized that he was in for a long legal battle—one that required competent legal help and ample funds. He knew that the State of Pennsylvania expected to outwait him until he gave up in despair. But Olmsted was a determined man. He retained one of the leading lawyers of the Philadelphia Bar, William Lewis, to represent him in his claim. Lewis was the great criminal lawyer of his day and was described as the "Senior of the Bar." He, with Edward Tilghman, William Rawle, Jared Ingersoll, and Alexander J. Dallas, handled most of the cases in the Federal Court. He later represented John Fries with great courage in the case which led to the impeachment in 1805 of Judge Chase, of the United States Supreme Court.

Thus settling his affairs, Olmsted returned to the sea, wreaking havoc on the British as a privateer. After seizing six British vessels, he was again captured by the British and at the end of the Revolution he was released as a prisoner of war.

Once again Olmsted returned to Philadelphia and the fray. His main difficulty was that there was no basic law he could rely on to enforce his rights. In the meantime, he contented himself by nibbling at the state's defenses.

Judge Joseph Reed died in 1785. Olmsted, by default, obtained a judgment against Reed's executors for the amount withheld from him under his claim. The estate was much too small, however, to satisfy judgment. Olmsted then arranged for the executors to sue Rittenhouse, the state treasurer, to the use of Olmsted, upon the bond of indemnity, in the State Supreme Court. After protracted delay Chief Justice Thomas McKean, a signer of the Declaration of Independence, non-suited the plaintiff in 1792, on the ground that the state court lacked jurisdiction over admiralty matters.

ONCE AGAIN, OLMSTED WAS SET BACK but only temporarily. His first real break came in 1795. In the case of *Penhallow v. Doane*, the Supreme Court of the United States held that the federal district courts were authorized to enforce the decrees of the old Court of Appeals. But still he needed funds to pursue his objective legally. It was not until 1803 that he took his next legal step. In the meantime, David Rittenhouse had died in 1796 of yellow fever, leaving two daughters, Mrs. Elizabeth Sergeant and Mrs. Esther Waters. As his executrices they received the United States loan certificates he had been keeping privately as stakeholder in the Olmsted claim. Attached to the certificate was a memorandum in his handwriting which declared the certificates to be the property of the State of Pennsylvania, but only on the condition that he be released by the State from the bond he had given Judge Ross.

On May 27, 1802, Olmsted petitioned Judge Richard Peters, United States District Judge for Pennsylvania, for a decree against the executrices of David Rittenhouse, directing them to turn the certificates over to him. On January 14, 1803, Judge Peters ruled in favor of Olmsted as he had requested. The State legislature of Pennsylvania immediately accepted the challenge of the federal court and enacted a law on April 2, 1803, which ordered the Governor of Pennsylvania to "protect the just rights of the state . . . from any process whatever issued out of any federal court" on the theory that Judge Peters had "usurped" jurisdiction. It also authorized the Attorney General to force the executrices to pay the money over to the state treasury "without regard to the decree of the district court," and also "to protect the persons and properties of those ladies from any process which might issue out of the Federal court, in consequence of their obedience to this requisition . . ."

Judge Peters was an excellent judge who had had a distinguished career during the Revolution, being the first Secretary of War. He was very much embarrassed, however, by the sharp defiance of the Pennsylvania General Assembly. Before causing a clash between the governments of Pennsylvania and the United States, he wanted to be absolutely sure that his legal position was correct. He preferred that the Supreme Court of the United States consider the case too. Under the circumstances he refused to grant Olmsted a mandamus order against the executrices of Rittenhouse. Once again Olmsted was frustrated.

Time dragged on. It appeared that Olmsted would never recover from the State of Pennsylvania. The Pennsylvania authorities hoped that the "incident" would be resolved by the passage of time. Perhaps Olmsted would die—clearing up the entire mess. But Olmsted in 1807, at the age of 59, was strong and virile. That year he petitioned the Pennsylvania General Assembly for redress —appearing personally before it. The Legislature in an effort to dispose of this irritating affair offered him a token payment of $1000 and a grant of land. He replied:

"I AM POOR, IT IS TRUE, and that or any money would be of service to me; but I am come to the house of representatives not to ask anything of them but justice. I wish the house to examine into the merits of my claim. If I am entitled to anything, I am entitled to the whole. If my claim is not just, I ought not to get anything."

The legislature refused to act.

Once again Olmsted worked and saved and collected sufficient funds to appeal to the United States Supreme Court. It is interesting to note the fees he paid; he kept a careful diary of his expenses. The total expenses charged up against the Case of the Sloop Active by Captain Olmsted was $22,873.44.

On March 5, 1808, Olmsted applied to the Supreme Court of the United States for a mandamus to be directed to Judge Peters commanding him to issue proper process to enforce obedience to the sentence of his court. Judge Peters in his return explained that in view of the action taken by the General Assembly of Pennsylvania, he had not issued any process of his decree "from prudential, more than other motives . . . to avoid embroiling the government of the United States and that of Pennsylvania on a question that has rested on his single opinion. . . ."

The case of *United States v. Judge Peters* was argued in 1809 by Attorney-General Caesar A. Rodney, William Lewis, and Francis Scott Key against John Sergeant. Chief Justice Marshall rendered his opinion on February 20, 1809. He emphasized that he made his decision "with great attention and with serious concern," and he had every reason to do so, for he realized that the safety of the nation was involved.

This was the period of the Embargo and the Force Acts. A bitter struggle was going on between President Jefferson and the commercial interests of New England; the charge was made by the Federalists that American shipping was being ruined. In New England particularly, the reaction was violent. Characteristic of the times was the denouncement of the Force Act by the Massachusetts legislature and its decree that enforcement of its provisions by an officer would make him guilty of a high misdemeanor, punishable by fine and imprisonment. Sedition, rioting and threats of secession became more prevalent. The Federalist view was that the Force Act and other extreme portions of the Embargo Laws were "so violently and palpably unconstitutional, as to render a reference to the judiciary absurd." It was "the inherent right of the people to resist measures fundamentally inconsistent with the principles of just liberty and the social compact."

MARSHALL WAS A FEDERALIST, but he cared little for talk of secession and resistance to law and order. He recognized that much more was involved in the case before him than a mere legal conflict between the State of Pennsylvania and a federal judge. Marshall knew he had to address his thoughts to the Federalists, and to all those who advocated sedition and secession. This was the dramatic background for Marshall's opinion in *United States v. Peters*, and he met the challenge squarely. Commenting that the act of the legislature of Pennsylvania challenged the very life of the National Government he asserted:

"If the legislature of the several states may at will, annul the judgments of the courts of the United States, and destroy the rights acquired under those judgments, the constitution itself becomes a solemn mockery; and the nation is deprived of the means of enforcing its laws by the instrumentality of its own tribunals. . . .

"These clear strong words" wrote Beveridge, in his

life of Marshall, "were addressed to Massachusetts and Connecticut no less than to Pennsylvania. They were meant for Marshall's Federalist comrades and friends, for Pickering and Gore, and Morris, and Otis, as much for the State officials in Lancaster. His opinion was not confined to the case before him; it was meant for the whole country and especially for those localities where national laws were being denounced and violated and national authority defied and planted. Considering the depth and fervor of Marshall's feelings on the whole policy of the Republican régime, his opinion in *U.S. v. Judge Peters* was signally brave and noble."

"It will be readily conceived," he concluded, "that the order which this court is enjoined to make by the high obligations of duty and of law, is not made without extreme regret at the necessity which has induced the application. But it is a solemn duty, and therefore must be performed." He then awarded a peremptory mandamus in favor of Olmsted.

Marshall's opinion received immediate attention throughout the states. When word of it reached Pennsylvania, Governor Synder of Pennsylvania, a Republican, requested and was granted authority from the state legislature to use State militia in order to prevent enforcement of Judge Peter's decree. The reaction throughout the country was one of great anxiety. "Had a message like this come from a New England governor, the cries of treason and rebellion would have filled every Democratic paper in the land," wrote one Federalist paper.

On March 24, 1809, pursuant to Marshall's peremptory mandamus, Judge Peters issued a writ to John Smith, United States marshal "to attach and arrest the bodies of the executrices of David Rittenhouse . . . and to keep and detain them under safe and secure arrest until they shall in all things comply with and perform the final sentence and decree pronounced in this cause on the 14th of January 1803."

THE CONFLICT BETWEEN THE STATE of Pennsylvania and the United States came to a head on March 25th, 1809, when Marshall Smith attempted to serve the writ on the ladies. When he approached the Rittenhouse home, he was met by a detachment of state troops under the command of General Michael Bright, who with fixed bayonets refused to allow the marshal to enter. Public excitement grew to an intense pitch and a tremendous crowd gathered in the streets around "Fort Rittenhouse," as the house was called.

Obtaining a chair, Marshal Smith stood on it, and lectured them on the duty of obedience. "In the name and by authority of the United States," he added, "I command you to lay down your arms and permit me to proceed."

The state soldiers looked to their officer. "In the name and by the authority of the Commonwealth of Pennsylvania, I command you to resist him," replied General Bright. The troops stood firm, bayonets pointed at the marshal.

Marshal Smith at last decided to leave without serving the writ. But he had one final ace to play. He announced a date two weeks hence to serve his papers and served notice that he planned to raise a *posse comitatus* of 2000 citizens to help him. This announcement came as a bombshell. A United States armed posse in conflict with state militia meant bloodshed! No one knew where it would end.

Here was a serious crisis. The Pennsylvania legislature, disturbed and considerably alarmed, sought a way out. "It had been supposed," wrote a correspondent, "that the marshal, good, easy man, would make but a faint attempt to enforce the service of the process. The active attempt made by him has awakened serious apprehensions. The Attorney General is here. The voice of prudence at length is heard, and it is understood that measures will be taken to compromise matters . . . ."

On April 6, Governor Snyder wrote to President Madison voicing the hope that an honorable solution could be found and that the President would "justly discriminate between opposition to the Constitution and laws of the United States and that of resisting the decree of a judge founded as it is conceived, on a usurpation of power . . ." In office but a few months, Madison refused to weaken the federal government's position. His tone was conciliatory but firm.

"It is sufficient, in the actual posture of the case, to remark, that the Executive is not only unauthorized to prevent the execution of a decree sanctioned by the Supreme Court of the United States, but is expressly enjoined by statute, to carry into effect any such decree, where opposition may be made to it."

The president's message was the final straw. Although presenting a bold front by issuing spirited resolutions, the legislature's resistance collapsed. One of the resolutions adopted is significant to this day. It proposed an amendment to the United States Constitution for the establishment of "an important tribunal" to decide upon controversies between States and the Nation. Very quietly, however, a law was enacted which authorized the payment of Olmsted's claim, if necessary. In the meantime, by a stratagem, the marshal managed to serve his writ, thus avoiding the necessity of a posse.

One of the executrices, Mrs. Sergeant, sued out a Writ of Habeas Corpus in the State Supreme Court, but Chief Justice Tilghman dismissed the writ, ruling that she was properly in federal custody. The Supreme Court decree had to be obeyed!

A DRAMATIC AFTERMATH of the Olmsted Case occurred when General Bright and his eight militiamen were tried and convicted for resisting an officer of the United States and forcibly preventing an officer of the United States to serve a legal process of a federal court. The trial took place on April 25, 1809 before Supreme Court Justice Bushrod Washington and Judge Richard Peters and a jury in the Circuit Court of the United States for the District of Pennsylvania. Both the nation and the city of Philadelphia became greatly excited over its implications. The *Aurora*, a newspaper which had strongly opposed the Federal Judiciary, spiritedly editorialized:

"The great evil of this case is the impression it must make . . . The question is, however, so important to the public safety and to the security of the federation of states that it required to be settled. . . . This issue is . . . whether the Constitution of the United States is to remain in force or become a dead letter. The plain question is shall the laws of the Union be violated or maintained. We have heard much talk of the independence of the Judiciary, from those who wish to create a tyranny under the name of that independence . . . but here is a point at which the independence of the Judiciary, in its strict and Constitutional sense, exists and demands to be supported and maintained, and in which it must be maintained, or there is an end to government."

Mr. Justice Douglas has noted that Judge Washington's charge to the jury in that case "is a hornbook on federalism, as we know it." The question the jury struggled with concerned whether the state militia had knowingly opposed the lawful authority of the United States or had merely followed orders of duly constituted state officials. After Judge Washington had held the jury for two days and nights refusing to release them until they brought in a verdict, the defendants were found guilty. The General was sentenced to three months imprisonment and a fine of $200, his soldiers to one month in jail and a fine of $50 each. Judge Washington, in imposing sentence explained that, he believed the defendants had opposed the laws of the United States under the mistaken impression, they were performing their duty to the state of Pennsylvania.

SATISFIED THAT THE FEDERAL GOVERNMENT had gained the victory, President Madison four days later on May 6, 1809, pardoned the defendants and remitted the fines.

It is most interesting to note that in January, 1810, the General Assembly of Virginia adopted resolutions praising the Supreme Court Judges for their understanding of federal-state relations and acknowledging that the Supreme Court of the United States had been created "to decide disputes between the State and Federal Judiciary." A posture quite alien to its thinking afterwards.

It has been said that Olmsted's victory was a "vindication of the national power." Warren aptly concludes that the Olmsted episode presents "an interesting illustration of the fact that throughout American history, devotion to State-Rights and opposition to the jurisdiction of the Federal government and the Federal Judiciary, whether in the South or in the North, has been based, not so much on dogmatic, political theories or beliefs, as upon the particular economic, political or social legislation which the decisions of the Court happened to sustain or overthrow. No state and no section of the Union has found any difficulty in adopting or opposing the State-Rights Theory, whenever its interest lay that way . . . In 1809 . . . these States (Eastern) were more nearly prepared than were the Southern States to endorse the extreme views of Pennsylvania as to State sovereignty."

Interestingly too, the Supreme Court has so rarely issued a Writ of Mandamus ordering a lower federal court judge to enforce a judgment that, when in October, 1962, it appeared the Supreme Court would issue such a Mandamus Order to Judge Davidson of the Federal District Court of Texas, *The New York Times* reported:

> "It is most unusual for the Supreme Court to admonish a lower court judge to carry out its orders. Long-experienced justice department aides said that . . . they could not recall any case in which the Court had come this close to issuing a Writ of Mandamus to a federal district judge."

Of course, they had forgotten the case of *United States vs. Judge Peters* in which Chief Justice Marshall, speaking for the Supreme Court, issued a Mandamus against Judge Peters to enforce Gideon Olmsted's judgment.

Thus, we come to the end of the Olmsted saga. Olmsted enjoyed the fruits of his victory for many years. He lived until his 96th birthday and died in East Hartford, Connecticut, on February 8, 1845. His will recites an additional claim against the state of Pennsylvania for $30,000, of which he devised $10,000. The remainder he gave to the state of Pennsylvania. *Noblesse oblige.*

McCulloch
v.
Maryland

National Power Versus
State Sovereignty

"MR. PINKNEY ROSE on Monday to conclude the argument; he spoke all that day and yesterday, and will probably conclude today. I never, in my whole life, heard a greater speech; it was worth a journey from Salem to hear it; his elocution was excessively vehement, but his eloquence was overwhelming. His language, his style, his figures, his arguments were most brilliant and sparkling. He spoke like a great statesman and patriot, and a sound constitutional lawyer. All the cob-webs of sophistry and metaphysics about State rights and State sovereignty he brushed away with a mighty besom."

This description of one of the most impressive and colorful arguments ever presented in the Supreme Court of the United States, written by Justice Story on March 3, 1819, marked the culmination of an epoch in the annals of American jurisprudence. Not only did it result in probably the most renowned and ablest of the opinions of Chief Justice Marshall but it also made an historic and permanent contribution to the principles of American constitutional law.

It has been said that no decision of Marshall was of

more transcendent importance than that rendered in the case of *McCulloch v. Maryland*. Certainly it is a case which no one who would understand the Constitution of the United States can avoid reading. Yet, its import really cannot be fully understood without an appreciation of the troublesome and agitated period out of which it arose. It is for this reason, among others, that Beveridge, Marshall's biographer, concluded that Marshall's opinion in this case "cannot be understood at all unless you look at [it] from the point of view of statesmanship. You might as well read nothing at all as to read Marshall's opinion and decision as a mere law opinion."

McCulloch v. Maryland represented another round in the acrimonious debate then being waged between the political disciples of Hamilton and Jefferson. The Democratic-Republicans, influenced by the thinking of Jefferson, contended that the Constitution of the United States had to be construed strictly, so that the sovereign rights of the several states could be guaranteed. The Federalists on the other hand, following the Hamiltonian line, believed in a strong, national government to insure the success of the great American experiment in democracy. This could be achieved only if implied powers could be assumed by the national government when necessary.

In a sense, the issue in controversy was rather simple. It involved the question of whether the adoption of the Constitution, and the form of government set forth therein, represented a compact between independent states in which each had surrendered a portion of its sovereignty to a national government, and had reserved all other powers not so granted. "If this be so," argued the Democratic-Republicans, "then the Constitution could not be construed as granting the national government general powers, but rather specific powers – and only those specific powers enumerated in Section 8 of Article I of the Constitution." The Federalists retorted that this was not so, "For doesn't the same Section 8, in addition to the powers enumerated provide the following: "To make all laws which shall be *necessary and proper* for carrying into execution the foregoing powers, and all powers vested by this Constitution in the government of the United States, or in any Department or officer thereof?" This then was the great constitutional issue—should the Constitution be interpreted so that the powers of Congress could be expanded to meet the changing needs of government—or could Congress exercise only the powers actually enumerated in Article I of the Constitution? How it was resolved proved to be as dramatic and exciting as the circumstances that led to it.

ONE OF THE MORE significant reasons for the failure of the United States government to thrive under the Articles of Confederation was the instability of its financial system. In addition to the trade barriers imposed by the 13 states, each state also issued its own currency with fluctuating and different values. In 1791, Hamilton proposed that a National Bank be chartered by Congress to ameliorate the financial disorder resulting from this chaotic condition. Jefferson and Madison objected strenuously, recognizing that a National Bank would concentrate enormous financial power in the federal government and weaken the sovereignty of the states. More than that, they contended, the United States Constitution did not grant such specific authority to the Congress, and as the Constitution had to be strictly construed, Congress could not charter a National Bank. Hamilton replied that Congress was merely exercising one of its implied powers in chartering the Bank and hence the act would be constitutional. If Congress could charter a Bank, rejoined Jefferson, then there would be no limitation on the power of Congress. Where would it end? The Federalists were in control of Congress, however, and in 1791 a charter was granted to the Bank of the United States for a period of 20 years.

Unfortunately, the Bank attracted the animosity of a majority of the people. They called it a "monopoly" and an "octopus" and resented its tight money policy. The state banks, eager to garner the profits made by the National Bank, conspired closely with the press in perpetuating this unpopular image. Although the Bank had fulfilled its mission admirably as a stabilizer of the economy, it had aroused such opposition by 1811 that Congress refused to renew its charter.

Then came the War of 1812! Business drew to a standstill. Without the restraining influence of the conservative policies of the National Bank, local banks "began a course that ended in a mad carnival of roguery, to the ruin of legitimate business and the impoverishment and bankruptcy of hundreds and thousands of the general public." Every kind of banking institution, even turnpike companies, began to issue currency and sell it at a discount. They would accept mortgages in payment and foreclose expeditiously even though their own specie had deteriorated in value or payments thereon had been suspended. The financial situation became so bad that President Madison, who had opposed the rechartering of the Bank, found it impossible to finance the war effort of the United States government. The state banks refused to accept the war loans floated by the Government, and, by 1814, the Treasury had insufficient funds to redeem its notes. The situation became intolerable when the War Department could not meet a $3,500 obligation! This turn of events became too embarassing, even for the followers of Madison and Jefferson. Many deserted their leaders. President Madison reversed himself and announced his support for a second National Bank. Despite the violent disagreement of the Southern and Western members of Congress, Congress reconstituted the Bank for another 20 years, by Act of April 10, 1816.

THE SECOND UNITED STATES BANK, however, was not managed as well as the first. It engaged in rash speculation and fraud, and overexpanded its credit to state banks. The financial crisis deepened, and, as the depression intensified, the Bank desperately attempted to recoup its losses. It called upon the state banks to repay their loans. The state banks, however, had overextended their own credit and could only meet their obligations by foreclosing on their outstanding mortgages and restricting credit. The result was catastrophic. Many people, especially in the South and West, lost their homesteads and businesses. At one time it was reported that the Bank of the United States actually owned a substantial part of the city of Cincinnati. Quite a few of the state banks were forced into bankruptcy, and by 1818 the complete collapse of the economy appeared imminent. Hostility to the Bank swept the nation. It was blamed for all the country's financial ills. Some states enacted legislation limiting the Bank's activities. Others levied heavy taxes on the branches of the Bank in their borders. Kentucky imposed a tax of $60,000 a year on the Bank's branch in that state; Tennessee $50,000 per year; and Georgia attempted to tax the Bank's stock at the rate of $31\frac{1}{4}$ cents per 100 dollars. Maryland enacted a statute imposing a tax on all banks located in Maryland not chartered by the legislature. Such banks were required to issue their currency on stamped paper supplied by the State or relieve itself of this tax by paying annually in advance the sum of $15,000. A forfeit of $500 was imposed for every offense, one-half to the informer and one-half to the state.

James W. McCulloch, cashier of the Baltimore branch of the Bank of the United States, continued to issue bank notes on unstamped paper in violation of the law. McCulloch was sued by an informer in the Baltimore County Court, in behalf of himself and the State, for the recovery of $2500 in penalties for five issuances of unstamped currency. The County Court rendered judgment in favor of the State. That the Bank's eventual destruction was inevitable if the judgment were upheld was obvious. The contending parties prepared for a long legal battle.

It is ironic to note that the Maryland branch of the Bank of the United States was notorious for its fraudulent practices and unsound administration. James McCulloch, the cashier, whose name now helps to identify a leading constitutional principle, was himself deeply involved in the Bank management's aberrations. Although he began his financial career in poverty, he embezzled such huge sums of money from the Bank that in 1819 while the Bank case was pending he actually was indicted for misappropriating $3,497,700 from it.

From its very inception the case of *McCulloch v. Maryland* was recognized as a "cause célèbre." Several tremendously important questions were involved and its implications were heatedly debated in newspapers and other public forums. Transcending all other issues was the constitutionality of the Maryland law which challenged the very power of the Federal government. For, in taxing the Maryland branch of the Bank of the United States, Maryland was actually interfering with an instrumentality of the Government itself. But did the Congress have the authority to establish such an instrumentality? It all depended on how the Constitution was to be construed—and there was the vexing problem to be determined!

The Attorney General of Maryland and the Attorney General of the United States, recognizing the great public importance of the constitutional question involved, agreed upon a statement of facts and argued the appeal to the Maryland Court of Appeals. The constitutionality of the Maryland law was upheld in June,1818, by that Court and the cause was brought, by writ of error, to the Supreme Court of the United States in September, 1818. Argument was set down for Washington's Birthday, February 22, 1819. Marshall had been a stockholder in the Bank of the United States for many years. As soon as he realized that the appeal to the Supreme Court would be taken, he immediately disposed of his holdings to avoid any suspicion of a conflict of interest.

In the words of Lord Craigmyle, *McCulloch v. Maryland* was a case which "set agog not only all the politicians but all the financiers and the business men of the Union." Justice Story noted that when the Supreme Court convened to hear argument on it, the courtroom was "full almost to suffocation." There was a "crowded audience of ladies and gentlemen . . . and many went away for want of room." Still ringing in their ears were the heated arguments made a few days before in the House of Representatives on a bill to repeal the Bank's charter. It was generally believed in Congress that the Supreme Court would uphold the constitutionality of the bank even though the Court consisted of five Republicans (Johnson, Livingston, Todd, Duval and Story) and only two Federalists (Marshall and Washington). To avoid such a decision, the opponents of the Bank attempted to repeal the Bank's charter by legislation and thus make the issue in *McCulloch v. Maryland* moot. Congress, however, had refused to vote on the bill and now the time had come for the making of the fatal decision.

As THE JUSTICES, WEARING THEIR BLACK silk robes, filed in and took their seats on the Bench, an intense air of anticipation prevailed in the courtroom. The room, in the basement of the Capitol, had been newly renovated. It was the first time it had been used since 1814. Bushrod Washington, Johnson and Livingston sat on the right of Chief Justice Marshall; Duval and Story on his left. After the justices had settled themselves comfortably in their seats, Chief Justice Marshall leaned forward to announce that Justice Todd was indisposed and would be absent from the Court. He then turned to the attorneys for the petitioner in error. As an impressive silence descended on the room, Daniel Webster rose to open for the Bank.

An imposing array of the most distinguished counsel of the day had been retained to argue the appeal. As the sovereign rights of the United States and the State of Maryland were involved, and as the government of the United States had directed its Attorney General to appear for the plaintiff in error, the Court had dispensed with its general rule permitting only two counsel to argue for each party. Daniel Webster, William Pinkney, and William Wirt, the Attorney General of the United States, appeared for the Bank. Luther Martin, Joseph Hopkinson and Walter Jones represented Maryland. Wirt and Pinkney were noted for their eloquence.

Pinkney was the senior counsel for the Bank. Although he was foppish in appearance, he was the acknowledged leader of the American Bar. Marshall said of

William Pinkney.
From a painting by Rembrandt Peale.

him that he was the greatest man he had ever seen in a court of justice. Justice Story was a great admirer of Pinkney. "Everytime I hear him he rises higher and higher in my estimation," he wrote in 1814. "His clear and forcible manner of putting his case before the court, his powerful and commanding eloquence, occasionally illumined with sparkling lights but always logical and appropriate, and above all, his accurate and discriminating law knowledge, which he pours out with wonderful precision, give him in my opinion, a great superiority over every man whom I have known."

WEBSTER HAD ESTABLISHED his reputation as the "Expounder of the Constitution" by his superb constitutional argument in the *Dartmouth College Case* the year before. Only three weeks prior to Webster's appearance in *McCulloch v. Maryland,* Marshall had delivered his famous opinion in the *Dartmouth College Case,* which enhanced even further Webster's standing as a great constitutional lawyer. He was still comparatively young (37 years old) and that he should be retained as junior counsel to Pinkney by so prominent a client as the Bank, over other able lawyers, was a testimonial to the distinction which he had attained. Luther Martin, "The Federal Bull-Dog," Attorney General of Maryland, at 71 years of age was still the leader of the Maryland Bar and one of the ablest lawyers in the United States despite his many years of hard drinking and carousing. Joseph Hopkins was 49 years old, and already noted for his great learning. Walter Jones has been described by Beveridge as "a legal genius."

Webster was dressed in the height of fashion, wearing a blue dress coat with large brass buttons and tight breeches. His starched, white shirt bosom was widely exposed and he featured a high soft collar. Webster always dressed impeccably when he spoke on important occasions. He stated the issues of the case slowly and clearly, as was his style, becoming more animated as he progressed. The general proposition advanced by the attorneys for the plaintiff in error was that the power to establish a bank was to be implied from the general power given to Congress to administer the financial affairs of the nation. "If the states may tax the bank," he exclaimed, "to what extent shall they tax it and where shall they stop? *An unlimited power to tax involves necessarily a power to destroy.* [An argument which Marshall later used with telling effect.] There is a limit beyond which no institution and no property can bear taxation. . . . It is essential to the existence and preservation of the government, that Congress should be able to exercise its constitutional powers, at its own discretion, without being subject to the control of state legislation." Webster spoke with great confidence. Shortly before he argued the case he wrote to Jeremiah Mason, "of the decision I have no doubt."

Webster argued for a good portion of the day, and he was followed by Hopkinson for the State of Maryland who spoke for a whole day. Hopkinson had been associated with Webster in the *Dartmouth College Case.* The gist of the argument of the attorneys for the State of Maryland was that the Constitution was a compact between the sovereign states. The powers delegated to Congress had to be interpreted strictly. Not only did the Constitution not provide for the establishment of a Bank; actually it was not necessary to the functioning of those powers enumerated. Hence the act chartering the Bank was unconstitutional. Wirt and Jones followed on February 24 and 25, and then Martin argued all day Friday and Saturday, February 26 and 27. Martin made an impassioned speech in defense of the rights of his beloved state. At one point, Justice Story later related, Martin played what he considered to be his trump card. He told the Court he would prove his case out of the mouth of Marshall! He then read excerpts from Marshall's speeches in the debates in the Virginia Constitutional Convention on the adoption of the Constitution in which he had expounded on the limitations imposed on the powers of Congress by the Constitution. Marshall sat rather uneasily during this display of oratory and heaved a sigh of relief when it was over. Story questioned Marshall on it later and Marshall explained, "Why, to tell you the truth, I was afraid I had said some foolish things in the debate; but it was not so bad as I expected."

Pinkney began the final argument on Monday, March 1. The atmosphere in the overcrowded room was charged with expectation as this great lawyer started to speak. He attacked the arguments of the attorneys for Maryland with such great force, logic and eloquence that Story felt compelled to describe it as set forth in the opening paragraph of this chapter. He commented on the importance of the case, representing as it did a conflict between National and State sovereignty and then continued: "I meditate with exultation, not fear, upon the proud spectacle of a peaceful review of these conflicting sovereign claims by this more than Amphictyonic council. I see in it a pledge of the immortality of the Union, of a perpetuity of national strength and glory, increasing and brightening with age: of concord at home and reputation abroad."

In his peroration he concluded: "I have a deep and awful conviction that upon this judgment it will depend mainly whether the Constitution under which we live and prosper is to be considered like its precursor, a mere phantom of political power, a pageant of mimic sovereignty to deceive and mock us . . . or whether it is to be viewed as a competent guardian of all that is dear to us as a nation."

Pinkney spoke for three days. It was the greatest effort of his distinguished career and was received with acclaim. In all, the full argument took nine days.

ALTHOUGH MARSHALL WAS A FEDERALIST, he was not exactly a liberal constructionist. By the same token he was not a strict constructionist either. He was not prepared to accept the principle that the Constitution granted Congress certain special powers, until upon critical examination of the Constitution it could be so established. Once, however, such examination proved conclusively Congress had such powers, he firmly believed that all incidental powers necessary to effectuate them followed. Marshall was an astute politician as well as a wise statesman and learned jurist. He was well aware that he was confronted by such a basic conflict between National and State sovereignty, that the fate of the nation would eventually hinge on his decision. The political conflict was inextricably intertwined with the economic welfare of the country. If the industrial revolution were to take root and flourish in the United States it had to be encouraged by a strong national government unencumbered by limitations imposed by the states. The national government, however, needed the power to do what it considered necessary to encourage industrialism especially in areas such as banking, transportation and commerce. The meaning of the "necessary and proper" clause of Article I of the Constitution was the key to the problem, and he decided to establish the Constitution, as Justice Story later noted, "upon its great original principles."

Beveridge has written that John Marshall, in *McCulloch v. Maryland,* "rose to the loftiest heights of judicial statesmanship. If his fame rested solely on this one effort, it would be secure." Actually, he added, Marshall "rewrote the fundamental law of the Nation; or perhaps it may be more accurate to say, that he made a written instrument a living thing, capable of growth, capable of keeping pace with the advancement of the American people and ministering to their changing necessities."

Only three days after the conclusion of Pinkney's speech, Marshall delivered the unanimous judgment of the Court before a few attorneys gathered there to conduct their own appeals. Marshall had been very much impressed by the arguments of counsel on both sides, particularly those of Webster and Pinkney. In his opinion he went so far as to publicly acknowledge that ". . . both in maintaining the affirmative and negative, a splendor of eloquence, and strength of argument seldom, if ever, surpassed, have been displayed." That he could write his opinion in such a short period, however, would indicate that he had given much thought to the case prior to the argument and had probably resolved the issues independently.

Marshall's opinion is based on two questions. First, has Congress the power to incorporate a bank, and, second, whether the State of Maryland may, without violating the Constitution, tax it. "The Constitution of our country, in its most interesting and vital parts is to be considered," he commented with great solemnity and clairoyance. "The conflicting powers of the government of the Union and of its members as marked in that Constitution are to be discussed; and an opinion given which may essentially influence the great operations of the government. No tribunal can approach such a question without a deep sense of its importance, and of the awful responsibility involved in its decision. But it must be decided peacefully or remain a source of hostile legislation, perhaps, of hostility of a still more serious nature. . . ." The question whether Congress had the power to incorporate a bank, he stated "can scarcely be considered as an open question. . . . The principle . . . was introduced at a very early period of our history. . . ."

Marshall contended it would be difficult to maintain the proposition of the counsel for the State of Maryland that "in the construction of the Constitution, to consider that instrument, not as emanating from the people, but as the act of sovereign and independent states," and that "the powers of the general government . . . are delegated by the states, who alone are truly sovereign, and must be exercised in subordination to the states who alone possess supreme dominion." Marshall insisted that the Constitution was not a compact of states but a scheme of government created and accepted by all the people. "The government of the Union, then . . . is emphatically and truly a government of the people. In form and in substance, it emanates from them. Its powers are granted by them, and are to be exercised directly on them, and for their benefit." (It is interesting to note how similar this thought is to Lincoln's in his Gettysburg address: "a government of the people, by the people, for the people.") As the government proceeds directly from the people, "their act was final and did not require the affirmance, and could not be negatived, by the state governments."

ON THE QUESTION OF THE SUPREMACY of federal laws vis-a-vis state laws, Marshall maintained that the federal government "is supreme within its sphere of action." True, the powers of the national government are enumerated in the Constitution and there is no reference to creation of corporations. But "there is no phrase in the instrument, which . . . excludes incidental or implied powers; and which requires that everything granted shall be expressly and minutely described . . ." "We must never forget," he emphasized, "that it is a constitution we are expounding."

Marshall then construed the significance of the "necessary and proper" clause of the Constitution and concluded, "Let the end be legitimate, let it be within the scope of the Constitution, and all means which are appropriate, which are plainly adapted to that end, which are not prohibited, but consist with the letter and spirit of the Constitution, are constitutional." The Constitution specifically empowers Congress "to lay and collect taxes, to borrow money, to regulate commerce, to declare and conduct a war, and to raise and support armies and navies." The Bank was an appropriate means to those ends and hence the act of Congress chartering the Bank was constitutional.

Actually Marshall could have used as authority, although he did not do so, the case of *U. S. v. Fisher*, in which he had held that in construing the "necessary and proper" clause, "it would be incorrect and would produce endless difficulty, if the opinion should be maintained, that no law was authorized which was not indispensably necessary to give effect to a specified power . . . Congress must possess the choice of means, and must be empowered to use any means which are in fact conducive to the exercise of a power granted by the Constitution."

Marshall has been criticized for his answer to the second question he postulated in that in his eagerness to strengthen the central government he was led to make "a much more sweeping declaration of principles than was at all needful to cover the case in hand." Taking advantage of Webster's argument that "the power to tax involves the power to destroy," he added "that the power to destroy may defeat . . . the power to create; that there is a plain repugnance, in conferring on one government a power to control the constitutional measures of another, which other, with respect to those very measures, is declared to be supreme over that which exerts the control. . . . If the controlling power of the states be established, if their supremacy as to taxation be acknowledged, what is to restrain their exercising this control in any shape they may please to give it? . . . The question is in truth, a question of supremacy; and if the rights of the states to tax the means employed by the general government be conceded, the declaration that the Constitution and the laws made in pursuance thereof, shall be the Supreme law of the land is empty and unmeaning declamation."

THE CRITICISM LODGED AGAINST Marshall is that he recognized no alternative between destructive, confiscatory taxation and no taxation at all. Corwin aptly notes that "the terms in which the Maryland Statute was couched indicated clearly that it was directed specifically against the Bank, and it might easily have been set aside on that ground." As a result of Marshall's decision on this aspect of the case, the Supreme Court has ruled that government securities and state and municipal bonds are not subject to taxation.

Marshall's opinion in *McCulloch v. Maryland* has been highly praised by Corwin as giving "evidence in their highest form, of his . . . notable qualities as a judicial stylist, his 'tiger instinct for the jugular vein', his vigorous pursuit of logical consequences; his power of stating a case, wherein he is rivalled only by Mansfield; his scorn of the qualifying 'buts', 'ifs', and 'thoughs', the pith and balance of his phrasing a reminiscence of his early days with Pope, the developing momentum of his argument, above all, his audacious use of the *obiter dictum*. Marshall's later opinion in *Gibbons v. Ogden* is, it is true, in some respects a greater intellectual performance, but it does not equal this earlier opinion in those qualities of form which attract the amateur and stir the admiration of posterity."

McCulloch v. Maryland quickly became the storm

center of a bitter controversy. Writing to his wife on March 7, 1819, Mr. Justice Story noted: "We have decided the great question as to the right of the States to tax the Bank of the United States, and have declared that they have no such power. This decision excites great interest, and in a political view is of the deepest consequences to the nation. It goes to establish the Constitution upon its great original principles. You, perhaps, from your retired life, may hardly think it possible that such should be the case, but if you mingled with the busy circles of politics or took an interest in the objects of governments and statesmen, you would readily admit its fundamental importance to the existence of the government."

In the main Marshall's opinion was praised in the Eastern and Northern newspapers by those who believed in the Hamiltonian philosophy of government and condemned by the supporters of states' rights in the Southern and Western papers. *Niles' Register* of March 13, 1819, lamented that "a deadly blow has been struck at the sovereignty of the states, and from a quarter so far removed from the people as to be hardly accessible to public opinion. . . . We are awfully impressed with a conviction that the welfare of the Union has received a more dangerous wound than fifty Hartford Conventions, hateful as that assemblage was, could inflict . . . and which may be wielded to destroy the whole revenues and so do away with the sovereignties of the States."

Although Madison, commenting on the "necessary and proper" clause in the *Federalist,* believed that "without the substance of this power, the whole Constitution would be a dead letter," and even if it had been omitted the central government could assume such power by implication because "no axiom is more clearly established in law, or in reason, than that whenever the end is required, the means are authorized; wherever a general power to do a thing is given, every particular power necessary for doing it is included," he felt constrained to attack Marshall's construction of the "necessary and proper" clause. "It was anticipated . . . by few if any of the friends of the

Constitution," he wrote to Spencer Roane in September, 1819, "that a rule of construction would be introduced as broad and pliant as what has occurred." If this had been made clear in the State constitutional conventions he was persuaded, "the avowal of such a rule would have prevented its ratification."

Spencer Roane, Marshall's old nemesis, writing under pen names of "Amphictyon" and "Hampden," warned after a fiery condemnation of the decision that Virginia "never will employ force to support her doctrines till other measures have entirely failed." The big question presented by the decision, he added, was whether the people were prepared "to give carte blanche to our federal rulers?" "A man must be a deplorable idiot who does not see that there is no difference" between an "unlimited grant of power and a grant limited in its terms, but accompanied with unlimited means of carrying it into execution. . . ." Even Jefferson, the venerable sage of Monticello, was stirred into condemning the federal judiciary as "a subtle corps of sappers and miners constantly working underground to undermine the foundation of our confederated fabric."

MARSHALL ATTEMPTED TO DEFEND his decision in a series of articles he wrote under the name of "A Friend of the Union." The protests continued to mount, however, and the senators from Virginia, upon instruction from their state legislature, protested the decision in the chambers of the Senate. Extravagant criticism of the decision ran rampant in other Southern and Western states and strong resolutions condemning it were passed by several of the state legislatures. It was even recommended that Congress amend the Constitution "creating a tribunal" with jurisdiction to adjudicate all questions pertaining to the "powers of the general and state government, under the compact." (A proposal which has been echoed in recent days.)

The resistance to the decision in Ohio became so vehement that its state treasurer cavalierly ignored its import and forcibly collected the state tax from the Bank's Ohio branch.. The dramatic story behind *Osborne v. The Bank of the U. S.* which resolved this issue in favor of the Bank deserves telling elsewhere.

From 1816 to 1830, the Bank was involved in forty-one lawsuits. Daniel Webster represented the Bank when these cases were appealed to the Supreme Court and he won them all! He also received some handsome fees from the Bank for doing so. The curtain finally came down on the Bank in the 1830's when it was destroyed by President Jackson.

The principle pertaining to the implied powers of the federal government, as set forth in *McCulloch v. Maryland*, is now generally followed by the Courts. The other principle laid down by *McCulloch v. Maryland*, that the states may not tax instrumentalities of the federal government, has been extended to many areas other than taxation by the Supreme Court. When the federal government is acting or legislating within the confines of its constitutional powers, the states may not interfere or attempt to control. By the same token, the Supreme Court has held that the federal government similarly may not interfere with or control the instrumentalities of the states.

It is indeed a tribute to Marshall's genius that these important principles of government are now generally acknowledged. It is not without reason that Beveridge called it "that opinion of John Marshall which has done more for the American Nation than any single utterance of any other one man, excepting the Farewell Address of Washington."

To-day, the political liberals who claim to wear the mantle of Jefferson and his Democratic-Republican Party surely would not accept their States-Rights Theories, whereas our modern conservatives, who are closely affiliated in political spirit with the platforms of Hamilton and the Federalist Party, would strenuously contest the principle of a strong, nationally, centralized government, espoused by them.

The Reporter
and the
Supreme Court

Copyright
and
Government Publication

H ENRY WHEATON was a mild-mannered cultured gentleman, a lawyer and a scholar of international re-
pute. If he could have been master of his destiny, his main
thought would have been to avoid becoming enmeshed
personally in a law suit. Yet it was his misfortune not only
to become involved in a famous American *cause célébre*
—but also to embroil his family in another after his death.

Richard Peters, Jr., was the son of Judge Richard
Peters, lawyer and revolutionary patriot. Peters, Jr., was a
scholar and a lawyer, too, and as it turned out, a rather
shrewd one.

Wheaton and Peters barely knew each other. Nevertheless, their association with the Supreme Court of the
United States was so unique that, when Wheaton instituted
his famous action against Peters, it flared up to preoccupy
the leading luminaries of the American Bar and to make a
lasting contribution to our jurisprudence.

The circumstances which led to the landmark case of
Wheaton v. Peters can best be appreciated by recollecting
the early history of the Supreme Court of the United
States. When George Washington was inaugurated as

President of the United States, there was no Supreme Court or any other federal court and as a result, no federal judge available to administer the oath of office. This unusual situation was due to a peculiar train of events. Article III of the Constitution provides that "The judicial power of the United States shall be vested in one Supreme Court and in such inferior courts as Congress may from time to time ordain and establish." Article II, section 2, adds that the President shall nominate, and by and with the advice and consent of the Senate, shall appoint the justices of the Supreme Court. Until Congress enacted a judiciary law implementing the constitutional provisions, Washington was unable to appoint anyone to the Supreme Court bench. Although it had been planned for the first Congress to be in session and the President in office under the Constitution by March 4, 1789, a quorum could not be obtained in both houses until more than a month later. Washington did not officially take office until April 30, 1789. As the seat of government was located in New York City, Robert R. Livingston, Chancellor of the State of New York, was called upon to administer the oath to the new President.

The absence of a federal judge at the presidential inauguration accentuated the need to establish a federal judiciary, and on September 24, 1789, a Judiciary Act was enacted under which the Supreme Court was organized. It provided that the Court should consist of a Chief Justice and five Associate Justices, any four of whom would be a quorum. The Court was to hold two sessions annually at the seat of government, one commencing the first Monday of February and the other the first Monday of August. It is not without interest to note how the sessions were changed until the present October term was established. The August term was eliminated in 1802. In 1826, the second Monday of January was substituted for the first Monday of February as the beginning day. In 1844, the first Monday of December was substituted for the second Monday of January, and in 1873, the first Monday of October was set as the beginning of the term, a practice which continues to this day.

PRESIDENT WASHINGTON MADE EVERY EFFORT to appoint important legal personalities to the Supreme Court, but in its early history, the Court made little impression on the young nation. When the Court first convened on February 1, 1790, its minutes disclose that only Chief Justice John Jay, and Associate Justices William Cushing and James Wilson were present. Lacking a quorum, the Court had to adjourn until the following day! Associate Justice John Blair appeared the next day, and a quorum finally being present, the Court read and published letters patent to the Justices appointing them to the Court and to Edmund Randolph appointing him Attorney General for the United States. Richard Weinman was appointed "cryer" and the Court adjourned. In the ensuing days, the only business for the Court was to appoint its clerk, decide on its seal, admit a handful of counsel to practice before it, adopt rules for admission to its bar and sundry other items, and then for lack of business adjourn *sine die* until the August term. Interestingly, John Rutledge, who had also been appointed to the Court by Washington, thought so little of it, that he resigned without ever sitting. Similarly, Robert Hanson Harrison, five days after he had been confirmed by the Senate, preferred to accept the post of Chancellor of Maryland instead of a Supreme Court appointment. James Iredell, appointed in Harrison's place did not take his seat on the Supreme Court until the second term of the Court in August, 1790. A rather sad reflection on the position of the Supreme Court at the time. As the late Chief Justice Vanderbilt expressed it: "It is difficult for us today to realize how weak the judicial branch once was and why, for example, John Jay should prefer to be Governor of New York to being Chief Justice of the United States."

Very little else occurred in the second, and third session, and it was not until the fourth term commenced on August 1, 1791, that the Court had two cases on its docket. In its sixth term, the Court decided its first case, *Georgia v. Brailsford.* Every justice wrote an opinion in this case. The first opinion published, oddly enough, was the dissenting opinion of Justice Johnson. It should be noted that the

Supreme Court followed the English system in which each judge wrote his own opinion. When Marshall became Chief Justice, one Justice was selected to write the opinion for the Court. Justice Iredell noted in his opinion that he had sat in the Circuit Court which rendered judgment on the case below, but that he would not allow it to influence his judgment on appeal! Justice Wilson began his opinion as follows: "I confess that I have not been able to form an opinion which is perfectly satisfactory to my mind . . ." Mr. Justice Clark recently commented on this apologetic beginning, perhaps with tongue in cheek, "I am sure many opinions since that time have been handed down by authors who have suffered the same difficulty."

The dearth of Supreme Court business is reflected in its official reports. The first volume of the *United States Reports*, known as *1 Dallas*, and three fourths of *2 Dallas*, contain no Supreme Court opinions but rather Pennsylvania Supreme Court Proceedings and colonial and other cases going back to 1774. It is not until we reach the last quarter of *2 Dallas* that United States Supreme Court opinions appear.

Not only did the Court have very little to report of its activities in those early days, but the manner in which its opinions were reported left much to be desired. This was a period when official court reporting was conspicuous by its absence. Prior to 1790, only one volume of the written opinions of an American Court had been published and that was *Kirby's Cases Decided in the Supreme Court of Connecticut*. Judges rarely reduced their opinions to writing except in a few states, such as Massachusetts, Maryland and Pennsylvania, where the rules called for written opinions in the Ecclesiastical and Admiralty Courts.

The situation pertaining to court reporting in England was little different. If it were not for private enterprise, there would be no record today of English decisions from the last *Year Books* (1537) to the nineteenth century. Veeder has noted that toward the end of the 18th century, "These private reports become fairly accurate and complete, but the long period from 1537 to 1785 is precariously covered by more than one hundred reporters of various degrees of merit." Some of them were so bad that Chief Justice Holt referring to volume 4 of Modern Law Reports in *Slater v. May* was moved to exclaim: "See the inconveniences of these scrambling reports, they will make us to appear to posterity for a parcel of blockheads." Many of these cases were published from the incomplete notes of lawyers taken down in court or from the personal records of judges, originally written down without any thought of publication. Upon the death of these people, enterprising publishers would arrange for the publication and sale of these reports without checking their accuracy or completeness. It has been noted, for example, by Veeder, that the case of *Clerk v. Day* is reported by Croke, by Owen, by Moore, and is also reported in Rolle's Abridgment, "yet Lord Raymond asserts that it is not accurately reported in any of the books named, even as to the names of the parties."

VERY LITTLE IMPORTANCE WAS ATTACHED to the early volumes of *Supreme Court Reports*. As a matter of fact, there was a general lack of interest in the work of the Court itself. For those occasional cases arousing the nation's attention, the public, and even lawyers and judges depended mainly on the newspaper reports. A leading historian of the Court has stated that these newspaper publications and editorial commentary, were more influential in forming public opinion concerning the Court than anything else.

The first Court Reporter for the Supreme Court was Alexander J. Dallas, who had been Secretary of Pennsylvania and later became Secretary of the Treasury under President Madison. He published four volumes covering the period from 1790 to 1800. He was followed by William Cranch, who published nine volumes of reports for the period from 1801 to 1815. While serving as Court Reporter, Cranch also sat as a Judge of the Circuit Court of the District of Columbia and later as its Chief Justice. It is obvious therefore that these early Court Reporters were distinguished men in their own right and that the position itself was sought after for the prestige attached to it.

It is difficult to ascertain how Dallas and Cranch were appointed. Congress was not interested in the position and had passed no legislation establishing the office of Court Reporter. The minutes of the Clerk's office of the Supreme Court fail to reveal the appointments of either man, although it is known that Cranch was regularly appointed by the Court. The same cannot be said for Dallas. No salary was arranged for these reporters, and they had to depend on the sale of their published reports to reimburse them for their efforts. The lack of public interest and the scarcity of lawyers, however, made their sale quite unprofitable.

Another feature of Supreme Court reporting at this time warrants attention. Apparently the Justices did not write their opinions unless the case was unusually important. Actually, there was no rule of the Court requiring the Justices to file copies of their opinions with the Clerk of the Court until March 14, 1834. Officially therefore, it was not until the January term of 1835, that the Clerk began to receive and file the written opinions of the Justices. Incidentally, too, it was not until the December term of 1857 that the Court requested the submission of a printed record on appeal. It is believed, however, that after Cranch became reporter of the Court, the Justices began the custom of issuing written opinions.

When Judge Cranch decided to retire as Court Reporter, Chief Justice Marshall and his Associate Justices Bushrod Washington, William Johnston, Brockholst Livingston, Thomas Todd, Gabriel Duvall and Joseph Story, selected a man to succeed him who had their complete confidence — Henry Wheaton.

HENRY WHEATON HAD ALREADY distinguished himself as a scholar, newspaper editor, and lawyer. Born in Providence, Rhode Island, in 1785, he had been graduated with honors from Brown University at the age of 17. Three years later he was admitted to the Bar and shortly thereafter he translated the new Napoleonic Code into English. In 1812, he moved to New York City where he was appointed editor of the *National Advocate,* which had been established by Tammany Hall. Under his control the paper achieved distinction for its high editorial standards. During this period he also became associated on occasion with Daniel Webster and other leaders of the bar on appeals to the Supreme Court. In May, 1815, he was appointed Justice of the Marine Court in New York City, where he served until 1819.

Wheaton, as was also true of Dallas and Cranch, was offered no salary. The only income he could receive officially, therefore, was derived from the sale of his reports, and as has been indicated, Supreme Court Reports in those days were not in popular demand. Daniel Webster, reviewing volume III of Wheaton's Reports wrote: "The sale is not very rapid. The number of law libraries which contain a complete set is comparatively small." As late as 1830 it was authoritatively stated that "few copies were found in many large districts, not a single copy of the reports are in the possession of anyone." In fact, the sale of Cranch's reports was so slow that he had to withhold the publication of the volumes for the period from 1812 to 1815 until 1816 for lack of funds.

After it was evident from the poor sale of his first volume that Wheaton would need financial help, Congress stepped in and by the act of March 3, 1817, the office of Supreme Court Reporter was recognized and an annual salary of $1000 was arranged for the Reporter, in return for which he had to publish all opinions within 6 months after decision, and 80 copies thereof had to be supplied to the Secretary of State for distribution to government officials. During this period, the reports sold for $5.00 each. Wheaton, of course was entitled to a share of the profits, too, but little was expected there. In 1831, 4 years after he had retired, there was a stock of Wheaton's Reports in storage worth from $25,000 to $30,000, and still unsold.

Wheaton received an inducement from the Court not granted to his predecessors in office. The Justices gave him their memoranda and notes to assist him in reporting the opinions. Wheaton used them to good advantage, destroying them thereafter. His reports were very well received by the bench and bar. His supplementary notes, particularly, were recognized as a scholarly achievement.

During his employment as Court Reporter, Wheaton also grew in stature as an authority on law and as a practitioner. Strangely enough, he also argued appeals before the Supreme Court and of course later reported them. As soon as the Supreme Court term ended, he would return to New York where he had become influential in the affairs of that state. In 1821, he was appointed a member of the New York Constitutional Convention and in 1823 served in the state assembly. As a member of the Constitutional Convention he worked closely with Chancellor Kent, Van Buren, Chief Justice Ambrose Spencer and other leading figures. Later he was chosen by the Legislature to work with John Duer and Benjamin F. Butler (founder of the School of Law of N. Y. U. in 1835) on the Revision of the Laws of New York. Although there is very little trace of Wheaton's influence on the Revision, he did prepare one or two of the earlier Chapters and worked on the original draft of the *"General Arrangement"* of the Code. This work, known as the *Revised Statutes of 1828*, is considered one of the monumental achievements of the nineteenth century and set the pattern for codification followed later by many other jurisdictions.

By 1827, Wheaton was so highly regarded that President Adams offered him the diplomatic post of Chargé d'Affaires to Denmark. Wheaton accepted and resigned as Court Reporter, little realizing the difficulties in store for him. For Wheaton depended on the slow but steady sale of his Reports to supplement his inadequate income. Richard Peters, Jr., the next Reporter, however, had different plans.

PETERS RECOGNIZED THE NEED to stimulate sale of the Reports in order to increase his own profits. He was astute enough to realize that his own Reports would sell better, if the earlier volumes were purchased, for the owner of a set would want to keep it current. He also realized that there was a good market for the earlier volumes of Dallas, Cranch and Wheaton if they could be sold at a modest price. He therefore proposed to publish all the cases adjudged in the Supreme Court from 1790 to 1827 inclusive in *"Peters' Condensed Reports,"* which would consist of six volumes to be sold at a price of $36. He promised that the reports would be of sufficient authority and accuracy as to make it unnecessary to refer to the Reports of Dallas, Cranch and Wheaton. He stressed that he was offering a complete report of the opinions and not an abridgement. Of course, he added later, Peters' Reports would continue currently reporting Supreme Court cases as decided, at the regular $5.00 price.

REPORTS

OF

C A S E S

ARGUED AND ADJUDGED

IN

THE SUPREME COURT

OF

THE UNITED STATES.

February Term, 1816.

BY HENRY WHEATON,
Counsellor at Law.

VOLUME I.

PHILADELPHIA:
PUBLISHED BY MATHEW CAREY.
1816.

REPORTS

OF

CASES ARGUED AND ADJUDGED

IN

THE SUPREME COURT

OF

THE UNITED STATES.

JANUARY TERM, 1828.

By RICHARD PETERS Junior,
COUNSELLOR AT LAW, AND REPORTER OF THE DECISIONS OF THE
SUPREME COURT OF THE UNITED STATES.

VOL. I.

PHILADELPHIA:
PHILIP H. NICKLIN, LAW BOOKSELLER.
L. R. BAILEY, PRINTER.
1828.

As Cranch's reports were republished in *Peters' Condensed Reports* before *Wheaton's*, the initial reaction came from Judge Cranch who wrote to Peters on July 18, 1828:

"I have been informed that you propose to publish a new edition of my reports. It is with great reluctance that I deem it my duty to others to inform you that I have not yet been reimbursed the actual expense of publishing my three last volumes by $1000, and that I must insist upon all my legal rights."

Peters replied shortly thereafter indicating his proposed line of defense. "My plan is, to publish in a condensed form the decisions of the Supreme Court of the U.S., and as the opinions of the court cannot be the subject of copy-right, neither can the facts of the cases be the property of any one, my work will not be obnoxious to the laws protecting literary property. These are opinions, which have had high professional sanctions, and by which I am willing to abide."

That Peters' business judgment was correct was borne out by the results. Of the 1500 copies published by Peters of his Condensed Reports at least 900 were sold by subscription before the full six volumes were completed.

Judge Cranch, for reasons best known to himself, allowed the matter to rest. But as soon as Wheaton's publisher, Robert Donaldson, learned that the 3rd volume of the *Condensed Reports*, to be published in 1831, would contain the first volume of Wheaton, he threatened legal action against any bookseller who sold the set. Peters replied with a public circular, dated March 2, 1831, in which he proclaimed that Wheaton had failed to copyright his volume properly according to the Acts of Congress in that he had not deposited his volumes in the office of the Secretary of State for the purpose of securing a copyright. The omission was fatal and Wheaton had lost his copyright. He then promised "to indemnify and save harmless all who publish or sell the work and to take defense in any prosecution which may be instituted against them." Peters then continued on with his reports and completed the sixth and last volume in January, 1834.

In the meantime, Wheaton abroad in Copenhagen, was unable to take any action in the matter. It therefore fell on Donaldson, his publisher, to pick up the cudgels, and in May, 1831, he filed a bill in equity against Peters and his publisher John Grigg, praying an account of the profits of the 3rd volume of *Peters' Condensed Reports*, for infringement of Wheaton's copyright. The bill also prayed that the defendants might be restrained by injunction from any other sale of said third volume and from publishing in continuation the remaining eleven volumes of Wheaton's Reports. The injunction was granted, but after argument the District Judge dismissed the bill and dissolved the injunction. An appeal was taken to the Circuit Court of the U. S. for the Eastern District of Pennsylvania where Justice Hopkinson held that Wheaton had failed to observe the technical requirements of the copyright law and that no common law copyright existed in the United States.

THE CASE OF HENRY WHEATON and Robert Donaldson, citizens of the State of New York v. Richard Peters and John Grigg, citizens of the State of Pennsylvania, was appealed to the Supreme Court and was argued in the January term, 1834.

The appeal attracted great interest and stirred up many comments. Wheaton was granted a leave of absence, and rushed to Washington to attend the argument. He had served his country with honor and distinction and was showing promise as an outstanding authority on international law. It was obvious, too, that he was being wronged by Peters, no matter how correct his legal stand, and everyone was sympathetic to his cause. Another dramatic aspect of the case was the warm friendship and admiration Chief Justice Marshall and Justice Story bore for Wheaton. The other justices on the bench knew Wheaton well, too—and it was an embarrassing situation. The embarrassment was aggravated by the close relationship between the bench and Peters, who was the Court Reporter.

The case was argued at length and in great detail before the Court by Daniel Webster and Elijah Paine for

Wheaton and Charles J. Ingersoll and John Sergeant for Peters. The complainants' general argument was to the effect that Wheaton was the author of the law reports and these reports were, like other books, objects of literary property. Wheaton was therefore entitled to the copyright in them under the common law and by statute. The defendants argued that only the opinions of the judges were reprinted by Peters, Wheaton's notes being deleted. Wheaton as a reporter was an officer of the Court and his reports were therefore for public use. He was not an author in this sense but an officer, a public agent, selected, authorized and paid for making up the reports of the decisions of the Court. He therefore had no property right in the words of the reports or the facts of the cases. Counsel for both sides reviewed extensively the common law and statutory aspects of the copyright law with eloquence and erudition. The justices showed great interest in the case, interrupting often to ask piercing questions. It was one of those magnificent performances that occasionally take place before the Supreme Court and the many lawyers who sat in the audience were enthralled.

The decision of the Court was disappointing to Wheaton, but has made a lasting contribution to the American law of copyright. With Justices Thompson and Baldwin dissenting, a majority agreed with the conclusion of Justice McLean, who wrote the opinion of the Court, that Wheaton could not claim the benefit of common law copyright. "It is clear," he wrote, "there can be no common law of the United States. The Federal Government is composed of twenty-four sovereign and independent States, each of which may have its local usages, customs and common law. There is no principle which pervades the Union and has the authority of law that is not embodied in the Constitution or laws of the Union. The common law could be made a part of our Federal System only by legislative adoption." The only right therefore that Wheaton had acquired, if any, arose out of the copyright laws enacted by Congress. Whether he had perfected these rights needed further determination by the lower court. The Court was unanimous, however, when it added: "no reporter has or can have any copyright in the written opinions delivered by this Court; and that the judges thereof cannot confer on any reporter any such right." This final statement was a crushing blow to Wheaton. His case was finished and he had to bear his financial loss.

EX-CHANCELLOR KENT OF NEW YORK was not too happy with the decision. Writing to Judge Story on April 11, 1834, he complained: "I don't feel satisfied that you or the Ch. J. did not write an opinion on the copyright case, and discuss the grounds of the claim at criminal law. It would appear to me to have fairly presented itself as a new question for discussion in our American Jurisprudence. I don't complain of the decision on the point . . . but that imposing brief of Mr. Wheaton ought to have been met by one of the only two men who could have met it with a giant's force . . . To deny the common law right and to construe the statute right with such severity is not palatable to us humble authors . . ."

Story replied on May 17, 1834: "I am sorry for the controversy between Mr. Wheaton and Peters, and I did all I could to prevent a public discussion of the delicate subject of copyright. . . . The strict construction of the Statute of Congress we adopted with vast reluctance, but after turning it fully and freely to our minds, the majority of the Court did not see how they could give any other construction to it. I wish Congress would make some additional provision on the subject to protect authors, of whom I think no more meritorious than Mr. Wheaton. You as a Judge, have frequently had occasion to know how many bitter cups we are not at liberty to pass by . . ."

Peters, of course, was jubilant with the result. He reported it comprehensively in his eighth volume, where it runs from page 591 to 699. He even published an appendix to the same volume in which he reprinted the opinion of Judge Hopkinson in the circuit court. More than that, he published a separate report of the case in 1834 which he dedicated: "To the Honourable John Marshall, Chief Justice of the United States . . . as a tribute due to your unequalled ability and usefulness, to the greatness of your character; the purity of your motives; and the kindness of your judicial deportment."

Although Wheaton was disappointed by the decision, he felt no resentment against his old friends on the Court. He wrote: "I have seen my judges . . . the old Chief Justice received me with fraternal frankness. What a green old age! I have also had the pleasure of meeting many old friends of the Bar with cordial greeting. They are one and all against Peters, crying out that his conduct has been shameful. But he bears it off with brazen impudence . . . I don't envy him his feelings."

Wheaton returned to his country's foreign service as Chargé d'Affaires and later as Envoy Extraordinary and Minister Plenipotentiary to Berlin, serving there until 1847. That year he was retired by President Polk and he died in 1848 in the U. S. During this period he achieved renown as one of the outstanding authors of the nineteenth century on international law. His *Elements of International Law* appeared in many editions and was translated into French, Spanish and Chinese. After his death two editions of this work were authorized by his widow — one by William B. Lawrence and another by Richard Henry Dana, author of *Two Years Before the Mast*. This ended in a notorious plagiarism action brought by Lawrence against Dana that was commenced in 1867 and ended in 1893, although Lawrence died in 1881 and Dana in 1882!

PETERS CONTINUED AS REPORTER for the Court until 1843 when he was summarily dismissed by some of the justices but without the approval of Justices Story and McKinley. The other members of the Court, especially Baldwin, resented Peters' attitude and decided to replace him with Gen. Benjamin C. Howard. This is a story by itself and almost provoked the resignation of Justice Story from the bench. Since then the Curtis edition of the U. S. Reports has superseded the Condensed Reports of Peters, and librarians today avoid the purchase of the Condensed Reports, preferring other editions — especially the Wheaton originals. Poetic justice?

The
Dorr
Revolution

Civil War in Rhode Island
and the Guarantee Clause

O N APRIL 4, 1842, GOVERNOR Samuel Ward King of the
State of Rhode Island sent a letter by special courier
to President Tyler, which revealed a situation unique in
American history:

"The State of Rhode Island is threatened with domestic violence. Apprehending that the legislature cannot
be convened in sufficient season to apply to the Government of the United States for effective protection in this
case, I hereby apply to you, as the Executive of the State
of Rhode Island, for the protection which is required by
the Constitution of the United States."

The long protracted struggle which led to this unusual request is not widely known today. Its importance,
however, cannot be overemphasized, for it ended in a
bitter controversy, the solution of which made a lasting
contribution to the constitutional law of the United States.
The troublesome question was vehemently discussed in
the newspapers of the day and aroused the entire country
politically. Whigs and Democrats argued over its implications in the halls of Congress. Even Tammany Hall in New
York attemped to influence the outcome. Ultimately it

developed into a revolution—the Dorr Revolution—and the story behind it is as dramatic and striking as its dénouement.

Rhode Island enjoys the odd distinction of being the only state in the United States to have suffered a revolution of its own after the war for independence. That it occurred, appears quite understandable today; that it took so long in the making, however, requires an explanation.

Shortly after the American Revolution began, all the original colonies except Rhode Island and Connecticut not only declared their independence of the British crown, but also framed and adopted new state constitutions and formed new governments. The political leaders of Rhode Island and Connecticut, however, reacted differently. They had long had a tradition of not accounting to the British Government and they considered their original royal charters as being sufficiently liberal and democratic in form. Under the circumstances, instead of changing the organic form of their governments, they merely formally renounced their allegiance to Great Britain and made certain statutory alterations. Thus, the Rhode Island Act of May 4, 1776, which declared the independence of the State, in no way affected its Royal Charter of 1663. As the old charter was neither abandoned nor abolished, and as the government continued on, the elected officials of the State pledged their allegiance to the successor independent government and stoically carried on with its operation. No opposition arose from the people and the authority and legality of the new government were not questioned. In a sense then, both Rhode Island and Connecticut assumed statehood with unwritten constitutions. Connecticut remedied this situation in 1818 when it adopted a formal constitution, but not Rhode Island.

THE RHODE ISLAND CHARTER OF 1663 provided for a governor, ten assistants, and a General Assembly consisting of freemen chosen from the different towns. The power of the General Assembly was supreme. In addition to its legislative authority, it also controlled the judicial and executive branches of the government. The Governor had no authority except as an executive officer of the legislature and in effect merely executed its orders. All members of the judiciary were appointed annually by the General Assembly and as a result were subservient to it.

On suffrage, the Charter provided that the General Assembly "shall have . . . full power and authority, from time to time . . . to choose, nominate and appoint, such and so many other persons as they shall think fit and shall be willing to accept the same, to be free of the said company and body politic and them unto the same to admit." And here was the rub! The Charter did not actually specify the qualifications for suffrage. Instead—it became the sole province of the General Assembly to determine who should be admitted as a freeman eligible to vote.

The General Assembly established various qualifications for the suffrage privilege from time to time. In 1723–24, it passed an act granting freeman-status to any "freeholder of lands, tenements or hereditaments in such towns where he shall be admitted free, of the value of one hundred pounds, or to the value of forty shillings per annum, or the eldest son of such freeholder." Later, the value of property requisite for voting was increased to two hundred pounds and in 1746 to four hundred pounds. In 1760 it was reduced to forty pounds and in 1798 to one hundred and thirty-four dollars or a rental of seven dollars per annum.

Thus the situation remained in Rhode Island until 1840. By then, the qualifications for voting had disenfranchised approximately one half of the adult male population. It was estimated that about nineteen towns having a total population of only 3,500 voters, returned over half the members of the General Assembly, so that less than 1,800 voters controlled the policies of a state of 108,000 population. Another vexing feature established that a suit in debt or tort could be instituted only if the plaintiff were a freeholder or had one endorse his writ!

The non-voting population resented the inactive role they were required to play in the state's politics. There was much agitation for change. The General Assembly, however, was adamant. As is true in most crises, a leader arose who played a decisive part in resolving it. The leader this time was Thomas Wilson Dorr. Strangely enough, although he espoused the cause of the disenfranchised, he was a Federalist by birth and environment. The son of a prosperous manufacturer who occupied a good social position, he was born in 1805, attended Phillips Exeter Academy as a boy, and was graduated from Harvard in 1823. He then went to New York where he studied law under Chancellor Kent and was admitted to the bar. Kent later acknowledged that several of the changes made in his *Commentaries* were based on Dorr's recommendations. Returning to Providence to practice law, Dorr began his political career as a representative in the Rhode Island Assembly in 1834.

That same year a convention assembled at Providence to liberalize the franchise requirements. As a member of the Committee which reported to the people, Dorr became influential in the movement. The landowners in the General Assembly however, continuing their stubborn course, refused to allow any reform.

By 1840, Rhode Island was the only state in the union which did not practice universal free manhood suffrage. The disenfranchised decided finally that the situation was intolerable and had to be remedied. Under the leadership of Dorr, they therefore set their plans to achieve what the citizens of other colonies had accomplished after the Revolution—the adoption of a constitution and a new form of government. Immediately after the Revolution it had been a comparatively simple process to do this; but what was the effect of Rhode Island's failure to have done so for so many years? Had its residents conceded their right to change their form of government by reason of their default? The failure of the Charter of 1663 to provide for the calling of a constitutional convention obviously created many additional problems.

WITH DORR AS THE guiding force the Rhode Island Suffrage Association was formed, dedicated to achieving the vote for the disenfranchised. Popular meetings, parades, and agitation became the order of the day. "A peaceful revolution" was demanded. Ignore the constituted authorities — call a constitutional convention by popular vote — frame and adopt a new written constitution which would grant the suffrage to all males over twenty-one. Thus began the movement that led to the Dorr Revolution the following year.

More petitions were presented by the Dorrites to the General Assembly for the desired relief and for a constitutional convention. In 1841 the General Assembly attempted to appease the Dorrites by calling a convention to frame a constitution. To many people's chagrin, however, the adoption or rejection of the new constitution was left to those who were eligible to vote under the charter, namely, the landowners and their oldest sons. The Dorrites refused to accept this course; they continued their popular agitation for reform.

In April, 1841, after a grand parade and mass meeting to which thousands were attracted, the Dorrites arranged for a popular convention on election day at Newport. There a suffragists' constitutional convention was approved. With Dorr at the helm, a constitution was framed which extended the suffrage to all males over twenty-one. In the month of December, 1841, this Constitution was voted on by the people. Approximately 14,000 voted in favor, 100 against it. Of the ballots cast in favor, over 4,900 represented qualified voters, a majority even of the legal voters. The Convention then resolved:

"That said constitution rightfully ought to be and is, the paramount law and constitution of the State of Rhode Island and Providence Plantations, and we do further resolve and declare for ourselves and in behalf of the people whom we represent, that we will establish said Constitution and defend the same by all necessary means."

By this time, however, Charter Government officials,

who had offered little resistance to the Dorrite movement, became greatly concerned by the turn of events. They warned the people that their action was illegal and "that this General Assembly will maintain its own proper authority and protect and defend the legal and constitutional rights of the people." They then called their own convention which framed a constitution whose terms substantially complied with the demands of the Dorrites. Unfortunately, the Dorrites, believing they had already adopted a constitution voted against it, as did also the conservative landowners. The result was a defeat for the proposed constitution in March 1842 by 676 votes—8,013 to 8,689.

And now all realized that they were sitting on a powder keg. Excitement ran high and feeling became so bitter that it even divided members of families.

To add to the confusion, the justices of the Rhode Island Supreme Court rendered an advisory opinion that "the convention which formed the People's Constitution assembled without law; that the votes in favor of it were given without law; and however strong an expression of public opinion they might present, their constitution was not the paramount law of the land and was of no binding force whatever, and that any attempt to carry it into effect would be treason against the state if not against the United States."

The General Assembly then enacted a law declaring all acts of Dorr's Popular Party illegal and that anyone accepting office under its constitution would be guilty of treason. A local newspaper declared jocularly that even the Dey of Algiers could not enforce such a law and it became known as the "Algerine Law." The members of the Law and Order Party thereafter were scornfully called "Algerine" by the Dorrites.

THE SITUATION REACHED THE DANGER point when the Popular Party threw down the gauntlet and announced its constitution adopted and in effect. It then elected an entire slate of state officials with Dorr as Governor. In May, 1842, there were two governments and two Governors in the state of Rhode Island!

It was about this time that the Charter Governor, Samuel Ward King, wrote his letter to President Tyler seeking help. President Tyler replied that he regretted "the unhappy conditions of things in Rhode Island." The controversies, however, were "questions of municipal regulation . . . with which this Government can have nothing to do." As president of the United States he had no authority to anticipate a revolutionary movement. He did indicate that he would step in if insurrection broke out and that he would recognize the existing government of the state. This letter strengthened Governor King's hand and many leaders of the Populist Party who were elected to office under the Suffragist Constitution declined to accept.

On May 3rd, Dorr was inaugurated Governor at the first and only meeting of the Populist Legislature. The State Building being locked, they met in an unoccupied foundry building. As a result, it was called the "Foundry Legislature." Unfortunately for Dorr, he and his aides hesitated to take decisive action and failed to seize the state capital, although they had the military means to do so.

In the meantime, Governor King proclaimed Martial Law and offered a $5,000 reward for the capture of Dorr. He also arrested all the Dorrite officials he could seize. Dorr appealed to Washington for help. Though he received a sympathetic audience from the Democrats privately, President Tyler refused to encourage him. All over the country, the democratic newspapers poured out invective on Governor King and supported Dorr. Tammany Hall offered to help him with money and men!

Dorr then decided to fight. He appealed for help to the people of Rhode Island and urged them to join his troops. There were some minor clashes in which, although no mortalities occurred, there was plenty of excitement. Dorr's followers began to desert him and he was forced to flee to New Hampshire to avoid arrest.

The Charter Government, realizing that it had to appease the people eventually, called another constitutional convention. This time, however, it gave the vote to

TO THE CITIZENS
OF PROVIDENCE!!!
You are reqested FORTHWITH to repair to the
State Arsenal and TAKE ARMS.
SAMUEL W. KING.
Governor of the State of Rhode Island.
Providence, May 17, 1842, 6 o'clock P. M.

all native males twenty-one years of age or more, except Indians, convicts and paupers. The constitution framed by this convention was subsequently adopted in 1843, and has remained the constitution of Rhode Island to this day. This constitution justified Dorr's position, for it completely accepted the suffrage program of the Populist Party.

OUT OF THE DORR REBELLION arose a landmark case which stirred the country politically almost to a fever pitch. Martin Luther, a shoemaker was chosen moderator of a town meeting held under the Dorr Constitution. He was indicted for serving as a moderator and receiving votes contrary to the "Algerine Law." Luther escaped to Massachusetts when martial law was declared. His home was broken into and his family molested during his absence by some men headed by Luther Borden, under an order of arrest issued by the Charter Government. Upon his return after the 1843 Constitution had been adopted, he was arrested, tried and fined $500 and imprisoned for six months. Claiming that he was a resident of Massachusetts, Luther prior thereto brought an action for trespass against Borden and his men, in the United States Circuit Court in November, 1842. Borden justified his action as sanctioned by the Charter Government under a decree of martial law. Luther in rebuttal maintained that the charter government had expired on May 3rd when the People's Constitution became effective, and he moved the court to instruct the jury that this was so, and that "a majority of the free white male citizens of Rhode Island, of 21 years and upwards, had a right to reassume the powers of government and establish a written constitution and that having exercised such right, the preexisting charter government became null and void." In essence, he argued, his right to live under a republican form of government guaranteed by the Constitution had been denied him by the Charter Government and he asked the Circuit Court to enforce that right. Judge Story ruled in favor of the defendants, exceptions were taken, the jury found for the defendants and an appeal was taken to the Supreme Court of the United States. And thus the celebrated case of *Luther v. Borden* presented to the highest court of the land the question whether the right to a republican form of government in a state could be resolved by the federal courts.

Luther v. Borden, aroused much controversy in the leading papers of the country. "The decision," said a Democratic paper, "will determine whether the American doctrine proclaimed in the Declaration of Independence or the doctrine of the divine right of rulers avowed in the manifests of the holy alliances of Europe is the real theory of our institutions. A vast responsibility to the country and to all times rests upon the Supreme Court in this mighty cause."

Although counsel for both sides were prepared to argue the appeal in 1845, 1846, and 1847, argument was postponed until some vacancies on the bench were filled, as it was felt that the case was too important politically to be considered by less than its full membership. It was therefore not until January 22, 1848, that the argument took place. The argument lasted six days and the political excitement engendered by it was intense. The leading attorneys of the Democratic party represented the plaintiff. Daniel Webster and another leading Whig presented the case for the defendants.

A Whig paper commenting on Webster's argument stated: "Mr. Webster demolished what was left of Dorrism. His argument was alike brilliant and profound . . . his speech . . . is perhaps the best exposition of constitutional liberty ever made . . . The Courtroom was crowded with ladies and distinguished gentlemen to listen to the great effort."

Another aspect of this case bears comment. Most of the judges on the bench were politically chosen from the Democratic party. There was great fear that this political partisanship would be reflected in the Court's decision. A Whig paper stressed this point:

"As Loco-Focoism made some capital out of this question in the contest of 1844 . . . our tribunal of highest resort, which is about to settle the law of the matter authoritatively, is almost entirely Loco-Foco, the only Whig on the bench being John McLean of Ohio, and he a very moderate partisan. The case comes up as an appeal of the Dorrites from the District Court, and the first of their seven points is as follows: "That sovereignty of the People is supreme and may act in forming a government without the assent of the existing government . . . We can't believe they really think their case has a leg to stand upon. At all events, we rejoice that the decision rests with Judges of their own party, appointed by Presidents of their own choice; and we trust these Judges will meet it manfully, deciding the question on its merits . . . Let us have Dorrism fairly weighed and measured in the Supreme Court of the Union."

THE DEMOCRATIC PRESS WAS VICIOUS in its attack. A fundamental principle was involved in this case — Have the people the right to change their form of government? Webster's argument that a new constitution could be adopted by the people of a state only in a manner prescribed by statute or previous practice was ridiculed. It was "worthy of a monarchist and a despiser of everything democratic or republican. It is in the very face and eyes of the institutions of this country."

Chief Justice Taney read the opinion of the Court in the January, 1849 term before a highly partisan crowd. He held that Article IV, Section 4 of the United States Constitution, which guarantees a republican form of government when in issue, could not be resolved by the judiciary. It was primarily a political question and hence non-justiciable.

"Under this article of the Constitution," he declared, "it rests with Congress to decide what government is the established one in a State. For as the United States guarantee to each state a republican form of government, Congress must necessarily decide what government is established in the State before it can determine whether it is republican or not." Once Congress so decides "its decision is binding on every other department of the government, and could not be questioned in a judicial tribunal."

By an Act of 1795, the President of the United States had the power of deciding when to suppress an insurrection in a state to effectuate the Guaranty Clause of the Constitution. In the instant case, he had actually recognized the Governor of the Charter Government as the executive power of the State, promising to offer him military support when deemed necessary, although he had not called out the militia. "After the President has acted and called out the militia, is a Circuit Court of the United States authorized to inquire whether his decision was right? Could the court, while the parties were actually contending in arms for the possession of the government, call witnesses before it and inquire which party represented a majority of the people? If the judicial power extends so far, the guarantee contained in the Constitution of the United States is a guarantee of anarchy, and not of order."

Thus, as Mr. Justice Brennan, writing for the Court in the landmark case of *Baker v. Carr* a 113 years later, clearly expressed it, several factors were thought by Taney to make the question in *Luther v. Borden* "political." They were "The commitment to the other branches [of the government, such as the Congress and the President] of the decision as to which is the lawful state government; the unambiguous action by the President, in recognizing the charter government as the lawful authority; the need for finality in the executive's decision; and the lack of criteria by which a court could determine which form of government was republican."

Incidentally, Taney considered this case as one of first instance, which in a sense it was in its frame of reference. It has been pointed out, however, that *Luther v. Borden* was antedated by *Ware v. Hylton*, holding that the Supreme Court could not pass upon whether a treaty had been broken and *Martin v. Mott*, which held that the President had exclusive and unreviewable power to determine when the militia should be called out. Any of these could have been considered "political questions."

Judge Woodbury dissented with Taney on the issue whether the Supreme Court could examine the legality of the Rhode Island regime of martial law, but agreed with him on his holding that *Luther v. Borden* presented a political and not a judicial question. Judges Catron, Daniel and McKinley, for various reasons, did not sit.

THE INTEGRITY AND INDEPENDENCE of the Court was upheld by this decision for it was a defeat for the Democratic party by Democratic appointees to the bench. In this sense, it was influential in establishing the reputation of the Court as nonpartisan.

Dorr returned to Rhode Island voluntarily, was tried for treason before the State Supreme Court and sentenced to solitary confinement at hard labor for life. He was committed June 27, 1844. The severity of the sentence aroused great public sympathy for Dorr, the "Martyr Governor." Agitation for Dorr's release finally made itself felt and in 1845 an act of General Amnesty was passed and he was released from jail after having served 12 months of his term. He came out a disappointed, broken-hearted man. In poor health, he lived in retirement until his death on December 27, 1854. Although this was an ignoble end for so altruistic a person, Dorr at least lived long enough to know that his purpose had been accomplished and his position vindicated.

Chief Justice White considered *Luther v. Borden* to be "the leading and absolutely controlling case" on the justiciability of enforcement of Article IV, Section 4 of the Federal Constitution. Since *Luther v. Borden,* the Supreme Court has refused to allow the Guaranty Clause to be invoked "as the source of a constitutional standard for invalidating state action." In this respect, the Court has refused to consider whether the delegation by a state to an agency, of power to control milk prices violated republican government, or that invalidation of state reapportionment statute by referendum negates republican government, or that initiative and referendum negated republican government, or that the alleged improper determination by the Kentucky Legislature of a contested gubernatorial election deprived voters of republican government. These were all "political" issues and had to be resolved by the political departments of the government.

Until the historic case of *Baker v. Carr,* was decided in 1962, it was generally assumed that State legislative malapportionment plans were not justiciable in the federal courts as they involved "political questions." The 1946 case of *Colegrove v. Green* clearly stood for this proposition, the Supreme Court there holding that an Illinois State apportionment law which created Congressional districts of glaring population inequality was non-justiciable in the federal courts as it presented a question "of a peculiarly

78

BY HIS EXCELLENCY,

SAMUEL WARD KING,

GOVERNOR, CAPTAIN-GENERAL, AND COMMANDER-IN-CHIEF OF THE STATE OF
RHODE-ISLAND AND PROVIDENCE PLANTATIONS.

A PROCLAMATION.

WHEREAS on the eighth day of June instant, I issued a Proclamation, offering a reward of one thousand dollars for the delivery of the fugitive Traitor, THOMAS WILSON DORR, to the proper civil authority: and whereas the said Thomas Wilson Dorr having returned to this State and assumed the command of a numerous body of armed men, in open rebellion against the Government thereof, has again *fled* the summary justice which awaited him; I do therefore, by virtue of authority in me vested, and by advice of the Council, hereby offer an additional reward of four thousand dollars for the apprehension and delivery of the said Thomas Wilson Dorr to the Sheriff of the County of Newport or Providence, within three months from the date hereof.

L.S. GIVEN under my hand and the seal of said State, at the City of Providence, this twenty-ninth day of June, in the year of our Lord one thousand eight hundred and forty-two, and of the Independence of the United States of America the sixty-sixth.

SAMUEL WARD KING.

BY HIS EXCELLENCY'S COMMAND:
HENRY BOWEN, Secretary of State.

political nature and therefore not meet for judicial determination." The dissenting opinion, however, suggested that the question involved was "exactly the kind that the equal protection clause was intended to prohibit," a concept which was used with telling effect in *Baker v. Carr.*

In this case the issue of gross malapportionment alleged by voters in Tennessee was held by the Supreme Court to be justiciable in the federal courts as a violation of the equal protection clause of the 14th Amendment rather than the Guaranty Clause. Actually, the Court did not overrule *Luther v. Borden* or the *Colegrove* case. Writing for the Court, Mr. Justice Brennan said of *Luther v. Borden* that its significance in reapportionment cases is that "the Guaranty Clause is not a repository of judicially manageable standards which a court could utilize independently in order to identify a state's lawful government. The Court has since refused to resort to the Guaranty Clause — which alone has been invoked for the purpose — as the source of a constitutional standard for invalidating state action." The question of malapportionment on the other hand was not a "political" one. Rather the question involved was "the consistency of state action with the Federal Constitution. We have no question decided, or to be decided, by a political branch of government co-equal with this Court." No foreign embarrassment to the government, or grave disturbance at home would occur by the court's acceptance of the case. No policy determinations were involved for which judicially manageable standards were lacking. Only the judicial standards of the Equal Protection Clause of the 14th Amendment were involved and the appellants might conceivably have added a claim under the Guaranty Clause. But that in light of *Luther v. Borden* and other precedents, would have been "futile."

MR. JUSTICE BRENNAN, HOWEVER, ADDED the following caveat: "True, it must be clear that the Fourteenth Amendment Claim is not so enmeshed with those political question elements which render Guaranty Clause claims nonjusticiable as actually to present a political question itself. But we have found that not to be the case here."

Thus, the Court finally determined that the allegation of a denial of equal protection in malapportionment cases presents a justiciable constitutional cause of action. It is interesting to note that Mr. Justice Douglas, in his concurring opinion said: "The statements in *Luther v. Borden* that the guaranty (of a Republican Form of Government) is enforceable only by Congress or the Chief Executive is not maintainable. . . . The abdication of all judicial functions respecting voting rights, however justified by the peculiarities of the charter form of government in Rhode Island at the time of Dorr's Rebellion, states no general principle. It indeed is contrary to the cases discussed in the body of [Mr. Justice Brennan's] opinion—the modern decisions of the Court that give the full panoply of judicial protection to voting rights. Today, we would not say with Chief Justice Taney that it is no part of the judicial function to protect the right to vote of those "to whom it is denied by the written and established constitution and laws of the state."

Mr. Justice Frankfurter, on the contrary, in his dissenting opinion, maintained that *Baker v. Carr* "involves all of the elements that have made the Guarantee Clause cases non-justiciable. It is in effect, a Guarantee Clause masquerading under a different label."

Professor Frank has aptly summarized the concept of "political question". "It is," he complained, "measured by any of the normal responsibilities of a phrase or a definition, one of the least satisfactory terms known to the law." His conclusion well bears repetition: "It seems to me that the basic objective of a plan of government ought to be to put the responsibility for the decision of questions some place, and that the political question doctrine is useful when it operates to put responsibility at its best place, and is harmful when it puts the decision no place."

The
Dred Scott
Case

A Political Judgment
and a
Great Blunder

THE DRED SCOTT CASE HAS BEEN characterized as "a blunder—a blunder worse than a crime." It reflected a situation so untoward in the annals of the Supreme Court that the lesson it taught is indelibly impressed on the judicial mores of our country. How it all came to pass strains credulity—especially when one realizes that the case involved a poor, ignorant, negro slave, only mildly interested in the outcome and completely unconcerned with the tragic role he was playing in the history of his people. Dred Scott—the *person*—died as obscurely as he had lived. Yet he set the stage for one of the most dreadful debacles in the history of the Supreme Court and adumbrated a decision which "roused the country like a fire bell in the night."

Section eight of the Act of March 6, 1820 provided for the admission of Missouri into the United States. Popularly known as the Missouri Compromise, it prescribed that in all territory of the Louisiana Purchase north of 36° 30' north latitude, not included within the limits of Missouri, "slavery and involuntary servitude, otherwise than in the punishment of crimes, whereof the parties shall have been duly convicted, shall be, and is hereby, forever prohibited." The Missouri Compromise became a bone of contention between the North and the South from its very inception. In essence, it raised the inflammable question whether Congress could constitutionally legislate on the introduction or exclusion of slavery in the territories of the United States.

THIS TURBULENT PROBLEM festered and frequently erupted on the national scene. It came to a head shortly after the Mexican War. By then, Southern leaders, who formerly had favored the Missouri Compromise as a means of introducing slavery in Southern California, Arizona and New Mexico came to the conclusion that cotton and tobacco could not be grown profitably in most of the areas involved. The situation became more aggravated when California was admitted as a free state and when as a result of the Mexican War the boundless acres of the Northwest Territory were opened for settlement. Thoroughly dissatisfied with the effect of the Missouri Compromise, the South determined that it had to be repealed or declared unconstitutional. Only the Supreme Court, however, could resolve the constitutionality of the Missouri Compromise and as early as 1848 this was actually suggested in Congress. But whether the Supreme Court would assume jurisdiction of the problem even if presented in an actual case was doubted, for the Court generally had the reputation of avoiding political issues. Then came the Dred Scott case.

Dred Scott was a negro slave, whose parents had also been slaves. Born in Virginia, he was taken to Missouri by his master, Peter Blow, in 1827. An army surgeon, Dr. John Emerson, bought Scott from Blow in 1834 and took him the following year to Rock Island, Illinois, and a year or so later to Fort Snelling, which was located in that part of the Wisconsin Territory which later became Minnesota. By the time Dr. Emerson returned to St. Louis, Missouri, in 1838, Scott had been married to a negress owned by his master, and two children had been born of the union. Six years later, Dr. Emerson died, leaving a will in which he appointed his brother-in-law, John F. A. Stanford, his executor, and left his property to his wife in trust for his daughter.

Mrs. Emerson found ownership of the Scotts embarrassing. She was not interested in owning slaves; yet there was some question whether she could emancipate Scott, since she held him in trust. Again, selling a slave was not done in polite society in those days, except as a punishment. Hence, when she moved to Massachusetts, Mrs. Emerson simply abandoned Scott, leaving him to fend for himself. Poor Scott, left to his own devices, with a family to support, turned to the son of his former master for help. Scott not only lacked the desire to better himself, but in addition was unskilled and shiftless. As long as Blow took care of his family's needs, Scott was quite content with his lot. Blow, however, saw it differently. He was burdened with the financial problems of someone else's slaves and there seemed to be no end to it.

Blow consulted the law firm of Field and Hall, who, it is claimed, saw an unusual opportunity to test not only the constitutionality of the Missouri Compromise, but also earn a good fee. If Scott could establish in court that by reason of his residence in an area in which slavery had been prohibited, namely, Ft. Snelling, he had obtained his freedom by operation of law, he could then claim back wages from the Emerson estate for the years he had worked illegally as a slave.

The attorneys for the Emerson estate found it necessary to defend the action.

LITTLE DID SCOTT REALIZE when he placed his cross on a petition in 1846 seeking his freedom and that of his family, the historic consequences that would ensue. From these prosaic beginnings erupted one of the most dramatic and fascinating *causes célèbres* in American history, "fraught with more momentous consequences than ever came before an Anglo-Saxon Tribunal."

Scott's action sought his freedom on the theory that he had been taken from slave territory into free territory by Dr. Emerson, and as a result he had become a free man under the Northwest Territory Ordinance of 1787 and under the Missouri Compromise Act of 1820. Once having attained this status, he alleged, he could not be returned to slavery, despite his return to a slave state (Missouri).

The case of "Scott (a man of color) v. Emerson" was heard by a jury in the Circuit Court of Missouri in April 1847. The Circuit Judge instructed the jury to find for the defendant, and the jury dutifully complied. Scott's attorneys instituted a new action, however, and this time (January, 1850) he was successful, the jury bringing in a verdict in his favor. The Emerson estate promptly appealed the verdict to the Supreme Court of Missouri, where it rested for more than two years. In March, 1852, the Supreme Court of Missouri by a vote of two to one finally decided to reverse the trial court. It held that under the laws of Missouri, no matter what status he had attained in free territory, upon Scott's return to Missouri, he reverted once again to slavedom.

A noted anti-slavery lawyer, and a leader of the Missouri bar, Roswell M. Field, was persuaded to take an interest in the case. He decided to abandon the original suit and institute an action of trespass *vi et armis* in the United States Circuit Court for the district of Missouri, in St. Louis, on Scott's behalf, alleging a technical assault by the defendant on Scott, his wife, and his children. By this time, a new defendant had been introduced into the case, one John Sandford. Mrs. Emerson's new husband, Dr. C. C. Chaffee, a Republican Congressman from Massachusetts and a well-known abolitionist, either embarrassed by the proceedings, or perhaps encouraged to believe that he was helping his cause by keeping the case before the public eye, arranged for a dummy sale of the Scott slaves to his wife's brother-in-law, John F. A. Sandford (or Sanford) of New York, who was also an executor of the Emerson estate.

The landmark case of *Dred Scott v. Sandford,* was commenced on November 2, 1853, Scott and his family claiming $9,000 in damages. As the action was for a technical assault, it was understood that if the Scott family were slaves of the defendant, the action could not be maintained. Scott also alleged that he was a citizen of

Missouri in order to give the federal court jurisdiction based on diversity of citizenship (Sandford being a citizen of New York). Pleading in abatement, Sandford interposed that the Court lacked jurisdiction, as Scott was a descendant of Negro slaves of pure African blood and hence could not be a citizen of Missouri. When the Court sustained Scott's demurrer to this plea, Sandford pleaded in bar that Scott was his slave and that the assault could thus be justified. The case went to trial and on May 15, 1854, the jury returned a verdict in favor of the defendant, finding that Scott was Sandford's slave. Scott took a writ of error to the Supreme Court of the United States.

On May 30, 1854, even before the Dred Scott case was docketed in the Supreme Court, Congress enacted the Kansas-Nebraska Act, repealing the Missouri Compromise Act and establishing the "intent of Congress not to legislate slavery into any Territory or State nor to exclude it therefrom." This was a terrible blow to the anti-slavery people, and in seeking a new avenue of attack, they hit upon the potentialities pregnant in the Scott case. They had nothing to lose in light of the Kansas-Nebraska Act, and yet morally they could gain great momentum if the Supreme Court reversed the findings below. Especially important to them was the possibility that the Supreme Court, in arriving at a decision, would declare the constitutional authority of Congress to legislate on slavery. On the other hand, the Southern leaders, very much disturbed by the unrest stirred up by their adversaries, seized upon the Scott Case as a splendid opportunity for an assertion by the Supreme Court of the unconstitutionality of any Congressional action restricting slavery.

AWARE OF THE IMPORTANCE of the case, Southern leaders enlisted the aid of leading members of the Supreme Court Bar to represent Sandford. U. S. Senator Henry S. Geyer of Missouri, the ranking lawyer of the St. Louis Bar, and Reverdy Johnson, former Attorney-General of the U. S., noted nationally for receiving the largest fees of any member of the American Bar, volunteered their services.

In desperation, Scott's lawyer wrote on December 24,

1854, to Montgomery Blair, a well-known St. Louis lawyer, for help. Blair was then in Washington.

"A year ago," Field stated, "I was employed to bring a suit in favor of one Dred Scott, a black man held in slavery. . . . The question involved is the much vexed one whether the removal by the master of his slave to Illinois or Wisconsin marks an absolute emancipation. . . . If you or any other gentleman at W. should feel interest enough in the case to give it such attention as to bring it to a hearing and decision by the Court, the course of humanity may perhaps be subserved. At all events a much disputed question would be settled by the highest court of the nation. . . . It is so late on the docket that it will hardly be reached this term." Blair consented.

The case was argued in great detail from February 11th to February 14th, 1856. Scott's appeal was based primarily on three points: 1) That he became a free man when he was taken by his master to Illinois and Ft. Snelling under the provisions of the Missouri Compromise. 2) That he could not be again enslaved on his return to Missouri. 3) That as a free man he was a "citizen" within the meaning of that word as used in article III, section 2 of the Constitution of the United States extending the jurisdiction of the Supreme Court and other Federal Courts established by Congress to controversies "between citizens of different states." Geyer and Johnson argued to the contrary and also attacked the constitutionality of the eighth section of the Missouri Compromise, prohibiting slavery north of 36° 30'.

The Supreme Court of the United States was held in the highest esteem by the American public and the Bar at the time of the appeal. It was regarded as the last judicial refuge of impartiality and conservatism, respected not only for its learning and sincerity but for its mental vigor as well. This reputation the Court had earned by reason of its careful and prudent approach to the sectional problems and political controversies stirring the country. The Court had meticulously circumvented any appearance of partiality in the slave case of *Prigg* in 1842 and *Van Zandt* in

1847, by basing its decisions purely on legal construction of Consitutional provisions. On the whole it appeared to be perpetuating the traditional concepts set for the Court by Marshall. Only a revolution in the Court's attitude toward Constitutional interpretation could have upset its Olympian image, and this was not anticipated. True, some opinions were expressed that the Court's decision might be influenced by the majority of Southerners on the Bench, Chief Justice Taney of Maryland, Wayne of Georgia, Catron of Tennessee, Campbell of Alabama, and Daniel of Virginia. Then again, although Grier came from Pennsylvania and Nelson from New York, they were known for the states-rights position they invariably followed. Only McLlean, of Ohio, and Curtis, of Massachusetts were considered as "safe" by the anti-slavery elements. Be that as it may have been, however, the Court was expected to carry on as cautiously in the Scott case as it had done in the past.

Actually the Supreme Court was presented with a comparatively simple problem, one in which with ease it could have avoided the political difficulties apparent in the case. For the Federal Circuit Court had held below that, since the highest Missouri Court had ruled that Scott as a Negro descended from Negro slaves could not become a citizen, it was bound by precedent to follow its decision, and hence the Court lacked jurisdiction, there being no diversity of citizenship. All the Supreme Court had to do, therefore, was to follow the rule laid down by Chief Justice Taney in *Strader v. Graham*, decided in 1851, that "every state has an undoubted right to determine the *status*, or domestic and social condition of the persons domiciled within its territory," not inconsistent with the Constitution of the United States. It could then dismiss the writ of error for failure of jurisdiction.

As a matter of fact, this was the first reaction of the justices in their private conference. Avoidance of the major controversy was uppermost in their thinking. But the Court found it quite difficult to avoid the Constitutional problem. The bitter and inflammatory political situation that followed the repeal of the Missouri Compromise drew the Court into the vortex of the great debate on whether Congress could constitutionally exclude slavery from federal territory. Rumors and speculations as to the justices' thinking were published by Horace Greeley's New York *Tribune* and other abolitionist papers. Southern leaders subtly attempted to "brain wash" the more sympathetic judges on the bench at social functions and by other means. A presidential election was being held that year and it was important that the election of their candidate, James Buchanan not be jeopardized by any action taken by the Supreme Court.

For a while it appeared that the court would manage to avoid involvement in the political struggle over slavery. Nelson was assigned to write a brief opinion avoiding all reference to the Constitutional aspects of the case and deciding it on technical grounds. The justices' conferences, however, provoked such disagreement that it appeared as though each justice would write an independent opinion. Taney feared that their failure to agree would be reflected in the presidential campaign debates to the detriment of the country and the Court's prestige. He therefore, quickly accepted Nelson's request for a reargument of the case on the technical question whether the Court could consider Scott's citizenship plea. Taney announced on May 12, 1856, with obvious relief, that reargument of the case would be heard by the Court in the December term, thus neatly withholding the Court's decision until after the Presidential election.

The Court's action was hailed by the press as a wise and diplomatic course to take. The *New York Courier*, for example, wrote: "The great tribunal to which the country has been taught for nearly three quarters of a century to look to for the dispensation of justice upon the principles of law, is not prepared to rush into the political arena, and ruffle its ermine in the strife of politicans and the squabbles of demagogues." The *New York Tribune*, however, characteristically commented that "the black gowns have come to be artful dodgers."

When the Court convened on December 12, 1856, for

the reargument, it was confronted by an important new development. Buchanan, a Southern sympathizer, had been elected; and the case which had till then received little notice in the press suddenly blossomed into a *cause célèbre*. Both the slavery and anti-slavery interests now fully realized how significant the Court's decision might be. Partisan newspapers devoted many columns to discussing its implication. "Taking into consideration the state of the country," predicted the *New York Courier,* "it may well be regarded as the most important that has ever been brought before that Tribunal. . . . The issue is of vast importance in itself, but there is another problem connected with it of far greater consequence. It is, whether the Supreme Court is a political Court made up of political judges. . . . How will the Judges abide the test now before them? . . . The Court, in trying this case, is itself on trial—a trial as vitally involving its character before the American people, as a confidence in its impartiality is vital to its authority. . . ."

This time Montgomery Blair had the assistance of George Tickner Curtis, of Boston, brother of Justice Curtis, to argue the constitutional points. Geyer and Reverdy Johnson appeared for Sandford again. The courtroom was filled to capacity with lawyers, jurists, Washington correspondents and political leaders. Blair's argument was described by an observer, as that of "a close, logical reasoner, a man of diligent and careful research, strong power of thought, but of a very poor pleader." Reverdy Johnson's effort was that of "an old stager in the elecutionary list. . . . The learned barrister entered into his argument, with all the fervor and power of appeal that has characterized the most ultra-congressional and stump speeches for slavery. . . . The passions of his audience, the prejudices of the Judges were appealed to, until I came to the realization of the fact that our Supreme Court is composed of men, mere men after all, with the like passions and prejudices of the masses. . . . The closing argument of Mr. Curtis of Boston was able, clear and, to me, conclusive." Curtis's was the briefest of all the arguments (which had continued for four days), as the Court had limited him to one hour and 15 minutes. Judge Catron later told Judge Curtis that his brother's argument was the best he had heard in the Court. Curtis was even congratulated by several Southern Senators.

FOR REASONS OF TANEY'S HEALTH (he was then close to eighty years of age), the illness of Judge Wayne, and the grief of Judge Daniels for the death of his young wife by accidental burning, the case was not taken up in the judges' private conference until late in February. Despite the lack of a conference, however, the newspapers maintained the country's intense interest by reporting rumors about the judges' thinking and continuing to stress the importance of the decision to the national welfare. Dred Scott himself took a philosophical attitude toward his case, treating it all with unpretentious humor. The *Washington Union*, a St. Louis paper, described him as laughing heartily when talking of "de fuss dey made dar in Washington" about him.

Then the case took a new and dramatic turn. Shortly before the judges' conference, President-elect Buchanan arrived in Washington to arrange his affairs before the inauguration, scheduled for March 4, 1857. Buchanan was sincerely dedicated to settling the acrimonious debate on slavery, in the interest of peace; but as a Southern sympathizer he could see no other course than to vindicate the policies of the slavery interests and defeat the abolitionists. What the Supreme Court did in the case was of vital interest to him, as he was then writing his inaugural address; and he was concerned with making a definite proposal on the introduction of slavery in the territories. He wrote to Justice Catron, who had been an intimate friend of his for many years, seeking information as to when the Court's decision might be made public. Although such leaks would be censured today, it was not unusual in those days for a Supreme Court justice to reveal in confidence to a close friend or relative, some background of a case being considered by the Court.

Catron replied: "It rests entirely with the Chief Justice to move in the matter. So far he has not said anything to me on the subject of Scott's case. It was before the judges in conference on two separate occasions about a year ago, when the judges expressed their views pretty much at large. All our opinions were published in the *New York Tribune,* the next day after the opinions were expressed. This was of course a gross breach of confidence, as the information could only come from a judge who was present. That circumstance I think, has made the chief more wary than usual."

He then continued that he would advise Buchanan as soon as he received more definite information. Some days later, he informed Buchanan that in all probability the case would be decided in conference a few days hence, the decision to be announced at the end of the month. Inasmuch as the opinion would avoid the constitutional issue, however, he regretted that Buchanan would not be able to use it favorably in his inaugural address.

When the judges met in conference, the majority appeared to be still determined to follow the precedent of the *Strader Case,* and thus to be governed by the law of Missouri on Scott's status as a slave. Nelson, of New York, was appointed to write an opinion sustaining the decision of the Circuit Court. And this he actually did write. But then came one of those imponderable developments, foreseen but not reckoned with by the majority of the Court. First McLean, who had presidential aspirations, and then Curtis announced that they planned to write extended dissenting opinions, the former giving a history of slavery in the United States from the biased viewpoint of the "Free Soilers," the latter on the Constitutionality of the Missouri Compromise.

Then Judge Wayne, of Georgia, perhaps influenced by the pressures exerted on him by Southern leaders, and sincerely imbued with the idea that the time had come in the interest of the country for the Supreme Court to decide the issue of slavery once and for all — in favor of slavery — assumed the mantle of leadership, determined to use

Engraved by Liman Brothers.

the Scott case as a vehicle for denying the authority of Congress to regulate slavery. Wayne's suggestion received added strength from Taney, Campbell, Daniel and Catron's realization that the dissenting opinions had to be answered lest their effect on the public would lead to more agitation. Above all, they reasoned, as Wayne did, that perhaps a forthright Olympian declaration by the Supreme Court on the slavery issue, even though it meant meddling in politics, might permanently settle the terrible crisis the country was undergoing. Judge Grier, however, remained unpersuaded that this was the proper course to take.

Hence Catron wrote to Buchanan on February 19, 1857, asking him to use his influence with Grier, to persuade him to join his Southern brethren.

"The Dred Scott case has been before the Judges several times since last Saturday," he advised Buchanan in confidence, "and I think you may safely say in your Inaugural: 'that the question involving the Constitutionality of the Missouri Compromise line is presented to the appropriate Tribunal to decide: to wit, to the Supreme Court of the United States. It is due to its high and independent character to suppose that it will decide and settle a controversy which has so long and seriously agitated the country, and which *must* ultimately be decided by the Supreme Court. And until the case now before it (on two arguments) presenting the direct question is disposed of, I would deem it improper to express any opinion on the subject.' A majority of my brethren will be forced up to this point by two dissentients. Will you drop [Justice] Grier a line saying how necessary it is, and how good the opportunity is to settle the agitation by an affirmative decision of the Supreme Court, the one way or the other. . . . He has no doubt about the question on the main contest, but has been persuaded to take the smooth handle for the sake of repose."

BUCHANAN REPLIED that he hoped the decision would be announced before his Inaugural—especially as he now knew what it would contain. Catron responded he would do everything possible as most of the judges were prepared to act. But, he added, "I want Grier *speeded*."

Upon Buchanan's urging, Grier replied: "Your letter came to hand this morning. I have taken the liberty to show it, in confidence to our mutual friends, Judge Wayne, and the Chief Justice. We fully appreciate and concur in your views as to the desirableness at this time of having an expression of the opinion of the Court on this troublesome question. With their concurrence, I will give you in confidence the history of the case before us, with the probable result."

After indicating the arguments that took place in conference, he added: "Those who hold a different opinion from Messrs. McLean and Curtis on the power of Congress and the validity of the Compromise Act feel compelled to express their opinions on the subject. Nelson and myself refusing to commit ourselves. A majority including all the Judges south of Mason and Dixon's line, agreeing in the result, but not in their reasons — as the question will be thus forced upon us, I am anxious that it should not appear that the line of latitude should mark the line of division in the Court. I feel also that the opinion of the majority will fail of much of its effect if founded on clashing and inconsistent arguments. On conversation with the Chief Justice, I have agreed to concur with him. Brother Wayne and myself will also use our endeavors to get Brothers Daniel and Campbell and Catron to do the same. So that if the question must be met there will be an opinion of the Court upon it, if possible, without the contradictory views which would weaken its force. . . . There will therefore be six, if not seven (perhaps Nelson will remain neutral) who will decide the Compromise law of 1820 to be of *non-effect*. But the opinions will not be delivered before Friday the 6th of March. . . ."

AFTER THE SOUTHERN JUSTICES and Grier were prevailed upon by Wayne to adopt his plan, a motion was approved that Taney should write the Court's opinion "upon all questions involved," instead of Nelson. Hot and spirited arguments took place during the conference sessions.

Curtis later related that, at one time the judges' tempers became so frayed, Taney was compelled to reprimand them. "Brothers," he caustically admonished, "this is the Supreme Court of the United States. Take your seats." Curtis added: "We sat down like rebuked schoolboys." It became readily apparent that unanimity would never be achieved, and all the judges prepared to write their own opinions.

Buchanan was sworn in as President on March 4, 1857. It was a cold and blustery day. Shortly before Taney administered the oath of office, he had occasion to talk casually with the President-Elect. This was most unfortunate, for it started the rumor that Taney had given Buchanan advance information on the Dred Scott decision, thus offering Buchanan the opportunity to use it effectively in his inaugural address. Buchanan stated that although he recognized "a difference of opinion has arisen in regard to the point of time when the people of a Territory shall decide the question [of slavery] for themselves, this is happily a matter of but little practical importance." "Besides" he benignly added, paraphrasing Catron's suggestion, "it is a judicial question which legitimately belongs to the Supreme Court of the United States before whom it is now pending, and will, it is understood, be speedily and finally settled. To their decision, in common with all good citizens, I shall cheerfully submit, whatever this may be . . ." The *New York Tribune*, however, voicing the reaction of the anti-slavery people, replied editorially to Buchanan: "You may 'cheerfully submit,' of course you will, to whatever the five slaveholders and two or three dough-faces on the bench of the Supreme Court may be ready to utter on this subject. But not one man who really desires the triumph of Freedom over slavery in the territories will do so. We may be constrained to obey as law, whatever that tribunal shall put forth; but happily this is a country in which the people make both laws and judges, and they will try their strength on the issue here presented."

Suffering from a cold he caught while standing bareheaded in the raw wind while he administered the oath to

Buchanan, Taney remained at home on March 5, putting the finishing touches to his opinion. On Friday, March 6th, while still weak from his illness, the aged Chief Justice read the opinion of the Court in the historic case of *Scott v. Sandford.* It took him almost two hours to deliver it. A jam-packed crowd listened with somber and respectful interest, apparently profoundly aware of the significance of the occasion. Judges Nelson and Catron then read separate opinions. Judges McLean and Curtis delivered their dissenting opinions the following day. Then separate opinions were read by Judges Daniel, Grier, Campbell, and Wayne. The court-room was packed once again that Saturday, reflecting the intense hold the fateful case had taken on the public.

Writing in 1928, Chief Justice Hughes commented that "it remains true that in three notable instances the Court has suffered from self-inflicted wounds. The first of these was the Dred Scott case." Carson in his history of the Supreme Court added "Upon this fair record but one blot appears. The 'damned spot' of the Dred Scott decision will not out . . ." The Dred Scott case is an example of how the majority of a Court can be influenced by a strong dissent to take a more extreme position than their better judgment dictates.

INSTEAD OF FOLLOWING the initial resolution to decide the Scott case on a technicality and thus to avoid political pitfalls, Taney attempted to settle a strong political controversy and failed horribly. Seeking to settle the slavery issue once and for all, he reasoned as follows in his opinion: A Negro could not become a citizen no matter what action a state might take, for the Constitution pertained only to members of the white race. This thesis he sought to prove by an elaborate exegesis on the history of slavery; an exegesis in which he adopted the thinking of Southern protagonists on slavery as an institution. Quoting from the Declaration of Independence's "We hold these truths to be self-evident: that all men are created equal . . .," he said: "the general words above quoted would seem to embrace the whole human family, and if they were used in a similar instrument at this day, would be so understood. But is too clear for dispute, that the enslaved African race were not intended to be included, and formed no part of the people who framed and adopted this declaration. . . . No one, we presume, supposes that any change in public opinion or feeling, in relation to this unfortunate race . . . should induce the court to give to the words of the Constitution a more liberal construction in their favor than they were intended to bear when the instrument was framed and adopted. If any of its provisions are deemed unjust, there is a mode prescribed in the instrument itself by which it may be amended; but while it remains unaltered, it must be construed now as it was understood at the time of its adoption. . . ."

Lincoln subsequently attacked this argument with telling effect in his debate with Douglas: "I think," he replied, "the authors of that notable instrument [the Declaration of Independence] intended to include all men, but they did not intend to declare all men equal in all respects. They did not mean to say all were equal in color, size, intellect, moral developments, or social capacity. They defined with tolerable distinctness in what respects they did consider all men created equal—equal in 'certain inalienable rights, among which are life, liberty, and the pursuit of happiness.' This they said and this they meant . . . they meant to set up a standard maxim for free society . . ."

The late Charles P. Curtis, commenting on the Taney and Lincoln approach to this problem aptly noted that "Though Taney and Lincoln were talking about the Declaration, they were both construing the Constitution. The difference between them is not only that Taney was wrong and Lincoln right. It is that Taney was ascribing to the words what he thought their authors intended and Lincoln was giving the authors credit for what their words meant. Men intend, words mean, though our language uses both terms indiscriminately Lincoln saw the difference, Taney did not."

Taney, in concluding this part of his essay on slavery

used an unfortunate expression which subjected him later to indignant attacks by the anti-slavery press. He wrote that at the time the Constitution was adopted Negroes were considered to be "so far inferior that they had no rights which the white man was bound to respect," but this was perverted into the assertion that "Negroes had no rights which the white man was bound to respect." Many were horrified that such an attitude should be expressed by the Chief Justice of the United States. No attempt was made to explain that it had been taken out of context. Of course the publication of this lie injured Taney's reputation and contributed heavily to the discrediting of the Court and of the Dred Scott opinion.

TANEY REASONED that since Dred Scott was not a citizen of Missouri he could not maintain an action in the federal circuit court. If Taney had stopped at this point, which he could easily have done under the circumstances and dismissed the case for lack of jurisdiction, he would have perhaps avoided the extreme derision and contempt directed at the Court and preserved its standing before the American public. But instead, he took the fatal plunge and considered the constitutionality of the Missouri Compromise, relating it to the question of Scott's freedom as affected by residence in Ft. Snelling and Illinois.

Taney held that the Missouri Compromise violated the Fifth Amendment to the Constitution for it deprived slaveowners of their property without due process of law. Therefore Scott never attained his freedom when he was taken to "free" territory, despite the Missouri Compromise. Although Taney suffered the bitterest criticism for this holding, it is doubly significant to us today.

Prior to Dred Scott, the Supreme Court had considered the due process clause as procedural due process. In *Murray's Lessee v. Hoboken Land and Improvement Co.* for example, in which a taxpayer challenged the sale of his property for unpaid taxes on the ground that he was not given notice, the court held in sustaining his argument that "we must look to those settled usages and modes of proceeding existing in the common and statute law of England before the emigration of our ancestors and which are shown not to have been unsuited to their civil and political condition by having been acted on after the settlement of this country." In the Dred Scott case, however, Taney gave a substantive effect to the due process clause for the first time, holding that the "due process" clause limited the power of Congress to confiscate property rights, no matter what procedure was set forth. "Thus the rights of property," he maintained, "are united with the rights of person, and placed on the same ground by the Fifth Amendment to the Constitution, which provides that no person shall be deprived of life, liberty, and property, without due process of law. And an Act of Congress which deprives a citizen of the United States of his liberty or property, merely because he came himself or brought his property into a particular territory of the United States, and who had committed no offense against the laws, could hardly be dignified with the name of due process of law."

When Taney declared the Missouri Compromise unconstitutional, it was the first time the Supreme Court had held an Act of Congress unconstitutional since *Marbury v. Madison,* in 1803.

Taney's third and final point was that Scott's status was governed by the decision of the Missouri court. As it had declared him a slave after his return from "free" territory, he was not a citizen and had no standing in court. The writ of error was therefore dismissed.

THE LACK OF UNANIMITY of the Court seriously damaged the authority of the decision despite its length and erudition. Only two judges concurred with him in his holding that a Negro could not become a citizen; one dissented; and the other five pointedly refrained from discussing the point. Taney received more support on the unconstitutionality of the Missouri Compromise in that six judges concurred with him, although Catron did so on different grounds. On Taney's third point, that the law of Missouri on Scott's status had to be followed, Nelson submitted the

Court's opinion and Taney and four other judges concurred.

McLean and Curtis of course dissented. McLean's dissent was of little importance, for he was seeking a presidential nomination and mainly used it as a sounding board for his political views. Curtis's dissent, however, was widely hailed for its refutation of all the points in Taney's opinion. Categorically stressing that Taney's opinion on the constitutionality of the Missouri Compromise was an *obiter dictum*, he emphatically stated: it was "an exertion of judicial power [transcending] the limits of the authority of the Court. . . . I do not consider it to be within the scope of the judicial power of the court to pass upon any question respecting the plaintiff's citizenship in Missouri save that raised by the plea to the jurisdiction, and I do not hold an opinion of this court, or of any court, binding when expressed on a question not legitimately before it." The Missouri Compromise, he argued was constitutional and negroes could become citizens. Curtis's dissent was given a great play in the abolitionist newspapers as an anti-slavery document. He had a reputation for conservatism, earned by defending the right of a slave owner to bring his slave into Massachusetts. Even later when Chief Judge Lemuel Shaw had upheld the Fugitive Slave Law in Massachusetts he had publicly concurred. That he should reverse himself was hailed by the anti-slavery advocates as an "honest" act.

From the moment the press reported the decision in the Scott case it was condemned in the North not only as a political tract, but also as part of a political scheme to deprive Congress of the authority to legislate on slavery. The mistake Taney made was to attempt to solve a political and economic problem while the nation was undergoing a major crisis on slavery. How else could one explain Taney's invalidation of the Missouri Act, when it had already been repealed by the Kansas-Nebraska Act of 1854? When Marshall declared an act of Congress unconstitutional in *Marbury v. Madison*, he did not attempt to settle a basic political question which had aroused the nation to a fever pitch. Rather he had discreetly limited his reasoning to the theoretical relationship of the Executive, Judicial and the Legislative powers in the American scheme of government. He had acted as a judicial statesman and his invoking of the "judicial review" power of the Supreme Court had served a valuable end. Taney had done otherwise, and soon therafter the court reaped the harvest it had sown.

An interesting by-play took place between Taney and Curtis. All the judges' opinion had been read in open court. Curtis filed his opinion with the clerk and then immediately sent a copy of his dissent to a Massachusetts paper for publication. Upon his return to Massachusetts, after a vacation, he learned that the opinions of the judges, including Taney's, had still not been published. He wrote to the clerk of the Court for a copy, for he had been advised that Taney intended to revise his opinion, substantially. The clerk replied that Taney, Wayne and Daniel, who had all remained in Washington, had ruled that none of the opinions would be released until they had officially appeared in Howard's Reports. This action rankled Curtis, for if Taney's opinion had been extensively altered, he wanted the opportunity to revise his dissent, if necessary. The correspondence that ensued between Taney and Curtis became so bitter, that soon thereafter Curtis resigned from the bench.

SOUTHERN LEADERS HAILED the Dred Scott decision as a great victory for their cause. "The nation has achieved a triumph," editorialized the *Richmond Enquirer*, "sectionalism" has been rebuked and abolitionism has been staggered. Another supporting pillar has been added to our institutions." The *New York Tribune* voiced the shocked reaction of the North: "Alas, that the character of the Supreme Court of the United States as an impartial judicial body has gone!" it exclaimed. "It has abdicated its just functions and descended into the political mire. It has sullied the ermine; it has dragged and polluted its garments in the filth of pro-slavery politics." The abuse and vilification heaped upon the judges by the wrathful anti-slavery elements has never been surpassed in the history of the Supreme Court. "If the people obey this decision" cried one newspaper, "they disobey God." A Washington correspondent wrote: "If epithets and denunciation could sink a judicial body, the Supreme Court of the United States would never be heard of again."

The Northern leaders boldly invented false and scurrilous stories about the decision and the judges in a desperate effort to discredit them. They accused the judges of engaging in a dastardly political conspiracy with the President and the leaders of the Democratic party, who, they claimed, had actually arranged for the case to be brought to the Supreme Court and decided in favor of the slavery protagonists. In the Senate, Seward denounced the decision as a nefarious plot devised by Buchanan and the Supreme Court. Later, in his debates with Douglas, Lincoln charged that Douglas, Pierce, Taney and Buchanan were specifically involved in the plot. "When we see a lot of framed timbers, different positions of which we know to have been gotten out at different times and places by different workmen—Stephen, Franklin, Roger and James [their first names] for instance—and when we see these timbers joined together and see that they exactly make the frame of a house . . . in such a case, we find it impossible not to believe that Stephen, and Franklin and Roger and James all understood one another from the beginning and all worked upon a common plan or draft drawn up before the first blow was struck." The conversation between Buchanan and Taney at the inaugural ceremony and Buchanan's reference to the forthcoming decision were pointed to as evidence of the Court's willingness to advise the President in advance of its decision.

Meanwhile Sandford died and Scott and his family were freed in May, 1857. Scott tragically died of consumption on Sept. 17, 1858, in dire poverty, completely neglected and ignored by the many vociferous champions who were fighting his people's cause.

Timothy Farrar prophesied in the *North American*

Review in October, 1857: "The country will feel the consequences of the decision more deeply and more permanently, in the loss of confidence in the sound judicial integrity and strictly legal character of their tribunals, than in anything beside; and this perhaps may well be accounted the greatest political calamity which this country, under our form of government, could sustain."

The serious damage to the prestige of the Supreme Court which resulted from the Dred Scott decision was reflected in this very "loss of confidence." The popular support the Court had enjoyed over the years was gone. In this sense, as Justice Hughes later concluded, its action was "a public calamity." Once again the doctrine of nullification raised its head. Now, however, in the North rather than in the South.

The judgments of the Supreme Court began to be challenged in the North. The Wisconsin Supreme Court, for example, ordered the release of a defendant held in federal custody for assisting a fugitive slave in violation of the federal Fugitive Slave law. When the federal authorities appealed to the Supreme Court, which then ordered the state officials to cease interfering with the operation of federal law (*Ableman v. Booth*) and return the defendant to custody, the decision was violently attacked not only in Wisconsin but throughout all the States in the North. With this encouragement, Wisconsin cavalierly ignored the Supreme Court decision, and nothing further was done about it. Twenty-two states passed resolutions declaring the Dred Scott opinion null and void, and many in addition enacted laws to the same effect. Thus, shortly after the Dred Scott case the influence of the Supreme Court in the Northern states reached its nadir.

Douglas attacked Lincoln in their series of debates for publicly resisting and deriding a decision of the Supreme Court. Lincoln countered by denying any resistance to the decision or desire to interfere with property rights. "All that I am doing," he continued, however, "is refusing to obey it as a political rule. If I were in Congress and a vote should come up on a question whether slavery should be prohibited in a new territory, in spite of the Dred Scott decision, I would vote that it should. . . . Sombody has to reverse that decision, since it is made, and we mean to reverse it, and we mean to do it peaceably." Lincoln said he believed in obedience to the Court and that its decisions on constitutional matters should control, subject only to constitutional amendment. "More than this would be a revolution. But we think the Dred Scott decision is erroneous. We know the court that made it has often overruled its decisions, and we shall do what we can to overrule this. We offer no resistance to it."

As A RESULT OF ITS LOSS OF PRESTIGE, the Court played a very weak role during the Civil War, interfering as little as possible with the encroachments on civil liberties made by the Lincoln administration. It avoided passing on many constitutional questions and often found by self-denial that it lacked the jurisdiction or power to contest a congressional enactment in violation of the Constitution. A notable example was *Ex Parte McCardle*. There the court meekly acquiesced when Congress deprived it of appellate jurisdiction in the case, even though it had actually come to a decision in private conference. Many years were to pass before the court retrieved its position as an integral part of the American system of checks and balances.

The Dred Scott case, many think, bears a contemporary message. Carl Brent Swisher has stated the lesson it teaches as lying "in the conclusion that when the people are fundamentally divided on basic issues, the judiciary will act at its peril if it intervenes unnecessarily to impose a judgment of higher law in support of one political faction and to aid in the defeat of another."

Lincoln
and
Civil Liberties

Ex Parte Merryman
Ex Parte Vallandigham
Ex Parte Milligan

"MY LORD, I CAN TOUCH A BELL on my right and order the arrest of a citizen of Ohio; I can touch a bell again and order the arrest of a citizen of New York; and no power on earth except that of the President can release them. Can the Queen of England do so much?"

This comment allegedly made by Lincoln's Secretary of State, William H. Seward, to the British Ambassador, Lord Lyons, reflects one of the most tragic and unique constitutional problems that ever confronted the American people. Before it was resolved the Civil War had to be fought and thousands of American citizens had to suffer and languish in prisons. The question it posed was this: Does a state of war suspend the Constitution?

Fort Sumter was attacked by the South on April 12, 1861. President Lincoln and his cabinet, fully aware of the desperate plight of the nation, placed its preservation uppermost in their decisions. They realized that support of the Union cause was far from unanimous in the North. Many Northerners sympathized with the South and even members of the Congress, the courts, the army and the government were suspect. Espionage and political and religious opposition to the war were other dangers that had to be met. Conscription was resisted violently in some sections of the North and further defections of states such as Maryland were dire possibilities. Obviously, Lincoln believed, the most effective means to curtail and prevent such activities was the use of force. The civil rights of the people had to be made subservient to military control. Unfortunately this meant the suspension of constitutional privileges, but Lincoln was a realist, and although he regretted the necessity of such action, he reluctantly decided to violate the Constitution in order to preserve it.

"My oath to preserve the Constitution," he later wrote, "imposed on me the duty of preserving by every indispensable means that government, that nation, of which the Constitution was the organic law. Was it possible to lose the nation, and yet preserve the Constitution? By general law, life and limb must be protected, yet often a limb must be amputated to save a life, but a life is never wisely given to save a limb. I felt that measures otherwise unconstitutional might become lawful by becoming indispensable to the preservation of the Constitution through the preservation of the nation. Right or wrong I assumed this ground and I now avow it. I could not feel that to the best of my ability I had even tried to save the Constitution, if to save slavery, or any minor matter, I should permit the wreck of the government, country, and Constitution, together."

Shortly after the firing on Fort Sumter, the clash between the expanded power of the military and the civil process of the courts came to a dramatic climax.

LINCOLN WAS VERY MUCH CONCERNED with the secessionist movement in Maryland, a strategic state by reason of its proximity to the capital. On April 27, 1861, he authorized General Winfield Scott or any of his commanding officers to suspend the writ of habeas corpus between Philadelphia and Washington whenever the resistance warranted it. Later, he extended the area north to New York. He used the authority of Article 1, section 9 of the Constitution to justify this extraordinary action: *"The privilege of the Writ of Habeas Corpus shall not be suspended, unless when in Cases of Rebellion or Invasion the public safety may require it."*

Maryland was a hot-bed of rebellion. The Maryland legislature, reflecting the popular will, prepared to vote for secession. Anticipating imminent revolt, General Benjamin F. Butler, commanding Union troops in the area, was ordered to deploy them in strategic positions around Baltimore. On May 25, 1861, prominent members of the government and others suspected as Southern sympathizers were arbitrarily thrown into prison by the military. John Merryman, a wealthy citizen of Baltimore and a leading Southern agitator, was one of those arrested and committed to the custody of General George Cadwalader, commander of Fort McHenry. Merryman petitioned Chief Justice Taney, who presided over the federal circuit which included Maryland, for a writ of habeas corpus. Taney directed General Cadwalader to produce his prisoner before the Circuit Court the next day. The writ was returned "served" but General Cadwalader refused to bring Merryman into court on the ground that the prisoner had been arrested on suspicion of treason and that the President of the United States had authorized him to suspend the writ of habeas corpus in cases involving the public safety. Taney immediately ordered that an attachment issue against the General for contempt of court. The marshal, however, was denied admission to the fort by the military guards stationed there. General Cadwalder simply ignored the order. Despite his great age — for he was then 84 years old — Taney fought back. *Ex Parte Merryman* was the last important case he decided. Taney was aware that the marshal could summon a *posse comitatus* to enforce his order. He excused him nevertheless for failing to do so, as the military power was obviously superior to that of the civil authority. Delivering his opinion orally from the bench, he reduced it to writing two days later, filed it with the clerk of the circuit court, and directed that a copy of the entire record be sent to President Lincoln.

Taney's opinion has been described as one which "will long remain among the most touching in American judicial literature." Taney maintained, after analyzing the Constitutional provisions, that the power to suspend the writ of habeas corpus was lodged only in the legislative branch of the Constitution. "If the President of the United States may suspend the writ," he declared, "then the Constitution of the United States has conferred upon him more regal and absolute power over the liberty of the citizen than the people of England have thought it safe to entrust to the Crown . . .," for in England only Parliament could do so. Commenting on the authority of the military to suspend the writ of habeas corpus, he said: "if the authority which the Constitution has confided to the judiciary department and judicial officers, may thus, upon any pretext or circumstances, be usurped by the military power, at its discretion, the people of the United States are no longer living under a government of laws, but every citizen holds life, liberty and property at the will and pleasure of the army officer in whose military district he may happen to be found." He then concluded that although he had exercised all the power which the Constitution and laws conferred upon him, "that power has been resisted by a force too strong for me to overcome. . . ." Indicating that he was sending the record of the case to the President, he then appealed to him as the highest officer of the nation "in fulfilment of his constitutional obligation to 'take care that the laws be faithfully executed,' to determine what measures he will take to cause the civil process of the United States to be respected and enforced."

ALTHOUGH TANEY WAS THE CHIEF JUSTICE of the United States, he expected to be arrested by General Cadwalader's troops on the day the return to Merryman's writ was to be made. Taney attended court anyway. Shortly after his opinion was delivered, the Chief Justice was congratulated by Mayor Brown of Baltimore for his action. Taney replied: "Mr. Brown, I am an old man, a very old man, but perhaps I was preserved for this occasion." The Merry-man case aroused the nation. Taney was bitterly de-nounced once again as he had been for his opinion in the Dred Scott case. The *New York Tribune* wrote "The Chief Justice takes sides with traitors, throwing around them the sheltering protection of the ermine . . . when treason stalks abroad in arms, let decrepit Judges give place to men capable of detecting and crushing it." Taney was accused of perverting the uses of the writ and prostituting its purposes. ". . . Treason will find a place of refuge, and its abettors encouragement and sympathy, in the Supreme Court." Other papers admitted that Taney was probably correct in his interpretation of the law but that he should have considered the revolutionary state of the nation. Taney also had his defenders. Obviously he had seen his duty as a judge and had acted accordingly. Mer-ryman had acted heinously, but, "it does appear to us that he could have been held and punished by the civil power . . . let us have no dictation from the army, so long as we can have justice administered from her customary seat." "The plea of State-necessity may be advanced by the President to justify himself for so high handed an act as the suspension of the writ; . . . but it would not be well for the highest officer of the Government to justify a plain violation of the Constitution, while calling out troops to maintain that same Constitution inviolate . . ." editorial-ized the *Baltimore American*. A biographer of Taney has written that his "action in this case was worthy of the best traditions of the Anglo-Saxon Judiciary. There is no sub-limer picture in our history than this of the aged Chief Justice, the fires of Civil War kindling around him, the President usurping the powers of Congress and Congress itself a seething furnace of sectional animosities, serene and unafraid, while for a third time in his career, the storm of partisan fury broke over his devoted head, interposing the shield of the law in defense of the liberty of the citi-zen."

Lincoln did not reply directly to the venerable Chief Justice. When the situation abated later in Maryland, and

Lincoln could feel more secure there, Merryman was released from military custody and turned over to the civil authorities. He was then indicted for treason, but the charge was not pressed and he was granted his freedom. Apparently this policy was adopted by the Government in many other cases of military arrest, especially when the prisoner could do no further harm to the Union cause. Perhaps it reflected a certain uneasiness about the constitutional problems involved and the tyrannical methods used.

Lincoln felt, however, that he had to continue in his course even though he might possibly exceed his constitutional authority. Military arrests in apparent violation of constitutional liberties were necessary to insure the public safety. In a state of rebellion especially, they were actually constitutional. Unfortunately, Taney did not live long enough to see his position vindicated. Four years later in *Ex Parte Milligan,* it was!

Despite the uncertainty of the legal situation, thousands of persons were arbitrarily taken into custody by the military authorities. Many were prominent in their communities and when the House of Representatives demanded a report on the prisoners in Fort McHenry, Lincoln replied, it would be "incompatible with the public interest at this time to furnish the information." Most of these arrests were made by Secretary of State Seward and Secretary of War Stanton. Stanton claimed Seward had no authority to do so and persuaded Lincoln early in 1862 to release political prisoners unless they were still dangerous to the Union cause and to grant the War Department the power to order "extraordinary arrests." Stanton then proceeded with even greater vigor than Seward had displayed to arbitrarily arrest citizens and deny them the writ of habeas corpus. Any civil judge who issued the writ was ignored when deemed necessary. If the judge persisted, the prisoner would be removed from his jurisdiction. Finally as the war situation became more desperate, even the civil judges refused to grant the writ.

On September 24, 1862, two days after the Emancipation Proclamation had been promulgated, President Lincoln proclaimed that whereas "disloyal persons are not adequately restrained by the ordinary processes of law from hindering" the execution of the draft measure, he therefore was compelled to order that:

"During the existing insurrection . . . all rebels and insurgents, their aiders and abettors, within the United States, and all persons discouraging voluntary enlistments, resisting military drafts, or guilty of any disloyal practices . . . shall be subject to martial law and liable to trials and punishments by courtsmartial or military commission;

"Second, that the writ of habeas corpus is suspended in respect to all persons arrested, or who are now, or hereafter during the rebellion shall be, imprisoned in any fort, camp, arsenal, military prison, or other place of confinement, by any military authority, or by the sentence of any court martial or military commission."

HERE INDEED WAS A LANDMARK in the subversion of civil rights—for not only did it subordinate the civil authority to the military but it also subjected the nebulous crime of "any disloyal practice" to martial law. Under this proclamation, military commissions were to be established, without the safeguards of civil trials, to try those arrested by the army. Appeal after conviction to the civil courts on the ground of illegal procedure or bias of the commission was also to be denied, and only the clemency of the President could avoid a miscarriage of justice. Dunning has properly characterized this document as "a perfect platform for a military despotism."

A controversy arose whether the President or the Congress had the authority to suspend the writ of habeas corpus. Then again—could the writ be suspended in areas in which the civil courts were functioning and the civil government was in control without fear of invasion or rebellion?

The ablest lawyers of the country debated the issue. The Nestor of the Philadelphia Bar, 82 year old Horace

Binney, supported the President's power to suspend the writ. Other distinguished jurists held that only Congress had the constitutional authority to do so. But Congress passed an act of indemnity for all violations of constitutional rights by executive officers who were sued for ordering or making arrests.

Much indignation was publicly expressed over the great numbers of citizens who were arrested by the military. An act of March 3, 1863, showed Congress's concern over the possible interpretation that it had ceded its power to suspend the writ to the President and had established no control over executive action in this field. It authorized the President, during the rebellion, to suspend the writ in any case throughout the United States, whenever in his judgment the public safety required it. It also required the Secretaries of State and of War to furnish to judges of United States Circuit and District Courts lists of citizens of states in which the administration of law remained unimpaired, who were held as state or political prisoners. That is, other than as prisoners of war. After such lists had been furnished and no grand jury indicted these persons, they were to be brought before the District or Circuit judge to be discharged, provided they took an oath of allegiance to the United States and put up a bond if required, and swore not to help the rebellion. Should such a list not be furnished by the Secretary of War or the Secretary of State as to those already under arrest and should a grand jury terminate its session without indicting a prisoner, he could petition the court for discharge.

The law also provided that any order of the President, or made under his authority, during the rebellion, would be a defense in all courts to any action, civil or criminal, pending or to be commenced, for any search, seizure, arrest, or imprisonment.

With this broad sweep of power granted to him by Congress, Lincoln on September 15, 1863, suspended the writ once again for the duration of the war. There was a weakness in the act, however, that soon became apparent. Its purpose mainly was to prevent imprisonment indefinitely without trial. It failed, however, to outlaw trials of civilians by military commissions. Lincoln's Proclamation of 1862 did provide for such trials. Hence if a military commission sentenced a prisoner to death rather than to imprisonment, he could be executed in the period between the trial and the meeting of the grand jury. The officials involved had no fear of reprisal for they were protected by the congressional act of 1863 which permitted the President's authority to be interposed as a defense to their actions.

Although many prisoners were released after military arrest, by taking the oath, many others suffered a different fate. At first civilians charged with violations coming broadly under the military code in regions hostile to the Union (as for destruction of railroad tracks and bridges), were tried by military commissions. This method was preferred by the government as the military commission was not subject to the laws of evidence or to jury trials and could expeditiously dispose of the prisoner. This was especially important when the civil law did not tolerate severe punishment for such acts. The public did not particularly object to such trials, as they were deemed necessary and were always subject to review by the President. Lincoln was noted for his clemency in these cases and saved many condemned civilians.

The situation changed radically, however, when citizens in areas free from military action and not under martial law were seized and tried by military commission. These people were often charged with interfering with recruitment of soldiers or acting disloyally. Soon many civilians began to be arrested by United States marshals and local magistrates in those areas, reported to the Judge Advocate General and then tried by military commissions. It is difficult to believe how many civilians were so arrested. The records are not clear nor complete but it has been estimated that many thousands were involved. The records of the provost-marshal's office in Washington bear out that there were at least 38,000 military political prisoners reported during the Civil War. The records of the

Commissary-General of prisoners from February, 1862 to the close of the war contain the names of 13,535 similarly arrested. At times the military arrest was used to prevent certain political leaders of the Democratic Party from attaining public office by election.

EVENTUALLY TRIAL BY MILITARY commission became a national scandal. Opposition to it arose from all quarters. Its legality was questioned and some lawyers refused to appear before these bodies, regarding the entire proceeding as unconstitutional. Then came the trials of Clement L. Vallandigham and Lambdin P. Milligan and the festering sore came to a head!

Part II
Ex Parte Vallandigham

"Must I shoot a simple-minded soldier boy who deserts, while I must not touch a hair of a wily agitator who induces him to desert? This is none the less injurious when effected by getting a father, or brother, or friend, into a public meeting, and there working upon his feelings till he is persuaded to write the soldier boy that he is fighting in a bad cause, for a wicked Administration of a contemptible Government, too weak to arrest and punish him if he shall desert. I think that, in such a case, to silence the agitator and save the boy is not only Constitutional, but withal a great mercy."

This shrewd and adroit observation by President Lincoln in 1863 on the trial by military commission of Clement Laird Vallandigham, not only dramatically highlighted the effect of the war between the states upon civil liberties, but also set the stage for one of the most extraordinary series of strange and pseudo-comic events in American legal history. For a moment, the very outcome of the War appeared to be affected. Despite the blunders and misplays that occasioned it, had the story developed otherwise, the cause of civil supremacy would have lacked the catalyst that triggered the great landmark decision in the *Milligan Case!*

Vallandigham was a handsome man with a domineering personality. A former Congressman from Ohio, he had been the leader of the Anti-Administration party and had lost to a Republican in 1862 after a bitter and hotly contested campaign. Actually his defeat was due to a desperate gerrymandering maneuver by which a strong Republican county was added to his old district. Noted for his prowess as an orator and a dynamic political leader, Vallandigham, unfortunately, had another side to his character which created many difficulties. Rhodes states that his contemporaries considered him "cold, calculating, selfish, ambitious and vindictive." Vallandigham was a schemer, and his main ambition was to become head of the Copperheads of the west. This he believed he could accomplish "by a violent and sensational antagonism and by making himself the spokesman for the extreme Democrats of Ohio, Indiana and Illinois." His followers idolized him, and his popularity in the Northwest, combined with his anti-war program, made him a dangerous man to the Union cause.

VALLANDIGHAM HAD TO BE STOPPED, SOON! Defeated for Congress, yet aware of his political strength, Vallandigham began to campaign for the governorship of Ohio. He stumped the state, violently attacking Lincoln and his conduct of the war. Better that the war be lost rather than victory be won by unconstitutional means, he argued, referring particularly to the suspension of the writ of habeas corpus and Lincoln's Emancipation Proclamation. And this was at a time when the Northern prospects appeared none too promising. In fact, early in 1863, the war had almost approached a stalemate; many Northerners, appalled by the dreadful bloodletting taking place on the battlefields, were becoming discouraged and ready to settle for peace at any price.

At this crucial moment, a new aggravating element was introduced in the person of Major General Ambrose E. Burnside, from whose characteristic overgenerous growth of side whiskers we have the word today "burnsides" or "sideburns." General Burnside was put in command of the "Department of The Ohio," consisting of the states of Ohio, Indiana, Illinois and Kentucky, by Secretary of War Stanton who was very much concerned by Vallandigham's activities. Burnside was a "military firebrand," rather insensitive politically, who was anxious to ingratiate himself with the Republican administration in Washington after his humiliating defeat at Fredericksburg. From his headquarters at Cincinnati he promulgated in rapid succession a series of military orders designed to weaken the strong opposition to the war prevailing in his command. It was obvious from these orders that he was out "to get" Vallandigham. On April 13, 1863, the famous General Order No. 38 was issued which soon brought the whole situation to a head.

"The Commanding general publishes," it decreed, "for the information of all concerned, that all persons found within our lines who commit acts for the benefit of the enemies of our country will be tried as spies or traitors, and if convicted, will suffer death. . . . The habit of declaring sympathies for the enemy will no longer be tolerated in this department. Persons committing such offenses will be at once arrested; with a view to being tried as above stated or sent beyond our lines into the lines of their friends. It must be distinctly understood that treason, expressed or implied will not be tolerated in this department. All officers and soldiers are strictly charged with the execution of this order." Thus, by denying freedom of speech to the people in "The Ohio Department" and devising the unique crime of "implied treason," Burnside prepared the trap for Vallandingham. Horace Greeley commented that "whether this (order) was specially aimed at Vallandigham or not, it was easily foreseen that he would be one of the first to expose himself to its penalties."

Unconcerned by the stunned and indignant reaction to his "order," Burnside went ahead with his plans. First he established a military commission to try violators of General Order No. 38. Then, anticipating that Vallandigham would be one of his first victims, and realizing that the Commission would be criticized as biased, he appointed Major James L. Van Buren, a relative of the then late Democratic President Van Buren, to add "Democratic flavor" to its membership. Burnside did not have long to wait.

A Democratic mass-meeting was held on May 1, 1863, at Mount Vernon, Ohio, and Vallandigham was invited to speak. Vallandigham was in fine form. Inspired by the enthusiasm of the great numbers of noisy Democrats who turned out — "the gay buntings — the pretty girls in decorated wagons — the hickory poles for Jackson and the

many butternut badges and Copperhead pins displayed"
—he gave them a real rabble rousing speech, fiery and
eloquent. "King Lincoln" had to be booted off his throne
by being voted out of office, he shouted. As for General
Order No. 38—he spat upon it. The inflamed crowd shouted
its approval as he denounced it. He then attacked the
President's usurpation of power, concluding that it would
destroy freedom and set up a despotic monarchy. Not
far from the speaker's platform, however, were two officers
in civilian clothes from General Burnside's staff who took
notes of what Vallandingham said. They hurried back to
headquarters—and after the notes had been studied it
was clear Vallandingham had violated General Order No.
38. The trap could now be snapped!

ON MAY 3RD, GENERAL BURNSIDE sent a company of soldiers on a special train to Dayton, Ohio, where Vallandigham lived, and about 2:30 in the morning of the next day,
they broke into his house and arrested him. Before res-
cuers could arrive, Vallandigham was forced to dress,
rushed to the train, and taken to Burnside's headquarters
in Cincinnati. There he was thrown into a military prison.
But Burnside this time had gone too far. This was military
despotism of the worst sort. From his prison cell, Vallandigham smuggled out a letter to Ohio Democrats which
received wide publicity.

"I am here in a military bastille for no other offense
than my political opinions, and the defense of them, and of
the rights of the people, and of your Constitutional liberties. . . . I am a Democrat—for the Constitution, for law,
for Union, for liberty—this is my only crime. . . . Be firm,
be true to your principles, to the Union, to the Constitution, and all will yet be well."

Vallandigham was a fanatic and a demagogue, but he
was also a prominent and important Democratic leader of
Ohio and the fact that he could be imprisoned by the military in such an obviously unconstitutional manner brought
immediate and violent reaction. Riots ensued and Democratic protest meetings were held not only in Ohio but in

other parts of the north as well. Excitement ran high over the case. Rhodes in his *History* clearly indicated the issues involved:

> "From the beginning to the end of these proceedings law and justice were set at naught. . . . The right of General Burnside even to make the arrest may be questioned. The majority of the United States Supreme Court in the Milligan case [later] maintained that the suspension of the writ of habeas corpus did not authorize the arrest of anyone. The argument that Southern Ohio was the theater of war and therefore under martial law cannot be maintained. . . . The United States courts were regularly open in the Southern district of Ohio."

Undeterred, Burnside convened the military Commission on May 6th to hear the charges brought against Vallandigham. He was charged by the court with "publicly expressing, in violation of General Order No. 38 . . . his sympathies for those in arms against the Government of the United States, declaring disloyal sentiments and opinions, with the object and purpose of weakening the power of the government in its efforts to suppress an unlawful rebellion."

The specifications indicated that Burnside's officers had not missed much in Vallandigham's speech at Mount Vernon. Vallandigham, they specified, had publicly stated that "The present war is a cruel, wicked, and unnecessary war . . . a war not being waged for the preservation of the Union . . . a war for the purpose of crushing out liberty and erecting a despotism . . . a war for the freedom of the blacks and the enslavement of the whites. . . . If the administration had so wished, the war could have been honorably terminated months ago. . . . The Government of the United States was about to appoint military marshals in every district to restrain the people of their liberties, to deprive them of their rights and privileges. . . . Order No. 38 was a base usurpation of arbitrary authority. . . . The sooner the people inform the minions of usurped power that they will not submit to such restrictions upon their liberty, the better. . . . [He] firmly

The Supreme Court of the United States in 1866.
(l. to r. David Davis, Nathan Swayne, Robert C. Grier, James M. Wayne, Salmon P. Chase, Samuel Nelson, Nathan Clifford, Samuel F. Miller, Stephen J. Field)

believed that the men in power are attempting to establish a despotism in this country, more cruel and more oppressive than ever existed before."

Vallandigham, the specifications added by innuendo, well knew that all of these opinions and sentiments "did aid, comfort, and encourage those in arms against the Government and could but induce in his hearers a distrust of their own Government, sympathy for those in arms against it, and a disposition to resist the laws of the land."

Vallandigham refused to plead until counsel had been assigned to him. The military tribunal insisted that he plead first. Vallandigham then excepted to the court's jurisdiction, whereupon the Judge Advocate was directed to enter a plea of "not guilty" on his behalf. Although allowed counsel, Vallandigham personally conducted the cross-examination of witnesses. He did not present a formal defense, however, preferring instead to read a "protest" in which he again objected to the court's jurisdiction and asserted his constitutional guarantees of due process.

"I am not in the land or naval forces," he declared, "not in the militia in actual service, and therefore am not triable for any cause by such a court, but am subject by the express terms of the Constitution, to arrest only by judicial warrant . . . and am now entitled to speedy and public trial by an impartial jury of the State of Ohio . . . and evidence and arguments according to the common law and ways of Judicial Courts.

"And all these I here demand as my right as a citizen of the United States. . . . The alleged 'offence' is not known to the Constitution nor to any law thereof. It is words spoken to the people of Ohio in open and public political meeting, lawfully and peaceably assembled. It is the words of criticism of the public policy of public servants of the people by which policy it was alleged that the welfare of the country was not promoted. It was an appeal to change that policy, not by force, but by free election and the ballot box. It is not pretended that I counselled disobedience to the Constitution or resistance to laws and lawful authority. I never have."

TO NO ONE'S SURPRISE the Military Commission soon found Vallandigham guilty and he was sentenced to close confinement in some fortress of the United States for the duration of the war. While the trial had been in session, a former Democratic United States Senator, George E. Pugh, applied to the United States Circuit Court for a writ of habeas corpus for Vallandigham. The petition was addressed to the judges of the Circuit Court, but as Mr. Justice Swayne of the U.S. Supreme Court was absent, the District Judge, Humphrey H. Leavitt held court for the circuit. A distinguished lawyer, A. F. Perry, was invited by the Judge to represent General Burnside, along with the U. S. District Attorney, Flamen Ball. Judge Leavitt followed an unusual course in deciding whether to grant the writ. Instead of promptly issuing it as "of right" he decided to obtain a statement from General Burnside on the army's position before taking action on it. Apparently it was the settled practice of the court to give notice to the defendant, in cases of military arrest, before issuing a writ of habeas corpus. Burnside submitted a statement to the court explaining the necessity for the issuance of General Order No. 38. He argued:

"If I were to find a man from the enemy's country, distributing in my camps, speeches of their public men that tended to demoralize the troops or to destroy their confidence in the constituted authorities of the Government, I would have him tried, and hung if found guilty and all the rules of modern warfare would sustain me. Why should such speeches from our own public men be allowed? . . . They create dissensions and discord which, just now, amounts to treason. . . . We are in a state of Civil War, and an emergency is upon us which requires the operations of some power that moves more quickly than the civil. There never was a war carried on successfully without that power. [Vallandigham should not be permitted to] use license, and plead that [he is] exercising liberty. [It was his duty] to stop license and intemperate discussions which tend to weaken the authority of the Government and the Army."

After the motion had been argued at great length, Judge Leavitt refused to issue the writ. He held that he was bound by the precedent of an unreported case pertaining to one Bethuel Rupert decided on circuit in the October term of 1862 by Justice Swayne, with Leavitt's concurrence. There the facts were similar to those in the Vallandigham petition and the Court had held that "this Court would not grant the writ of Habeas Corpus, when it appeared that the detention or imprisonment was under military authority." As a District Judge, even though sitting on a Circuit Court, it would be embarrassing if he were to reverse a decision of the Circuit Court, made when both judges were on the bench.

Referring to Vallandigham's argument that a person not in the military or naval service of the government was not liable to arrest under or by military power, he inquired whether the Court should not be "imperatively bound to regard the present state of the country, and, in the light which it throws upon the subject, to decide upon the expediency of interfering with the exercise of the military power as invoked in the pending application. . . . In my judgment, when the life of the Republic is imperiled, he mistakes his duty and obligation as a patriot who is not willing to concede to the Constitution such a capacity of adaptation to circumstances as may be necessary to meet a great emergency to save the nation from hopeless ruin. . . . It is clearly not a time when any one connected with the judicial department of the government should allow himself, except from the most stringent obligations of duty, to embarrass or thwart the Executive in his efforts to deliver the country from the dangers which press so heavily upon it . . ."

ASSUMING THAT BURNSIDE AS COMMANDER in Chief had been authorized to act as he had done by the President he added the enigmatic thought that "The precise extent of his authority, in this responsible position is not known to the Court." Judge Leavitt, however, failed to prescribe the actual constitutional limits that should have applied. He found the arrest to be legal and even though illegal it was "morally certain that the writ would not be obeyed, and I confess I am somewhat reluctant to authorize a process, knowing it would not be respected, and that the court is powerless to enforce obedience."

Vallandigham was sent to Fort Warren, in Boston Harbor, to serve his sentence. When news of this became known the effect on the North was explosive. Governor Seymour of New York wrote that Vallandigham's treatment was "cowardly, brutal and infamous." Later he told a Democratic mass meeting protesting the affair that it consisted of "a series of offenses against our most sacred rights. It interfered with the freedom of speech; it violated our rights to be secure in our homes against unreasonable searches and seizures; it pronounced sentence without trial, save one which was a mockery, which insulted as well as wronged. "The perpetrators now seek to impose punishment, not for an offense against law, but for the disregard of an invalid order put forth in the utter disregard of the principles of civil liberty." Then solemnly calling the Administration to task he gave it notice that "The people of this country now wait with the deepest anxiety the decisions of the Administration upon these acts. Having given it a generous support in the conduct of the war, we pause to see what kind of government it is for which we are asked to pour out our blood and our treasures." Was the war being fought "to put down rebellion at the South or destroy free institutions at the North?"

The reaction to Governor Seymour's letter was tremendous. With a great outpouring of emotion, resolutions were adopted censuring all those involved and squarely holding the administration responsible for what had occurred. Copies were sent to Democrats in all the Northern States and a special copy was forwarded to President Lincoln with a letter which added that the "meeting was one of the most respectable as to numbers and character, and one of the most earnest in support of the Union ever held in [Albany]."

As feelings ran high over the Vallandigham affair, Lincoln began to worry, for he realized he had to contend with an election the following year. Suddenly it had become a personal matter with his own political future at stake — and all due to Burnside's bungling action. As Commander-in-Chief of the Army and head of the civil government only he could make the final decision as to Vallandigham's fate. What should now be done with him?

Actually this *cause célèbre* had come as a surprise to Lincoln, for he had been deeply involved in the military stalemate, and when he finally learned the facts he had been greatly distressed. Vallandigham's was not an isolated case. Similar arbitrary arrests and trials were taking place all over the country — and even public newspapers were being raided and suppressed by the military at the insistence of Secretaries Stanton and Seward. An editorial in *Harpers' Weekly*, which was loyal to the Union read: "Of the arrests which have been made by the government within the past eighteen months a few were probably wise and useful; but the great bulk were foolish and injurious. . . . Obscure editors and noisy talkers have been locked up, and the wrongs they have endured have given an influence to their disloyalty which it would never have otherwise acquired. . . . In circles likely to be tolerably well informed, it is openly boasted that Mr. Stanton dare not come to New York and Mr. Seward himself has been similarly threatened . . ."

EVEN WHILE LINCOLN WAS STRUGGLING with a solution to the Vallandigham mess, General Burnside continued in his ruthless and despotic way, suppressing the *Chicago Times* and prohibiting the circulation of the *New York World* in his department. As a result, civil leaders in the Chicago area added their voices of official protest to those emanating from other parts of the country.

Alarmed at the stupidity of his military leaders, Lincoln discussed the situation with his cabinet. Gideon Welles' diary for June 3rd notes: "The arrest of Vallandigham and the order to suppress the circulation of the *Chicago Times* in his military district issued by General Burnside have created much feeling. It should not be otherwise. The proceedings were arbitrary and injudicious. It gives bad men the right of questions, an advantage of which they avail themselves. Good men, who wish to support the administration, find it difficult to defend these acts. They are Burnside's, unprompted, I think, by any member of the administration, and yet the responsibility is here unless they are disavowed and B. called to account, which cannot be done. The President—and I think every member of the cabinet—regrets what has been done, but as to the measures which should now be taken there are probably differences."

Later Welles wrote that the arbitrary seizures of some papers could be attributed to Secretary of State Stanton at "Seward's promptings, and the President in deference to Seward, yielded to it. . . . These things are to be regretted. . . . Yet the administration ought not to be condemned for the misdeeds of one, or at most two, of its members. They would not be if the President was less influenced by them."

But what could Lincoln do? He could not overrule Burnside. That would have weakened the authority of his Commanding Generals in the various military departments. To approve his action however, would have strengthened the hands of the conservative Democrats.

It was at this moment that he wrote his famous defense, in which he referred to shooting a deserting simple-minded soldier boy and protecting the "wily agitator who induces him to desert." He probably would not have arrested Vallandigham, he added; but while he could not "shift the responsibility from myself, I hold as a general rule, the commander in the field is the better judge of the necessity in any particular case . . ."

In light of the great outcry that followed his actions, Burnside offered his resignation. Lincoln refused to accept it. "When I shall wish to supersede you I will let you know. All the cabinet regretted the necessity for it, but being done, all were for seeing you through with it." Lincoln promised to release Vallandigham as soon as the public safety permitted it.

Lincoln finally decided that the best approach would be to cast a light, pseudo-comic complexion on the entire matter. Taking advantage of the wording of Burnside's Order No. 38 which provided as an alternate punishment that convicted violators could be "*sent beyond our lines into the lines of their friends*" he directed the War Department to send the following telegram to General Burnside.

"The President directs that without delay you send C. L. Vallandigham under secure guard to the headquarters of General Rosecrans, to be put by him beyond our military lines; and in case of his return within our lines he be arrested and kept in close custody for the term specified in his sentence." Thus Lincoln suggested that Vallandigham's sympathy for the South would be rewarded by deporting him there. By this means he hoped to deflate the importance Vallandigham had achieved by reason of his treatment.

GENERAL HALLECK SENT BURNSIDE a confidential letter expressing the cabinet's unhappiness with Burnside's precipitant actions. He then suggested that Burnside "interfere with the ordinary civil tribunals as little as possible." Burnside should be careful "against inciting opposition to the government by unnecessary arrests and military trials." In conclusion, Burnside was advised that he would soon be ordered to take command in the field.

Vallandigham, banished to the Confederacy, later went to Canada. While there, he directed an unsuccessful campaign for election as Governor of Ohio. During this period he was regarded as a martyr, and many Democratic resolutions were addressed to Lincoln demanding Vallandigham's return to Ohio.

Lincoln wrote a letter to a Committee of Citizens demanding Vallandigham's return, that he would be prepared to arrange it if they would admit that there was an insurrection, that the military forces of the United States were trying by constitutional means to suppress it, that the committee members would not do anything to lessen the efficiency of the armed forces in this endeavor, and that it would also support this effort financially. The Committee indignantly rejected these terms.

In the meantime, in 1864, Vallandigham's lawyers moved the United States Supreme Court for a writ of certiorari to review the sentence of the military commission. Although Taney, who had acted with such courage and independence in the Merryman Case was still Chief Justice, he did not sit on the case because of his ill-health. The Supreme Court denied the writ, dismissing the case. Justice Swayne delivering the opinion for a unanimous court held that it had no jurisdiction to review the proceedings of a military tribunal. "This court," he wrote, "cannot originate a writ of certiorari to review or pronounce any opinion upon the proceedings of a military commission." The court could do so only when a United States Court of the type indicated in section 14 of the Judiciary Act of 1789 was involved.

Thus the encroachment by the military upon civil authority continued during the Civil War with the sanction of the Supreme Court. Because it was almost impossible to obtain judicial review of the proceedings of a military tribunal very few appeals were addressed to the Supreme Court. With judicial review barred in these cases, only those attacking the constitutionality of the suspension of the writ of habeas corpus could potentially reach the Supreme Court. The Supreme Court refused to consider even such attacks until the hostilities had ceased. When the Supreme Court finally did break through its self-imposed barrier in *Ex Parte Milligan,* it did so under circumstances so peculiar and dramatic, that it changed the course of American history!

Part III
Ex Parte Milligan

SHORTLY AFTER LINCOLN'S TRAGIC assassination on April 14, 1865, which followed quickly in the wake of Lee's surrender at Appomattox, the Northwest was thrown into such a pitch of excitement over another unprecedented and highly inflammatory event that it appeared for the moment the Union was once again to be confronted by a national crisis. Caused by the publication of a letter sent by Maj. Gen. Alvin P. Hovey, Military Commander of the District of Indiana, to Col. A. J. Warner, commanding Indianapolis, the affair brought to the fore a cancer which had been aggravating the country from the very start of the Civil War.

"I have just received from the Department Headquarters an order," the letter read, "commanding me to carry into effect, 'without delay,' the sentence of the military commission in the cases of William A. Bowles, Lambdin P. Milligan and Stephen Horsey. The sentence of each is death. . . . From the language of my orders, I am compelled to fix Friday, the 19th instant (between the hours of 12 o'clock M. and 3 o'clock P.M.), as the most remote day within which the same can be properly obeyed. You will give the condemned every facility within your power, consistent with their safe-keeping, to settle up their worldly affairs and prepare for the future. These are sad duties for both of us, and more trying than the field of battle, but they are stern duties, that must be obeyed for our country's safety and future welfare. . . ."

Before the difficulties that ensued from this affair were finally resolved, the President of the United States was impeached and just barely escaped removal from his high office, and the whole conduct of the Reconstruction program was disastrously interrupted. Even more significant was the lasting effect it made on American civil liberties, for it eventually culminated in the famous case of *Ex Parte Milligan*, which, to this day, is recognized as one of the great landmark decisions of the Supreme Court of the United States. Although technically the *Milligan Case* presented different issues to the Supreme Court, the Court had in 1864 considered a similar fact pattern in *Ex Parte Vallandigham*. In that case, however, it had failed to decide the issues on the merits, preferring instead to avoid open conflict with the executive and legislative branches of the government.

It was not until the Civil War had come to a grinding close and hundreds of thousands of the flower of American manhood had been destroyed, that the Supreme Court found the strength and courage in the interest of justice to really grapple with the constitutional issues involved and to assert its will over the other branches of the government. The manner in which all this came to pass proved to be as tense and exciting as the dramatic ending.

Lambdin P. Milligan was a self-educated teacher and lawyer. Subject to epileptic fits as a youth and sickly in later life, he managed by his outstanding ability to become a prominent citizen of Huntington, Indiana. He was respected in Indiana as an intellectual and a leader of the Democratic party. Milligan was a peaceable man, certainly not a demagogue, but he was imbued with his own sense of righteousness. He was fearless in his denunciation of the tyrannical tendencies and acts of the Lincoln administration and he had to find an outlet for his passionate beliefs. He became a leader of the Sons of Liberty, one of the many Butternut or Copperhead secret orders in the Northwest, sympathetic to the Confederacy. Their purpose was to foment armed uprisings and resistance to the military drafts in the North and even, if possible, to smuggle supplies to the South and act as spies for the Confederacy.

THE SONS OF LIBERTY gave General Hovey much concern, for it was especially active in Indiana, Ohio and Illinois and numbered from 175,000 to 500,000 members at a time. Some of the hothead leaders of the Sons of Liberty decided to incite disorder in Chicago while the 1864 Democratic National Convention was in session. Their plan was to seize the federal and state arsenals, and bolster their own forces with the prisoners of war they would release. Thus reinforced they could invade Kentucky and Missouri, join other forces in those states sympathetic to the South and then attack loyal troops in the area. Rumors of the impending attack were rife and the many spies and informers employed by Secretary of War Stanton in the Northwest Territory meticulously reported to the federal authorities the dire ramifications of the plot.

On October 5, 1864, Milligan and several other leaders of the movement were arrested by order of General Hovey. They subsequently were tried by a military commission on charges of conspiracy against the government, inciting insurrections, affording aid and comfort to the rebels and violations of the laws of war. The specifications related to their roles in the plot to attack Union troops after seizing the arsenals and liberating the prisoners of war.

Milligan objected to the jurisdiction of the military commission. He was not in the military forces of the U.S., he argued, and as a citizen of Indiana, in which neither war nor insurrection existed and in which the civil courts, both state and federal, were functioning, he was entitled to a trial in a civil court, with all the attendant constitutional guarantees. The military commission decided differently, however, asserting that it was authorized by Presidential decree to try traitors like Milligan. All the prisoners were found guilty and three of the more important ones including Milligan were sentenced to death by hanging. The execution was set for May 19, 1865.

In January 1865, the death sentences of the military commission, having been approved by General Hovey, were forwarded to President Lincoln for his approval. The war was going well for the North at the time and Lincoln was disposed to grant clemency to the Indiana conspirators. He suggested that certain technical errors be corrected in the moving papers submitted by their friends and upon resubmission he would be lenient. Lincoln was reported as saying, "I'll keep them in prison awhile to keep them from killing the government." Then came Appomattox and Lincoln's assassination. Andrew Johnson was President of the United States when the papers were once again submitted.

JOHNSON BELIEVED THAT TREASON was a crime and "crime must be punished." On May 9, 1865, General Order No. 27 was issued at Indianapolis by General Hovey, in which he recited that the President of the United States had approved the sentences and directed that they be carried into execution "without delay." Therefore each prisoner was to "be hanged by the neck until he be dead on Friday, the 19th of May, 1865." It was then that General Hovey sent his letter to Colonel Warner, which stirred the Northwest to a fever pitch.

This was the first time a death sentence by a military commission was to be executed. Was it necessary now that the war had been won by the North? Why shouldn't the prisoners be tried by the civil courts in light of the circumstances? Local and ardent supporters of the administration were shocked by the impending execution of such prominent citizens. Was it for this that they had fought so bloody a war and with such great sacrifice—especially if the prisoners had been unlawfully convicted? Governor Morton of Indiana wrote to President Johnson recommending that the sentences be commuted to imprisonment. Johnson remained adamant! He was flooded with petitions for clemency, particularly so by the Indiana politicians. Even Judge David Davis of the United States Supreme Court, who was on circuit duty, wrote from Indianapolis along with the local circuit judge urgently appealing that the sentences be commuted to life imprisonment. An uneasy and brooding atmosphere began to build up in Indiana. The pressure became too much for the President to withstand. Three days before the 19th of May, he postponed the Milligan execution data until June 1st.

Milligan in the meantime had filed a petition for a writ of habeas corpus on May 10, 1865, to the Circuit Court of the United States for the District of Indiana. In this proceeding he demanded that he be either discharged or turned over to a civil court for trial, for the reasons he had given in objecting to the jurisdiction of the military commission. He also added that the grand jury of the United States Circuit Court which had met while he was in military custody had adjourned without having found any indictment or presentment against him. The circuit court judges divided on the issues. With the thought that this important case should be decided by the highest court in the land they certified the following questions to the Supreme Court: I) Ought a writ of habeas corpus be issued? II) Ought the petitioner to be discharged from custody? III) Had the military commission jurisdiction to try and to sentence Milligan?

Milligan's appeal to the Supreme Court could not have come at a more inopportune moment for the War Department in Washington. Secretary of War Stanton attempted desperately to persuade the President not to prevent the executions. Much more was at stake than the lives of some Indiana conspirators. Stanton was arranging at the time to try by military commission the assassins of President Lincoln, including Mrs. Mary Surratt, and he was determined that they and many other traitors incarcerated in the Old Capitol Prison in Washington should not escape the Republic's vengeance. No mercy should be shown to Milligan less it affect his own plans! General Hovey was advised to ignore any process of a civil court and to carry out the execution unless ordered to the contrary by the Bureau of Military Justice.

President Johnson was in a dilemma. He was still committed to the policies of the Republican Radicals, but he was slowly undergoing a change of heart. Reluctantly, overriding the objections of Stanton, he finally relented, and on May 30 he commuted the sentences of Milligan and his co-defendants from death to imprisonment for life at hard labor. The prisoners were sent to the penitentiary at Columbus, Ohio. It is interesting to note, in this respect, that Johnson suspended the writ of habeas corpus by special order for the execution of Mrs. Surrat just a month later. Despite the importunities of five members of the military commission that had found her guilty of complicity in the conspiracy which ended in Lincoln's assassination, he refused to commute her sentence to life imprisonment and she was subsequently hanged.

Ex Parte Milligan was argued in the March term of the Supreme Court in 1866. The state of the nation was so inflammatory at the time, and the issues of the case were so pertinent thereto that, it was clear the Court's decision would affect the history of the country for some time to come. It should be recalled that in 1866 the lines of battle had been sharply drawn between Johnson and the Congress over Reconstruction policies and a fight to the death was being waged between them. Johnson, by executive authority, had established military and civil state governments in the South. The Republican Radicals were exerting every effort to abolish them. Until the South was reconstructed, they insisted, military governments only should control the various states formerly in the Confederacy. These military governments, of course, were to obtain their authority by legislative sanction, thus reserving to Congress the power to impose its will on the Southern states. Later, after their governments had been reorganized to conform to the new order, they would be permitted to seek admission to the Union upon terms decreed by the Congress. How the Supreme Court would react to any situation pertaining to this proposed Congressional program was of vital importance to the extremists in Congress, for the military government plan was of doubtful constitutional validity. President Johnson added to the fears of these Congressional leaders by proclaiming that he would challenge in the courts any such legislation enacted by the Congress. With the Supreme Court suddenly taking on so important a role in the conflict between the radicals and the moderates, its decision in *Ex Parte Milligan* was eagerly awaited.

WITH THIS THOUGHT EVER PRESENT, both the government and the petitioners enlisted the finest legal minds in the country to argue the case before the Supreme Court.

Attorney General Speed called upon Henry Stanberry and Gen. Benjamin F. Butler to represent the government. For the prisoners appeared James A. Garfield, Joseph E. McDonald, Jeremiah S. Black and David Dudley Field. Butler had been a major general during the war who "in the conduct of tactical operations was almost uniformly unsuccessful." Yet he was a brilliant lawyer, one of the first really successful "corporation" lawyers in the modern sense. At the time of his death in 1893, his professional annual income as a lawyer was estimated at $100,000. Stanberry was a prominent lawyer in Ohio, who later succeeded to Attorney General Speed's position. Field, of course, was a leading member of the New York Bar, noted for the Field codes. Black had been a justice of the Supreme Court of Pennsylvania and was considered to be without peer as an appellate advocate. He was a former Attorney-General and Secretary of State. Garfield, a leading Union man, who later became President of the United States, staked his political reputation to defend Milligan. This was a celebrated case and as a rather young lawyer, known for his Republican leanings, he believed he had much to gain by participating in the argument with so many superior members of the Supreme Court Bar. On the other hand, his appearance on behalf of Milligan removed the stigma of partisanship from the defense. All the defense counsel served without fee!

Ex Parte Milligan was argued before the Supreme Court from March 5 to March 13, 1866. Counsel on both sides surpassed themselves, and a crowded courtroom of professional observers, lawyers and congressmen were highly impressed. Butler stated the position of the government: "We do not desire to exalt the martial above the civil law or to substitute the necessarily despotic rule of the one for the mild and healthy restraints of the other . . . [But] when the Nation is threatened . . . [with war] . . . when the bayonet is called in as the final arbiter; when on its armed forces the Government must rely for all it has of power, authority and dignity; when the citizen has to look to the same source for everything he has of right in the present, or hope in the future – then we ask that martial law may so prevail, that the civil law may again live, to the end that this may be a 'government of laws, and not of men.'"

The main argument for the petitioners was delivered by Black: "I am not afraid that you will underrate the importance of this case. It concerns the rights of the whole people. Such questions have generally been settled by armies. But since the beginning of the world no battle has ever been lost or won upon which the liberties of a nation were so distinctly staked as they are on the result of this argument. The pen that writes the judgment of the court will be mightier for good or for evil than any sword that ever was wielded by mortal arm . . . We submit that a person not in the military or naval service cannot be punished at all until he has had a fair, open, public trial before an impartial jury, in an ordained and established court, to which the jurisdiction has been given by law to try him for that specific offense . . ." Black attacked "with irresistible power, the constitutionality of the proceedings of the military commission." He argued for more than eight hours without respite, and during this entire period he did not refer to a single note, book or reference. An observer commented: "And yet he presented an array of law, fact and argument, with such remarkable force and eloquence, as startled and bewildered those who listened to him."

GARFIELD DELINEATED ON THE HISTORY and function of military law, concluding that the President had no right to suspend the writ of habeas corpus. This power was lodged in the Congress only, he maintained. He then submitted that no situation, no matter how desperate, could justify the trial of a civilian by a military commission, when the proper civil courts were still functioning.

The Court rendered its judgment on April 3, 1866. The worst fears of radical Republicans proved to be well-founded. A majority of the Court held that the writ of habeas corpus should be issued, as the President had no authority to try civilians by military commissions in areas where the civil courts were still functioning. The petitioners were therefore to be discharged as prayed for. The Chief Justice then announced: "The opinion of the Court in these cases will be read at the next term when such judges as see fit will state their grounds of dissent."

Upon learning of the Court's decision, Milligan filed a petition for a writ of habeas corpus on April 9th, which was granted on the 10th and immediately served on the warden of the prison. On the same day, however, Stanton ordered the release of Milligan and his co-defendants, as the President had remitted their sentences on the original application made on their behalf. Stanton's telegram was received by the warden at 4 p.m. The beneficence of the President came too late. Milligan had already been released on his own writ at 3 p.m. and discharged from prison by the warden!

Upon his return home Milligan was acclaimed as a hero. The federal courts in Indiana later indicted him on the old charges—but the case never came to trial. Milligan brought a civil suit for money damages in 1868 against the members of the military commission which had tried and convicted him. The case lingered in the courts until 1871, when it was heard. Milligan was given a verdict of $5 damages! In any event it was a moral victory for Milligan.

When the Court delivered its formal opinion in the Milligan Case on December 17, 1866, the full import of its significance was brought to the attention of the public. Warren notes that it was violently attacked and extravagantly praised. The majority opinion was read by Judge Davis, a personal friend of Lincoln, to a crowded room of lawyers and congressmen. An announcement was made by the clerk to the effect that no note taking would be permitted. To prevent any misunderstanding, reporters were directed to wait until the published opinions were made available. This was not done until January 1, 1867. Holding that the Supreme Court could review the action of a military commission if there were no law to justify the military trial, a position it had failed to take in the Vallandigham case, Judge Davis commented on the constitutional guarantees of Americans pertaining to their arrest, trial and punishment for crime. He then continued: "The Constitution of the United States is a law for rulers and people, equally in war and peace, and covers with the shield of its protection all classes of men, at all times, and under all circumstances." The Constitution cannot "be suspended during any of the great exigencies of government. Such a doctrine leads directly to anarchy or despotism . . . Martial rule can never exist where the courts are open, and in the proper and unobstructed exercise of their jurisdiction." It is "confined to the locality of actual war." Milligan's trial by military commission was therefore illegal. Milligan was ordered released. Justice Davis held, too, that Congress had no authority to establish military commissions even if it decided to do so. The concurring judges, however, refused to be so sweeping in the denial of this power to Congress and dissented on this point.

The Milligan decision, which "has so long been recognized as one of the bulwarks of American liberty," stirred up considerable difficulty. The Supreme Court, by interjecting itself in the struggle between the President and Congress, became a target for Radical Republican vituperation and vengeance. The attack on the Court eventually became so violent that in 1866 a law was enacted reducing the number of justices from nine to seven. The main reason for the opprobrium wreaked upon the Court was the realization of the Reconstructionists that their efforts to impose military rule upon the Southern States now could be frustrated. Johnson's moderate program had suddenly acquired a powerful ally, and they had to fight back. If the Court's doctrine had been imposed during the War, they indignantly maintained, the North would probably have lost. The *New York Times* editorialized: "In the conflict of principle thus evoked, the states which sustained the cause of the Union will recognize an old foe with a new face. . . . The Supreme Court, we regret to find, throws the great weight of its influence into the scale of those who assailed the Union and step after step impugned the constitutionality of nearly everything that was done to uphold it. . . ."

IN DEFENSE OF THE COURT came the *National Intelligencer:* "They are disloyal, who, under the pretense of preserving the liberties of the citizen, have disregarded the obligations of the organic law. . . ." The Democratic papers were jubilant in their comments. The *New York World* considered the decision "a triumphant vindication of the Democratic Party and a happy augury of the future!!"

Johnson, fortified by *Ex Parte Milligan,* proceeded to eliminate military governments in the South. He ordered the dismissal of all trials of civilians by military commission in those Southern States in which Congress had declared a state of war still existed. Federal Judges issued writs of habeas corpus to release prisoners held by the military. Johnson's policy finally led to his impeachment by Congress, and only one vote prevented his removal from office. Criticism of the Supreme Court continued. Impeachment of the judges was recommended and repeal of their appellate jurisdiction was also suggested. When the constitutionality of the Reconstruction Acts was appealed to the court, Congress withdrew the Court's jurisdiction over the case. In *Ex Parte McCardle,* the Court accepted this imposition and dismissed the case for lack of jurisdiction.

It is not without interest to note that to this day it is unclear whether the President of the United States may suspend the writ of habeas corpus in case of rebellion or invasion, or whether he must seek congressional authority to do so, as was held by Chief Justice Taney in Ex Parte Merryman. The question has never been resolved for congress ratified, by special enactment, Lincoln's action in suspending the writ.

The landmark decision of *Ex Parte Milligan,* according to Chief Justice Warren, "established firmly the principle that when civil courts are open and operating resort to military tribunals for the prosecution of civilians is impermissible." The Chief Justice, however, notes that although the Supreme Court will follow the doctrine of *Ex Parte Milligan,* some cases like *Hirabayashi v. U.S.* (detention of Japanese during World War II) must be considered differently. "These decisions demonstrate dramatically that there are some circumstances in which the court will, in effect, conclude that it is simply not in a position to reject descriptions by the Executive of the degree of military necessity. Thus, in a case like *Hirabayashi,* only the Executive is qualified to determine whether, for example, an invasion is imminent. . . . The consequence of the limitations under which the Court must sometimes operate in this area is that other agencies of government must bear the primary responsibility for determining whether specific actions they are taking are consonant with our Constitution. . . ."

Ex Parte McCardle

Reconstruction:
Congress versus
the Court.

O N MARCH 21, 1868, CONGRESSMAN Wilson of Iowa, made a speech in the House of Representatives, which reflected a situation so untoward in American jurisprudence that its repercussions are felt to this very day in the halls of Congress and even in the inner sanctum of the Supreme Court of the United States. Replying to Congressman Eldridge of Pennsylvania, in a heated debate on the implications of a bill affecting the appellate jurisdiction of the Supreme Court, he exclaimed:

"The gentleman from Pennsylvania says it is not proper for us to look into the courts and see what they propose to do — what cases they have to dispose of. Why, sir, we could not shut our eyes nor close our ears to the information which comes to us from all quarters, particularly in the press representing the party to which the gentleman belongs, that it was a thing certain that the *McCardle Case* was to be made use of to enable a majority of that court to determine the invalidity and unconstitutionality of the Reconstruction Laws of Congress . . . . When we were told day by day that the majority of the Court had practically made up its judgment, not only to pass upon the sufficiency of the return to the writ . . . . but also to do as the Court once did before in the Dred Scott Case, go outside of the record properly involving the questions really presented for its determination, undertaking to infringe upon the political power of Congress and declare the laws of the government of the rebel states in every respect unconstitutional, it was our duty to intervene by a repeal of the jurisdiction and prevent the threatened calamity falling upon the country."

THE OCCASION FOR THESE STRONG words and the manner in which the situation was resolved are so closely interwoven with the peculiar historical facts surrounding the remarkable *McCardle Case*, that they cannot be properly understood without a knowledge of the dramatic and eventful circumstances which led to their spectacular dénouement.

It has been noted that although the case represents one of those rare instances in the history of the Supreme Court when great strength and resolution were called for, yet the Court merely "quavered, faltered and failed!" Certainly the prestige and power of the Court were so terribly shattered by its implications that it still remains a bitter bone of contention among constitutional lawyers. Yet, ironically, the subject matter of the case was so far removed from the purpose of the statute upon which the decision turned that the litigation came as a shocking surprise!

William H. McCardle, editor of the *Vicksburg Times*, was a thorn in the side of Major-General E. O. C. Ord, the Commanding General of the Fourth Military District, comprising the states of Arkansas and Mississippi. The Fourth Military District was one of the five military districts into which the former Confederacy had been divided by the *Reconstruction Acts* of March, 1867, which superimposed a system of military government on the defeated Southerners. Thaddeus Stevens and his Radical Republicans, revengeful and deeply concerned with perpetuating themselves in power, were the driving force behind this legislation. A strongly worded veto by President Johnson protesting the unconstitutionality of the *Reconstruction Acts* had not deterred them.

Not only did the *Acts* prepare the stage for the dramatic struggle between President Johnson and the Radical Republicans, but they also ushered in a period of unsurpassed violence and rebellion in the South. The large, ignorant, Negro electorate which Reconstruction created was deeply resented, along with the corrupt "carpetbaggers" and "scalawags". McCardle and other editors of newspapers in the South, fought back by launching vitriolic attacks upon them and the military authorities. McCardle's editorials built up public resentment in Mississippi against Ord's military administration, picturing it as oppressive and unscrupulous, stressing the injustices of its policies and recommending aggressive resistance. When the Constitutional Convention then in session in Mississippi required additional funds, and General Ord's government imposed a tax to collect revenue for this purpose, McCardle fumed in his paper:

> "There is not a man who will pay any tax imposed by this convention, and if their tax collectors undertake to enforce collection by seizing and selling the property of the people, they will be shot down like dogs, as they are! They will deserve to be shot, and we advise every man to resist the payment of such a tax by all the means God has given him. The Mygotts and Orrs, the Hausers and Gibbs . . . . and all the other scavengers may make a note of it. The people of Mississippi are in no humor to be trifled with. They know that Ord's convention has no power or authority to tax them, and they are determined not to be robbed! The men who attempt it will certainly get hurt, for they will be treated as all robbers and highwaymen deserve to be treated.
>
> "The insolence and villany of this convention is boundless. The adventures from abroad, the renegades of home production, and the Negroes assembled with them seem to think that they are the masters of the people, and that they can rob them at pleasure. We advise a little caution. There are some things that flesh and blood will not bear. Let them go and concoct their villany; let them make their constitution so called, and when it is completed, the people — the

real people, not the omnibus full of vagrants and vaga-
bonds called Radicals—will rise in their might and trample
this constitution under their feet."

As MILITARY GOVERNOR of the District, General Ord was
responsible for preserving the peace, protecting life and
property and punishing all offenders. McCardle, he complained, was disturbing the peace, inciting insurrection,
impeding reconstruction in the South and publishing libels
about him and his associates in the military government.
Under the alleged authority of the *Reconstruction Acts* of
Congress, McCardle was arrested on November 8, 1867, by
order of General Ord, for trial by a military commission.

The charges against McCardle were founded upon his
publication of incendiary and libelous articles in the
Vicksburg Times. Thus, although McCardle was not in the
military service of the United States, he was held in custody by military authority for trial before a military commission. There was something fundamentally wrong, however, with this situation. Only two years before, in *Ex Parte
Milligan*, the Supreme Court had reversed the supine role
it had played during the Civil War and had courageously
decided that military trials of civilians were unconstitutional. Then again, many moderates felt as Mr. Justice
Douglas later expressed it, that the idea of a civilian being
tried by military authorities was "repulsive to the American scheme of justice."

Almost as soon as McCardle was arrested by the military, both the Radical Republicans and the opponents of
reconstruction recognized that a basic political issue had
been created by General Ord. For McCardle's arrest offered a golden opportunity to the enemies of Reconstruction and posed a problem for the Radical Republicans
which had to be resolved no matter at what cost!

The constitutionality of the Acts of March, 1867, had
been suspect from their very enactment. President Johnson, in vetoing them initially, had raised many constitutional objections to their passage. Then again, to many
constitutional lawyers, the provision for military trials of

Southern civilians was in direct violation of the Supreme Court's ruling in *Ex Parte Milligan.* The Radical Republicans, however, persisted in their course, determined to impose military rule on the helpless South to effectuate their Reconstruction goals.

Ex Parte Milligan was condemned by Charles Sumner, a Radical Republican leader, as "an alliance offensive and defensive between the Supreme Court and the President." Thaddeus Stevens had added that the *Milligan* opinion was "more dangerous than *Dred Scott,* placing the knife of the rebel at the throat of every man who now or ever had declared himself a loyal Union Man." Wendell Phillips went so far as to recommend that the Supreme Court be abolished. Actually, the Radical Republicans had good reason to fear the Supreme Court for it was generally believed that if the validity of the *Reconstruction Acts* were ever questioned before the Court, a majority, including Chief Justice Chase, would have ruled them unconstitutional.

HENCE, TO PRESERVE THEIR PROGRAM, the Radical Republicans believed the Supreme Court had to be silenced or at least be deprived of the opportunity to render judgment thereon. By the same token, the moderate and conservative opponents of the program realized that Reconstruction could only be effectively challenged by somehow arranging for the Supreme Court to apply the logic of the *Milligan* case to it. But how to do it?

A number of ways had already been tried, but unsuccessfully. Shortly after the Reconstruction Acts went into effect, a motion had been made before the Supreme Court to file an original bill in equity on behalf of the State of Mississippi, to enjoin "Andrew Johnson, a citizen of the State of Tennessee and President of the United States and his officers and agents appointed for that purpose, and especially E. O. C. Ord, assigned as military commander of the district . . . from executing or in any manner carrying out the acts of March 2 and 25, 1867."

After a great constitutional argument, the Court held,

in *Mississippi v. Johnson,* it could not receive the bill as the acts being questioned were not ministerial. Executive discretion was involved and the Supreme Court "has no jurisdiction of a bill to enjoin the President in the performance of his official duties.

Although highly disappointed by this defeat, counsel for Georgia and Mississippi had decided to try another tack. This time they asked the Supreme Court for leave to file bills enjoining Secretary of War Stanton and General Grant from executing the provision of the *Reconstruction Acts* as they annulled the existing State governments and subjected the civilian population to military rule. Dismissing the suits, ten days later, the Court held, *in Georgia v. Stanton,* that they presented questions calling for an adjudication of rights of a political nature pertaining to sovereignty and the corporate existence of a state, rather than of a person or property and that it had no jurisdiction over such issues.

The *Nation* had critically observed with reference to this decision:

> "Undoubtedly, it is no light matter that the highest court in the land should thus disclaim the power of enquiring into the constitutionality of an act of Congress destroying the government of ten states . . . No State in the Union, therefore, can rely upon the Supreme Court for protection against the usurpation of Congress . . . Notwithstanding all the perils of such a decision, it is clear that it is justified by reason and experience. . . . The immediate results of the decision . . . are unqualifiedly beneficial . . . We think that every intelligent Southerner — certainly every shrewd lawyer or politician feels relieved by the decision. Certainly, it is a cause for congratulations among all friends of regulated liberty. The speedy reorganization of the South under the *Reconstruction Act* is now made all but certain."

But the moderates still refused to concede defeat. True, they had suffered some jurisdictional checks, but they expectantly prepared for the next opportunity. Then came the *McCardle Case!*

MCCARDLE WAS ARRESTED on November 8, 1867. His counsel quickly seized the initiative—for here personal rights were involved—and perhaps this time the Supreme Court would assume jurisdiction over the case! But how could *McCardle's Case* be brought without delay to the Supreme Court? It was important to attack the *Reconstruction Acts* as soon as possible lest the Radical Republicans achieve their hostile purpose before the Supreme Court could act. For McCardle to bring his case on appeal to the Supreme Court through regular process and channels would have taken too long.

Then someone got a brilliant idea! In their haste to protect Federal officials and others loyal to the federal government, especially Negroes, from possible interference and arrest by the local courts and officials of the Southern States, the Radical Republicans on February 5, 1867 had carelessly amended the Judiciary Act of 1789 to authorize the Federal courts, "*to grant writs of habeas corpus in all cases where any person may be restrained of his or her liberty in violation of the Constitution, or of any treaty or law of the United States.*" The act then provided: "From the final decision of any judge, or court *inferior to the Circuit Court, appeal may be taken to the Circuit Court of the United States* for the district in which said cause is heard, and *from the judgment of said Circuit Court to the Supreme Court of the United States.*" Before this amendment, the Supreme Court could review such decisions only by issuing an original writ of habeas corpus.

Of course, this law had been enacted to enforce the Reconstruction program and had never been intended to relieve Southerners improperly deprived of their basic liberties thereby, but it was perfect for McCardle's case and seemed to be tailormade for his counsel's purpose.

On November 11, 1867, McCardle's counsel petitioned Judge Robert A. Hill of the United States Circuit Court for a writ of habeas corpus, challenging the constitutionality of the *Reconstruction Acts* which authorized military arrest and trial of civilians. In granting the writ, Judge Hill made it returnable on November 21, 1867. Before the return date, however, McCardle was arraigned before the military commission, but he refused to plead pending the outcome of his habeas corpus hearing. He was therefore held without bail until the return day when he was surrendered to the Circuit Court by Major-General Gillem, who commanded the sub-district of Mississippi.

ON HIS RETURN, GENERAL GILLEM set forth that McCardle had been arrested and held in custody for trial by a military commission under the authority of the *Reconstruction Acts* and that the charges against McCardle were (1) disturbance of the public peace; (2) inciting to insurrection, disorder, and violence; (3) libeling the character of General Ord and his subordinates; and (4) impeding reconstruction by adjuring the population not to vote on General Ord's program calling for a convention to frame a new Constitution for the State of Mississippi. On November 25, 1867, Judge Hill adjudged that the *Reconstruction Acts* were constitutional and that McCardle be remanded to the custody of General Gillem.

McCardle's counsel, however, had anticipated this decision and immediately moved for permission to appeal to the Supreme Court. Judge Hill granted the motion and admitted McCardle to bail on his own recognizance in the sum of one thousand dollars. McCardle was thus discharged from the custody of General Gillem, with the continuing liability however, under the recognizance, to be returned to military custody in the event his appeal to the Supreme Court was unsuccessful.

And now both sides prepared for a decisive legal struggle! The distinguished Jeremiah S. Black, one of the leading constitutional lawyers of his day, was retained as McCardle's counsel. He moved the Supreme Court on January 10, 1868, to advance the case on the calendar for a more immediate hearing. Black's speech was described as "an extremely bitter Copperhead harrangue on State-Rights and the unconstitutionality of the Reconstruction laws. He evidently argued the McCardle Case *con amore*." Then Attorney-General Stanberry made a dramatic announcement in Court. Firmly convinced that the *Reconstruction Acts* were unconstitutional, he had advised President Johnson he could not in good conscience represent the government. He therefore was withdrawing himself from the case and General Ord and General Gillem would have to have other counsel assigned to them. Seven days later the Supreme Court set the case for argument on the merits for the first Monday in March. According to the newspaper reports, Judges Grier, Clifford, Nelson, Davis and Field were for granting the motion and Chief Justice Chase, Judges Swayne and Miller were against it, and it was popularly believed that the Court would be similarly divided when the constitutionality of the *Reconstruction Acts* would be considered by the Court. Thus, it appeared, the first round, would go to McCardle – but then came the counterattack!

THE RADICAL REPUBLICANS WERE DEEPLY concerned with the damage the Supreme Court could do to their Reconstruction program. Although they were strongly entrenched in power politically, their fortunes did not appear to be too bright. Opposition to their program was growing in the North. Some states were having second thoughts on the Fourteenth Amendment. New Jersey's Legislature in a joint resolution had declared the amendment would result in "The disturbance of the harmony, if not the destruction of our system of government" and would "place new and unheard of powers in the hands of a faction." The Legislature of Ohio, in rescinding its approval of the Fourteenth Amendment, criticized the power it bestowed on Congress "to legislate on subjects foreign to the original objects of the Federal Compact."

With the political trend running against the Radicals in the North, if they could not impose their iron will on the South, they would lose out completely. The *McCardle Case* was therefore of the greatest import to the Radicals. What vexed them particularly was the fact that although five of the eight judges sitting on the Court had been appointed by President Lincoln, the Court was obviously unpartisan!

If the Court could not be depended on to preserve the Reconstruction program, then other measures would necessarily be adopted.

Senator Lyman Trumbull, an eminent Illinois lawyer, and Chairman of the Judiciary Committee of the United States Senate was retained to present the government's case. Although he was a United States Senator, Trumbull was given and accepted a fee of ten thousand dollars, for which he was severely criticized. There is no doubt, however, but that he tried diligently to earn his fee. Three days after he was retained, a bill was introduced in the House by the Judiciary Committee requiring a two-thirds vote of the judges before any law of Congress could be declared unconstitutional. A bitter debate ensued. Defending the Court, Congressman Marshall of Illinois denounced the bill as "revolutionary and dangerous". Its purpose, he continued, was "to prevent an adjudication of the validity of their motley Reconstruction Acts. . . . It is a confession of guilt on the part of the majority. It is evident that they feel and know in their hearts that their legislation will not bear investigation by a Legal Tribunal, made up now principally of members of their own party, placed there by their own favored President." In reply, Congressman Spalding of Ohio stressed that the Supreme Court owed its "Official life" to Congressional action. Ripping into the opposition, Congressman Bingham of Ohio flatly declared that, if Congress willed it, the Court could be limited to three members and even be required to have a quorum of two or even three members.

ALTHOUGH THE BILL PASSED the House and received enthusiastic support in the daily press, still many people had misgivings about the wisdom of such drastic action. The *Chicago Republican* summed up this opposition well: "Congress . . . must not meddle with the constitutional rights and privileges of the people, nor of their Executive or Supreme Judiciary . . . Regarding, as they do, the Supreme Court as the judicial bulwark against tyranny and injustice on the part of either President or Congress, they will never permit this safeguard against oppression to be swept away. The people will be found as prompt to resent usurpation on the part of Congress as of Johnson." Gideon Welles, writing in his diary reflected the fear of many moderates. "In the House," he noted for January 13, 1868, "under the discipline and stimulation of the Radical leaders, there is manifested a revolutionary and violent spirit. Part of the conspiracy is a scheme to change the character of the Supreme Court, which Stevens and his fellows find is against them."

The bill was finally dropped in the Senate. The Democrats, however, cynically suggested the bill was dropped because the Radicals feared that even the two-thirds requirements would not be sufficient to prevent the Supreme Court from finding the *Reconstruction Laws* unconstitutional. Another bill, introduced in the House by Thaddeus Stevens, depriving the Court of jurisdiction in any case involving the *Reconstruction Acts* was similarly dropped as politically inexpedient. The *Nation* commented: "If this game of 'exceptions' as an instrument of party warfare, be once fairly entered on, we venture to say that, in the course of the next twenty years, the constitutionality of half the *Statutes at Large* would be withdrawn from the cognizance of the Supreme Court."

Trumbull's next tactic was to move the Supreme Court on January 31, 1868, to dismiss McCardle's appeal for want of jurisdiction. James Hughes argued with him on the motion and Black, now joined by William L. Sharkey, another leading constitutional lawyer, opposed the motion. After a most thorough argument, which was continued on February 7th, the Court reserved decision. On February 17, 1868, Chief Justice Chase, speaking for a unanimous Court held that the *Act of February 5, 1867,* which amended the *Judiciary Act of 1789* gave the Court jurisdiction of appeals from the judgments of inferior courts in cases of habeas corpus. The motion to dismiss was therefore denied.

And now the case was to be argued on the merits! Many people had felt that the Court would never accept jurisdiction of the case. The fact that it had, presented a cold, sobering problem for the Radicals. Condemnation of the decision appeared in all their newspapers. The Conservatives and Democrats, however, rejoiced. The Radicals were quick to respond in Congress. Gideon Welles sadly noted in his diary on February 18th, that: "In their war upon the Court, the Radicals, under the lead of Trumball, have under consideration an act prohibiting the Court from passing judgment on political questions, and they have now a bill declaring what are political questions. These usurpations and intrigues strain our government."

DESPITE THE MACHINATIONS OF THE RADICALS in Congress, and the greatly aroused public interest in the *McCardle Case,* an uneasy quiet took over. Everyone concerned with the outcome of the Case appeared to be in arrested motion, awaiting the argument on the merits before the Supreme Court.

When it became clear to the Radicals that the case would have to be argued on the merits, Secretary of War Stanton, with the advice of General Grant, retained Matthew Hale Carpenter, an acknowledged leader of the American Bar, to work with Senator Trumbull on the government's brief. Writing to his wife on February 24, 1868, Carpenter revealed:

"I got my "big" brief into the hands of the government printer this morning. Stanton has ordered one thousand copies to be printed . . . Stanton sent for me this morning and said to me: 'You may as well understand that you are in for the whole fight.' He gave me a check for five thousand dollars as a retainer. What will come of all this fight I cannot predict."

When the Court opened on March 2, a crowded room of distinguished lawyers and government officials, awaited the argument with intense anticipation and excitement. Judge William L. Sharkey and Robert J. Walker of Mississippi, Charles O'Connor and David Dudley Field of New York, and Jeremiah S. Black of Pennsylvania appeared for McCardle, a most illustrious group of leading members of the American Bar. Senator Trumbull and Carpenter for the government, as well as James Hughes, were equally well known. A titanic legal struggle was anticipated, and the audience was not disappointed.

Justice Stephen J. Field, a brother of David Dudley Field, later described the arguments as he heard them from the bench: "Seldom has it been my fortune during my judicial life now of nearly twenty years, to listen to arguments equal in learning, ability and eloquence. The whole subject was exhausted. As the arguments were widely published in the public journals, and read throughout the country, they produced a profound effect. The impression was general that the *Reconstruction Acts* could not be sustained; that they were revolutionary and destructive of a republican form of government in the states, which the Constitution required the federal government to guarantee . . .

Counsel for McCardle also stressed the Constitutional guarantee of trial by jury, which was denied McCardle by the Military Commission, and made a great point of *Ex Parte Milligan*, in which the Supreme Court had held the trial of civilians by military commission unconstitutional.

CARPENTER ARGUED THE GOVERNMENT'S CASE on March 3d and 4th affirming the validity of the *Reconstruction Laws* and the legality of all rightful acts thereunder as an exercise of belligerent rights. In print, his effort comprised about 100 octavo pages. The Supreme Court, he maintained was not coordinate in power with Congress, and certainly was not above it. Actually, it was subordinate to Congress in the frame of reference of the Constitution. Although the Court could not organize and reorganize Congress, Congress could actually do this to the Supreme Court.

When Carpenter finished his speech, Secretary of War Stanton is alleged to have "clasped him in his arms, and, with tears in his eyes, exclaimed: "Carpenter, you have saved us!" Writing to his wife the same day, Carpenter exulted: "I spoke two and one-half hours today and did as well as I expected or hoped to do. I am praised nearly to death. I had more than half the Senate for an audience. Miller's face was 'as the face of an angel' radiant with light and joy. Davis and Field looked troubled; Nelson, Clifford and Grier dead against me. But I shook them up and rattled their dry bones."

While the argument was still continuing, an unprecedented event occurred. The Radical Republicans, desperately aware that the tide was turning against them, agreed on a two-pronged attack to protect their reconstruction program. President Johnson had to be removed from office and the Supreme Court had to be neutralized! First they impeached President Johnson, so that on March 5, Chief Justice Chase had to hasten to the Senate to sit there as the presiding officer during the trial. As a result, the argument on the *McCardle Case* was not completed until March 9th, when the Court took the case under advisement.

Then the Radicals turned their attention to the Court. They increased their pressure in Congress to prevent the Court from rendering a decision in the *McCardle Case*. With President Johnson practically removed from office, only the Supreme Court threatened to nullify the effect of the *Reconstruction Acts*. And the Radicals were very much concerned about the Court, for rumor had it, the Court would definitely invalidate the Reconstruction program.

The sensitivity of Congress to the Justice's reactions to the *McCardle Case* was interestingly related by Justice Field in his *Reminiscences* of a brilliant dinner he had attended in honor of the Secretary of the Treasury. "Some of the brightest spirits of Congress were present. As we took our seats at the table, I noticed on the menu a choice collection of wines, Johannisberg among others. The dinner was sumptuously and admirably served. Our host saw that the appropriate wine accompanied the successive courses. As the dinner progressed, and the wine circulated, the wit of the guests sparkled. At about eight, songs had been added to other manifestations of pleasure. I then concluded that I had better retire so I said to my host, that if he would excuse me, I would seek the open air." Shortly after he left, Rodman M. Price, former Governor of New Jersey, arrived, and he was given the place vacated by Field. After a while Price loudly exclaimed, that in his opinion, "The whole reconstruction measures would soon be 'smashed up' and sent to 'Kingdom come' by the Supreme Court." A reporter who had been listening closely to Price asked the waiter who he was. The waiter, checking the seating list said it was Justice Field. Delighted with this news beat, the reporter sent it to the *Evening Express*. The Radicals in Congress were so incensed by this "impropriety" that a resolution was passed directing the House Committee on the Judiciary to ascertain whether Field should be impeached.

RESENTFULLY COMMENTING ON THE RESOLUTION Field said: "The resolution was evidently intended to intimidate me, and to act as a warning to all the judges as to what they might expect if they presumed to question the wisdom of the validity of the reconstruction measures of Congress. What little effect it had on me my subsequent course in the *McCardle Case* probably showed to the House. I had only one feeling for the movement—that of profound contempt; and I believe that a similar feeling was entertained by every right-thinking person having any knowledge of the proceeding." It was not until several months later that the resolution was tabled even though the facts were disclosed soon after the incident. Many people considered it a wonderful joke on the Radical Republicans.

Although it appeared that the Court would not decide the *McCardle Case* until the following term, as Chase was preoccupied with the Johnson impeachment trial, the Radicals decided not to take any chances; they decided to intervene anyway. Hence on March 12th, a rider was attached to an inocuous bill in the House for which unanimous consent had been obtained by Congressman Schenck for action. (It is interesting to note that one of the drafters of this bill was Senator Lyman Trumbull, who appeared to be working overtime to earn his fee.) The rider repealed the section of the act of February 5, 1867, which authorized appeals of habeas corpus cases from the Circuit Court to the Supreme Court, *"or the exercise of any such jurisdiction by said Supreme Court, on appeals which have been, or may hereafter be taken."* Thus this surreptitious rider not only deprived the Court of appellate jurisdiction under the act of February 5, 1867, but actually took the *McCardle Case* away from it, even though the Court had already taken the case under advisement. Completely unaware of its import, the Democrats and Moderate Republicans permitted its passage without debate. It was not until the bill similarly passed the Senate the same day that the great deception was uncovered. The slick manner in which the rider had been passed and its effect on the Court shocked and angered many sections of the country.

Once again Welles lamented in his diary:

> *"March 14, 1868.* It is evident that the Radicals in Congress are in a conspiracy to overthrow not only the President but the Government. The impeachment is but a single act in the drama. . . . By trick, imposition and breach of courtesy, an *Act* was slipped through both houses, repealing the laws of 1867 and 1789, the effect of which is to take from the Supreme Court certain powers and which is designed to prevent a decision in the *McCardle Case.* Should the Court in that case, as it is supposed they will, pronounce the *Reconstruction Laws* unconstitutional, the military governments will fall and the whole Radical fabric will tumble with it. Only one course can prolong the miserable contrivance, and that is a President like Wade, who will maintain the military governments regardless of Courts, of law, or right. Hence, I have very little expectation that the President will escape conviction. His deposition is a party necessity, and the Senators have not individually the strength, ability, nor honesty, to resist the Radical caucus decision, which Stevens, Ben Butler, and other Chief conspirators sent out."

THE BIG QUESTION NOW WAS WHAT would the Supreme Court do in the face of this Congressional attack? President Johnson gave the Court every opportunity to grapple with the problem before the bill became a law. Instead of vetoing it immediately, he held on to it the full ten days allowed him by the Constitution. Thus he gave the Court ample time to decide the *McCardle Case* before its jurisdiction was withdrawn.

The Democrats and moderate Republicans hopefully awaited the Court's action. But as time passed and the Court failed to act, some Democrats accused it of avoiding its constitutional duty. Others, however, still continued to have faith in its integrity. It was unbelievable that the Court would not decide the *Case* said the *Boston Post*, if for no other reason but "in defense of its own dignity, and to show that the Court cannot be trifled with by reckless partisans who flippantly speak of 'clipping the wings of the Court'. It is well ascertained that Justices Chase, Nelson, Grier, Clifford, Davis and Field believe the *Reconstruction Acts* to be unconstitutional. . . . The decision is made up, and they have the power and the right to deliver it. Whether they have the nerve to be an independent Judiciary remains to be seen."

Would the Court stand up to the Radicals? That was the burning question—and it had to be answered before March 25th—the last day Johnson had to veto the bill. Still no word came from the Court! The Court held a second conference on the *McCardle Case* on March 21. Justice Field later commented that the case should have been "decided in regular course of proceedings when it was reached on the second subsequent consultation day, the 21st." More to the point was his revelation that *"The Judges had all formed their conclusions, and no excuse was urged that more times was wanted for examination."* Still the Court hesitated. Then once again reverting to the servile role it had played to Congress during the Civil War, it took cognizance of the pending bill and decided to postpone its decision until a disposition was made of it. Justices Field and Grier, however, valiantly objected, stating for the record that the decision should not be postponed.

President Johnson anxiously waited for the Court to

act, but in vain. As a Republican paper stated it, the Court had decided that it would not run a race with Congress . . . it would hardly have been consistent with the dignity of the country and the respect due to the other branches of the Government to proceed with the matter until the President had either approved or vetoed the bill, and the Congress had acted on the veto." March 25th came and finally Johnson could delay no longer. Even though he was undergoing the severest ordeal of his life in his impeachment trial, and it was obvious that his action would inflame his enemies even more—he courageously vetoed the bill. Moreover, in doing so, he sent a strong message back to Congress, in effect reading both it and the Court a lesson on their Constitutional duties.

> "The legislation proposed", he maintained, "establishes a precedent which, if followed, may eventually sweep away every check on arbitrary and unconstitutional legislation. Thus far during the existence of the Government, the Supreme Court of the United States has been viewed by the people as the true expounder of their Constitution, and in the most violent party conflicts, its judgments and decrees have always been sought and deferred to with confidence and respect. In public estimation, it combines judicial wisdom and impartiality in a greater degree than any other authority known to the Constitution; and any act which may be construed into, or mistaken for, an attempt to prevent or evade its decisions on a question which affects the liberty of the citizens and agitates the country cannot fail to be attended with unpropitious consequences. It will be justly held by a large portion of the people as an admission of the unconstitutionality of the act on which its judgment may be forbidden or forstalled, and may interfere with that willing acquiescence in its provisions which is necessary for the harmonious and efficient execution of any law."

RECOILING FROM THIS UNEXPECTED assault, the Radicals faltered for almost two days while the aroused Democrats engaged in an acrimonious and vicious debate on the purpose of the bill. They were taunted as being "afraid of the decision of the Court" even though five judges of the eight had been appointed by President Lincoln whose program the Radicals claimed they were effectuating. Senator Reverdy Johnson warned that it was "dangerous to inculcate the belief that Courts can be governed by political and party motives." There was no doubt that the Moderates had decisively beaten the Radicals in the debate, but the Radicals controlled Congress and on March 26, 1868, the bill passed the Senate over the President's veto with the necessary two-thirds vote and on March 27, it was enacted into law when the House passed it. Thus, Congress, prevented the Court from challenging the Constitutionality of the *Reconstruction Laws*.

Professor John W. Burgess accused it of perpetrating "an abominable subterfuge" and "a shameful abuse of its powers." Gideon Welles bemoaned in his diary that "The Judges of the Supreme Court have caved in, fallen through, failed in the *McCardle Case*. Only Grier and Field have held out like men, patriots, Judges of nerve and honest independence. These things look ominous and sadden me. I fear for my country when I see such abasement. Fear of the usurping Radicals in Congress had intimidated some of these Judges, or like reckless Democratic leaders, they are willing their party should triumph through Radical folly and wickedness. These are indeed evil times!"

And so—Congress had imposed its will on the Supreme Court. But what was the effect of the law depriving the Court of jurisdiction in the *McCardle Case*? Would the Supreme Court accept it docilely? There was no precedent to fall back on. As Swisher has noted "this is apparently the only instance in American History in which Congress has rushed to withdraw the appellate jurisdiction of the Supreme Court for the purpose of preventing a decision on the Constitutionality of a particular law." Although many Constitutional authorities asserted the Court now lacked jurisdiction to decide the case, others contended the repealing law was not binding on the Court as it had become effective after the Court had taken the case under advisement and hence, in essence, was an *ex post facto* measure.

March 30, 1868 was the Court's next opinion day. When no decision was announced on the *McCardle Case*, Jeremiah Black rose on behalf of McCardle, and suggested that one was due. He insisted that the repealing law was not binding on the Court and proposed that its effect should be formally argued. Despite the Government's opposition, the Justices, perhaps with some embarrassment, consented to set it down for April 2nd, if acceptable to both sides. Counsel for the Government, however, requested more time for preparation, and argument was then postponed until the December, 1868 term. This was too much for Justices Grier and Field. Unbeknownst to the other judges, they had been preparing a protest on the Court diffidence. To everyone's amazement, Justice Grier then read the following unprecedented protest in open court.

> "This case was fully argued in the beginning of this month. It is a case that involves the liberty and rights not only of the appellant, but of millions of our fellow citizens. The country and the parties had a right to expect that it would receive the immediate and solemn attention of this Court. By the postponement of the Case, we shall subject ourselves, whether justly or unjustly, to the imputation that we have evaded the performance of a duty imposed on us by the Constitution and waited for legislation to interpose and supersede our action and relieve us from our responsibility. I am not willing to be a partaker either of the eulogy or opprobrium that may follow; I can only say,
> *Pudet haec opprobria nobis,*
> *Et dici potuisse; et non putuisse repelli*"

The quotation from Ovid's Metamorphoses was translated by Field as "It fills us with shame that these reproaches can be uttered, and cannot be repelled."

JUSTICE FIELD, THEN ADDED to the Court's confusion by reading his own endorsement of Grier's excoriating indictment of his brethern:
"I am of the same opinion as my brother Grier, and unite in his protest."

Grier's "extra-judicial opinion" again aroused the nation. He and Field were subjected to abuse as well as praise. Former Justice Benjamin R. Curtis, who had himself strongly dissented in the Dred Scott Case, summed up the country's attitude well when he observed: "Congress, with the acquiescence of the country, has subdued the Supreme Court, as well as the President."

It is not without interest, however, to note the justification for the Court's action in the *McCardle Case* as expressed by Charles Warren in his *"Supreme Court in U. S. History."* After admitting that the Court "had not been firm in its stand," he sympathetically explains "it must be admitted that, in view of the fact that the Chief Justice was presiding in the Impeachment Trial of the President, it was probably wiser on the part of the Court to postpone arguments on so important an issue until there should be a full Court; and the intimations that its action was influenced by the political situation were clearly unfair, in view of its previous courageous action in sustaining its jurisdiction over the case."

Final argument on the *McCardle Case* took place on March 19, 1869. Sharkey, for the appellant, maintained that the Constitution vested judicial power in one Supreme Court. The Court therefore receives its jurisdiction directly from the Constitution and not from Congress. The jurisdiction being vested by the Constitution alone, Congress cannot abridge or take it away. If the Court could only exercise its judicial power by Congressional grant, what would be the Court's function if Congress refused to act thereon? The "judicial power" would cease to exist. The Court is coexistent and co-ordinate with Congress and must be able to exercise the whole judicial power of the U. S., though Congress passed no act on the subject. Suppose the *Judiciary Act of 1789* were repealed? Would the Court lose the power to pass on every case to which the judicial power of the U. S. extended? Although the Repealing Law took away the appellate power of the Court in cases of habeas corpus, he submitted Congress could not do so. Another point he stressed was that the Court had actually taken the *McCardle Case* under advisement. Can Congress thus interfere with cases on which the Court has passed, or is passing judgment? Is not legislation like this an exercise by the Congress of judicial power?

In reply, Trumbull and Carpenter argued that the Constitution gives to the Court appellate jurisdiction in any case like the *McCardle Case*, but only with such exceptions and under such regulations as Congress makes. The Court had no jurisdiction in this case – an appeal from the Circuit Court – until it was conferred by the Act of February 5, 1867. That Act, however, having been repealed, the jurisdiction ceased; and the Court had thereafter no authority to pronounce any opinion or render any judgment in the case.

ON APRIL 12, 1869, A UNANIMOUS Court handed down its decision. Chief Justice Chase read the opinion: The judges agreed with Sharkey, that the appellate jurisdiction of the Court was not derived from acts of Congress. "It is strictly speaking, conferred by the Constitution. But it is conferred 'with such exceptions and under such regulations as Congress shall make'." Whether the Court could have exercised general appellate jurisdiction under rules prescribed by itself if Congress had made no exceptions and no regulations was not pertinent to this case – for Congress actually had done so – as early as September 24, 1789, when it established the judiciary of the U. S. The Court agreed with the holding in *Durousseau v. U. S.* that although "The appellate powers of this Court are not given by the judicial act, but are given by the Constitution, they are nevertheless limited and regulated by that Act and by such other acts as have been passed on the subject." The *Judiciary Act* was an exercise of the power given by the Constitution to Congress "of making exceptions to the appellate jurisdiction of the Supreme Court." Under it Congress has affirmatively described the Court's jurisdiction, and hence, it is understood to imply a negation of the exercise of such appellate power as is not comprehended within it.

Here Congress has expressly repealed the appellate

jurisdiction of the Court in cases of habeas corpus. "We are not at liberty to inquire into the motives of the legislature. We can only examine into its power under the Constitution, and the power to make exceptions to the appellate jurisdiction of this Court is given by express words. What, then, is the effect of the repealing act upon the case before us? We cannot doubt as to this. Without jurisdiction the Court cannot proceed at all in any cause. Jurisdiction is power to declare the law, and when it ceases to exist, the only function remaining to the Court is that of announcing the fact and dismissing the cause. . . . It is quite clear, therefore, that this Court cannot proceed to pronounce judgment in this case, for it has no longer jurisdiction of the appeal; and judicial duty is not less fitly performed by declining ungranted jurisdiction than in exercising firmly that which the Constitution and the laws confer." The Court then dismissed the appeal of McCardle for want of jurisdiction, but it added that it still had jurisdiction over habeas corpus cases brought to the Court by the writ of certiorari as authorized by the original *Judiciary Act of 1789*.

Thus, although the Reconstruction Acts were patently unconstitutional, under the principle established by *Ex Parte Milligan*, the Radical Republicans forestalled their testing by the Supreme Court and gained the time to impose their program on the South. Professor Schwartz has aptly characterized the *McCardle Case* as a striking demonstration of "the fallen state of the Supreme Court in the post-Dred Scott Period." There is no doubt but the prestige of the Court reached its nadir by reason of its hesitancy and decision in the *McCardle Case*.

It has been suggested, however, by Dr. Eubank "that viewed in the light of history, one must conclude that its actions proved the wiser course. An adverse decision might have destroyed the effectiveness of the Court just as the Dred Scott decision had a decade earlier. As it was, the Court came through the rocky shoals of Reconstruction with its powers relatively unimpaired and with its prestige only temporarily weakened."

It should also be noted that the *Reconstruction Acts* were brought before the Supreme Court once again in 1869 in *Ex Parte Yerger* by another Southern editor, imprisoned, convicted and sentenced by a military commission on a charge of murder of a Colonel Crane. This time, however, he appealed for a writ of habeas corpus under the original *Judiciary Act* of 1789. For a moment it appeared that the classic conflict between the Court and Congress in *Ex Parte McCardle* would once again be resurrected, for after the Court assumed jurisdiction of the case, a bill was introduced in Congress specifically depriving the Court of jurisdiction in all cases involving the constitutionality of the *Reconstruction Laws*, and then by another more drastic one prohibiting the judicial review of any act of Congress. But fortunately, under an agreement between Yerger's counsel and the attorney general, Yerger was turned over to the civil authorities and his petition was withdrawn. The question therefore becoming moot, Congress took no further action on the bills and the last opportunity to test the Constitutionality of the *Reconstruction Laws* finally came to naught.

The *McCardle* and *Yerger* cases reflect the high mark of Congressional interference with the authority of the Supreme Court. Gradually the division of power between them became more balanced, especially after President Johnson escaped conviction by one vote in his impeachment trial and Thaddeus Stevens, the indomitable Radical leader died shortly thereafter. Slowly the Court regained its former prestige and independence. Never again did Congress attempt to interfere with a case actually pending before the Court.

It was not until 1954, that Congress became interested again in the appellate jurisdiction of the Court. This time, however, it was for the Court's benefit. A Senate Judiciary Committee proposed an amendment to the Constitution, sponsored by the American Bar Association, depriving Congress of any power to deny the Supreme Court jurisdiction "in all cases arising under the Constitution."

THE MCCARDLE DOCTRINE LAY DORMANT for many years until an unusually critical and resentful reaction to the Supreme Court's decisions in the *School Segregation Cases* led to its revival. Proposals were introduced in Congress to deprive the Supreme Court of jurisdiction in the subject areas covered by those cases. The Supreme Court Cases on the right to practice law in *Schware v. Bd. of Ex.*, and in *Konisberg v. State Bar of Calif.*, were also bitterly denounced.

To no one's surprise, the Judiciary Committee of the Senate favorably reported a bill depriving the Supreme Court of jurisdiction to review cases involving state regulations for admission to the practice of law. That same year a bill was introduced in Congress by Senator Jenner limiting the Court's appellate jurisdiction so as not to include cases involving the investigating power of Congress. This was in answer to the Court's decisions in cases concerning national security. Fortunately for the Court, these proposals were short lived. Later however, in reprisal for the Court's decisions in *Baker v. Carr* and other "malapportionment" cases, angered Congressmen passed a bill sponsored by Rep. William M. Tuck of Virginia withdrawing the appellate jurisdiction of the Court in state legislature reapportionment cases. In the Senate, Senator Everett Dirksen introduced a bill to delay the Court's action in these areas.

These Congressional attacks on the Court's appellate jurisdiction have brought to the fore once again the significance of the Court's holding in *Ex Parte McCardle*. Does Congress have the Constitutional power to limit the Court's appellate jurisdiction, "with such exceptions, and under such regulations as the Congress shall make"? It is recognized, of course, that a constitutional amendment to accomplish this purpose is undoubtedly legal and proper. The Eleventh Amendment nullified the holding of *Chisholm v. Georgia,* the Fourteenth Amendment, the *Dred Scott* decision and the Sixteenth, the *Income Tax Cases* decision. But can it also be done solely by Congressional fiat by reason of the *McCardle Case*? In other words, as Charles Curtis has stated it, is the Court's appellate jurisdiction "held and exercised at the pleasure of Congress?"

The Tuck Amendment (H. R. 11625) "That neither the Supreme Court of the U. S., nor any Federal Court inferior thereto, shall have jurisdiction, either original or appellate, to change,, modify, direct, or set aside any apportionment or reapportionment of legislative districts adopted by the lawmaking bodies of the respective states", has resurrected a constitutional question that has troubled lawyers from the beginnings of the *McCardle Case.*

On the one hand, we have the sweeping conclusion of Justice Douglas in his book, *"We The Judges,"* that *Ex Parte McCardle* remains the law today. "The power of Congress over the appellate jurisdiction of the Supreme Court is complete." We also have Justice Frankfurter's words dissenting in *Nat. Mutual Ins. Co. v. Tidewater* that Congress "may withdraw appellate jurisdiction once conferred, and it may do so even while a case is *sub judice.*" On the other, we have opinions rendered by constitutional lawyers, such as Dean Robert B. McKay that *Ex Parte McCardle* is "a case exceptional on its facts although never specifically overruled." McKay points out "that *McCardle* involved only Congressional withdrawal of jurisdiction from the Supreme Court as to appeals from lower federal courts. Congress had *not* attempted the much more critical interference with the judicial branch and with the functioning of the federal system that is now suggested, namely, a denial of appellate jurisdiction in review of *state* court decisions. To take away this power would negate what has always been considered the most important aspect of judicial review and to alter fundamentally the character of the federal system. "As Mr. Justice Holmes long ago observed," McKay continues, "I do not think the United States would come to an end if we lost our power to declare an Act of Congress void. I do think the Union would be imperiled if we could not make that declaration as to the laws of the federal states" . . . I would be very doubtful of the constitutionality of the proposal even assuming that McCardle was correctly decided on its facts. But even that is doubtful. Mr. Justice Douglas recently stated that in a dissenting opinion in *Glidden v. Zdanok:* "There is a serious question whether the *McCardle Case* could command a majority view today." Perhaps the Douglas evaluation of McCardle in the *Glidden Case* reflects his changing opinion of the doctrine therein espoused. Certainly it should be observed that Congress, later expunged the act denying the Court appellate jurisdiction in habeas corpus cases, and restored jurisdiction to the Court to hear habeas corpus appeals, perhaps reflecting its own doubt as to its constitutionality.

It is also not without interest to note that the Dirksen amendment currently being considered by Congress, which would require Federal Courts to delay action in all legislative apportionment cases for two to four years was decried by fifteen deans and professors of law as a dangerous threat to the integrity of our judicial process in that it would interfere with "the power and duty of the state courts to enforce the Federal Constitution and of the Supreme Court to insure uniformity of interpretation." Then referring to the *McCardle Case* as the one time "in our history Congress acted to prevent a Constitutional decision which it anticipated," they pointed out that "most historians and legal analysts have regarded the *McCardle* affair as an unfortunate episode in our history. It ought not to be repeated in this even more drastic form."

In essence, therefore, what must be resolved is whether the exceptions and regulations clause of the Constitution gives to Congress the power to negate the essential function of the Supreme Court, even though *Ex Parte McCardle* indicates that it does!

THAT PEPPERY REBEL, MAJOR WILLIAM H. MCCARDLE, formerly of the Confederate Army and Editor of the Vicksburg Times, must be smiling at all this "hoop-a-la" over his case. Certainly, he would have enjoyed it for he loved a good battle and an opportunity to use his vitriolic pen.

In 1962, a letter to the *American Bar Association Journal* asked "What happened to McCardle? Did the Yankees hang him?" After ascertaining that McCardle was alive in 1890, "which indicates, of course, he was not executed," the editor unearthed with the aid of Mrs. H. H. Bragg, President of The Vicksburg Historical Soceity, the fascinating fact that after the Supreme Court's decision in his case, McCardle was not brought to trial and that his case was dropped. "General Ord's purpose in arresting McCardle in Vicksburg in 1867 was to silence him. . . . When the Supreme Court dismissed his case in April 2, 1869, refusing to hear it, the government could have pressed its charges and brought him before a military commission for trial but they quietly let the matter drop. By this time General Ord had long since been removed from his command at Vicksburg and his successor was apparently not as sensitive to criticism as Ord had been."

"McCardle continued to wield his sharp pen on behalf of the South during the long and painful Reconstruction period. When that was over at last, he used his influence and ability in restoring peace and tranquility in Mississippi. McCardle died in Jackson, Miss. on April 28, 1893. He was at that time engaged in writing a history of Mississippi in collaboration with Governor Lowney of this State."

That McCardle was never subsequently tried by the military commission was substantiated by Professor Meador of the University of Virginia Law School, who wrote "Neither the Circuit Court Minute Book nor any other records at the Federal Records Center, in Georgia, reveals any proceedings subsequent to the Supreme Court decision."

Almost a century has passed since McCardle's case. It is not without reason that Professor Schwartz considers it as "a case more celebrated than understood." What is even more dismaying is the realization that the problems with which it dealt lie before us still unresolved today.

The
Slaughter House
Cases

*The Banded Butchers
and the
Supreme Court*

"THE BANDED BUTCHERS ARE BUSTED. MATT." This noted telegram, sent by Matt H. Carpenter to Louisiana state officials in New Orleans on April 14, 1873, not only advised them of a great legal triumph in a landmark case, but also highlighted a Supreme Court decision which "profoundly affected the course of the future history of the country." Known as the *Slaughter-House Cases*, its significance has become even more enduring by reason of the Supreme Court's reappraisal of the scope of the Fourteenth Amendment — a judicial process so intimately interwoven with the rise of due process and the concept of laissez-faire that it has been critically cited as a classic example of "government by judiciary." Actually, *The Slaughter-House Cases* cannot be properly appreciated without an understanding of the confusing and involved socio-legal issues from which they evolved. Yet, oddly enough, despite the national character the cases quickly assumed, they all began with ordinary, albeit highly defiant New Orleans butchers!

New Orleans in 1869 seethed with outraged emotion. A corrupt state legislature controlled by the carpetbaggers had passed an act on March 8, 1869, "To protect the health of the City of New Orleans, to locate the stock landings and slaughter houses and to incorporate 'The Crescent City Live-Stock Landing and Slaughter House Company'." In essence it granted the corporation, consisting of seventeen persons, the exclusive right for twenty five years to slaughter livestock in New Orleans, Jefferson and St. Bernard parishes, and maintain stock-landings, yards, wharves, stables, slaughterhouses, abattoirs, and other buildings for landings and keeping animals for sale and for slaughtering. All other persons were prohibited from carrying on such activity under penalty of heavy fines and imprisonment, and were required to pay the corporation certain fixed fees for the use of its facilities or services. Immediately affected by this most unpopular law were about 1000 persons employed daily in the slaughtering of livestock. When the bill had first been considered in the legislature, they had vigorously opposed it and even employed ridicule to defeat its passage. All attempts to block it in the legislature, however, including a filibuster, had been defeated, and the bill had passed with what appeared to be undue expedition. Shortly after its passage it became known that the legislators had been given the privilege to purchase shares of stock in the Corporation and pay for them at their convenience. The uproar against the monopoly was reflected in the local newspapers. The *Bee* editorialized that the bill would "become a by-word of reproach to all concerned in it." The *Picayune* exclaimed that the monopoly had to be set aside. "It may take time and a reformation of the polluted courts of justice to bring this about, but it will be done when the people awake to the necessity of driving the money changers and the false scribes and Pharisees from the Temple."

The independent butchers of New Orleans refused to accept such a brazen deprivation of their livelihoods without a battle. They maintained that the monopoly "was an invasion of their personal rights." After many protest meetings they organized the "Benevolent Butchers Association of New Orleans" on July 21, 1869 to redress their grievances. But what could the butchers do? Ordinarily their situation would have been helpless, for under the federal Constitution a state's powers in such matters were inviolable. But something new had been added to the federal Constitution—the Thirteenth and Fourteenth Amendments,—and based on their provisions, the butchers brought hundreds of suits against the Crescent City Corporation or "The Monopoly" as it was called, contending that the act of the Louisiana Legislature created a monopoly in violation of the Thirteenth and Fourteenth Amendments. In retaliation, the Attorney General of Louisiana brought suit, on behalf of the State, to enjoin the independent butchers from continuing to engage in their business in defiance of the law. In a countermove, the Butchers Benevolent Association then sought to enjoin "The Monopoly" from enforcing the provisions of the law.

As was anticipated, the Supreme Court of Louisiana upheld the validity of the law when these cases went up on appeal from the district courts. The butchers, however, prevailed upon Mr. Justice Bradley, sitting in the Federal Circuit Court, to enjoin the enforcement of the prohibitory provisions of the statute. In the meantime, they brought several of the causes to the Supreme Court of the United States by writ of error.

THE BUTCHERS THEN PLAYED their final ace. They retained John A. Campbell to argue their appeal before the Supreme Court. Campbell, at the time, was one of the leading attorneys in the South. Characteristic of the confidence he instilled in his clients was the saying, "Leave it to God and Mr. Campbell." He had formerly been an Associate Justice of the Supreme Court who had resigned from the bench on April 26, 1861, out of loyalty to his state, Alabama, when it had seceded from the Union. Although he firmly believed in states' rights, Campbell was not a secessionist. Campbell had lost most of his property during the Civil War, and had settled in New Orleans in 1865. Before long he had acquired a large practice and had assumed the leadership of the New Orleans Bar.

Campbell found himself in an unusual and novel situation. Although a staunch believer in states' rights and a loyal Southerner, in order to succeed in the appeal he necessarily had to argue that the federal judiciary could restrict the acts of a state government. To impose such a limitation upon states' rights went contrary to the essence of his political belief, and yet he had no alternative. For the position of the South had deteriorated to such an extent under the influence of corrupt Reconstruction governments, only federal intervention could resurrect it. In a letter written several years later, he described it as follows:

"The Southern communities will be a desolation until there is a thorough change of affairs in all the departments of the government. There is now no responsibility – and we are fast losing all of our ancient notions of what is becoming and fit in administration. The public is tolerant of corruption, maladministration, partiality in courts, worthlessness in juries, and regard government only as a means of exploitation. Indifference to anything wrong is the common sentiment. Hope is disappearing . . .

"Discontent, dissatisfaction, murmurings, complaints, even insurrection would be better than the insensibility that seems to prevail."

Campbell, however, had avidly followed the debates in Congress and in the state legislatures, on the ratification of the Thirteenth and Fourteenth Amendments, and was very much aware of their importance to the South. He recognized that they had been designed primarily to grant Congress authority to protect the rights of the newly enfranchised slaves from usurpation by the Southern states. But, he reasoned, why not apply them to the instant case, even though Negro civil rights were not involved.

The legal situation with which Campbell had to contend was one of first impression. As an aftermath of the Civil War, a strident demand had arisen for federal protection of the Negro from the abuses of state governments. The laws enacted by Congress to protect civil rights were considered to be of doubtful constitutional validity. Only a constitutional amendment could adequately protect the freedmen, and the Fourteenth and Fifteenth Amendments were the answer. But before they were finally adopted, many bitter and passionate debates had ensued in Congress on how the final drafts should read. One of the greatest concerns expressed pertained to the possibility that the traditional form of American government, in which the sovereignty of the states was recognized, would be destroyed by a constitutional provision granting federal restraint over state action.

Senator Orville H. Browning of Illinois in a letter published in *The Cincinnati Commercial* on October 26, 1866 emphasized this fear:

"If the proposed amendments of the Constitution be adopted, new and enormous power will be claimed and exercised by Congress, as warranted by such amendments, and the whole structure of our Government will perhaps gradually but yet surely be revolutionized. And so with the Judiciary. If the proposed amendments be adopted, they may and certainly will be used substantially to annihilate the State judiciaries . . . Be assured, if this new provision be engrafted in the Constitution, it will, in time, change the entire texture and structure of our government, and sweep away all the guarantees of safety devised and provided by our patriotic sires of the revolution . . ."

AS FINALLY ADOPTED, the first section of the Fourteenth Amendment, read as follows:

"All persons born or naturalized in the United States, and subject to the jurisdiction thereof, are citizens of the United States and of the State wherein they reside. No State shall make or enforce any law which shall abridge the privileges or immunities of citizens of the United States; nor shall any State deprive any person of life, liberty, or property, without due process of law; nor deny to any person within its jurisdiction the equal protection of the laws."

Section 5 added: "The Congress shall have the power to enforce, by appropriate legislation, the provisions of this article."

Mr. Justice Brennan has aptly brought out in his James Madison Lecture that, "That language, like the language of Article I, Section 10 of the Constitution, is language of limitation. On its face it appears simply to impose limits upon, and not to authorize Congress to displace, the states in the exercise of their traditional authority to legislate directly upon all their citizens in regard to life, liberty, and property. But Section 5 of the amendment does grant the Congress affirmative authority to enforce these prohibitions by appropriate legislation."

What then was the significance of the restraints set forth in the 14th Amendment as they pertained to the states? Campbell was familiar with *Barron v. Baltimore*, decided by the Supreme Court in 1833, which had held that the first eight amendments to the Constitution, popularly known as the Bill of Rights, were applicable only as restraints upon actions of the federal government and in no way abridged those of the states. True, the states were subject to the limitations imposed upon them by Article I, section 10 of the Constitution, which restrains the states from passing Bill of Attainder and Ex Post Facto laws, or laws impairing the obligation of contracts, but in areas such as freedom of speech or of the press, unreasonable searches and seizures, double jeopardy or deprivation of life, liberty, or property, without due process of law, only the conscience of the citizens of the state reflected in the actions of their elected officials governed.

After pondering on these aspects of the case for long hours in his library, Campbell hit upon a solution. Certainly he would present an argument that would shake the Court to its core. But he had to be careful of Matt Carpenter. There indeed was a brilliant advocate!

Matt. H. Carpenter, former Senator from Wisconsin, who had been influential in the drafting of the 14th Amendment as a member of the Senate, and Jeremiah S. Black, appeared with Thomas J. Durant in behalf of the "Monopoly" and the State of Louisiana. Carpenter was once asked by Senator Roscoe Conkling how he should handle a rather difficult legal question: "Employ a good lawyer!" was Carpenter's sage reply. Carpenter and Black were two of the most astute lawyers in the country and a veritable battle of giants was anticipated.

The records were filed in the Supreme Court in 1870, and because of the importance of the questions involved, were taken out of their order by permission of the court and argued in January, 1872. At that hearing, however, Judge Nelson, who was quite advanced in age and indisposed, was absent, and as there was a marked diversity of views of the Justices who were present, the Court, impressed with the gravity of the questions raised in argument, ordered that the cases be placed on the calendar and reargued before a full bench. Judge Nelson resigned on November 28, 1872, after 27 years service on the Court and President Grant appointed Ward Hunt, a Judge of the New York Court of Appeals, to fill the vacancy.

The Slaughter-House Cases were argued again on February 3rd, 4th, and 5th, 1873. The argument was as masterful a one as the Court had heard in many years. Campbell's powerful presentation was lengthy and scholarly, suggesting in a moment of clairvoyance how the principle of laissez-faire could be introduced into the American Constitution.

HE MAINTAINED THAT THE LOUISIANA statute created a monopoly conferring exclusive privileges upon a small number of persons at the expense of the great body of the community of New Orleans. It thus imposed servitudes on the plaintiffs in error through restrictions on the use of their property, contrary to the Thirteenth Amendment. The State statue also abridged their privileges and immunities as citizens of the United States, to engage in the lawful employment of butchering, denied them the equal protection of the laws and deprived them of their property without due process of law, in violation of the Fourteenth Amendment. Here indeed was a telling stroke! For Campbell asserted that the traditional form of the American Government had been changed by the Fourteenth Amendment in that the first eight amendments to the federal Constitution, i.e., the Bill of Rights, by reason thereof, now served as a restraint upon state action as well as federal action.

Expounding a nationalist interpretation of the Fourteenth Amendment he eloquently declaimed:

"The Fourteenth Amendment embodies all that the statesmanship of the country has ordained for accommodating the Constitution and the institutions of the country to the vast additions of territory, increase of the population . . . and the mighty changes produced by . . . social, industrial, and commercial development. . . . It is apparent that, by the first clause, the national principle has been indefinitely enlarged. The tie between the United States and every citizen in every part of its jurisdiction has been made intimate and to the same extent the Confederate features of the Government have been obliterated. The States, with their connection with the citizen, are placed under the oversight and enforcing hand of Congress. The purpose is manifest to establish, through the whole jurisdiction of the United States, one people, and that every member of the Empire shall understand and appreciate the Constitutional fact that his privileges and immunities cannot be abridged by State authority . . .

"The Fourteenth Amendment was not adopted as an act of hostility, nor designed to sow discord; nor to answer an ephemeral or unworthy purpose. Those who deprive the first clause of its vitality, and demand an interpretation which would leave the State Governments in possession of their powers over persons and property unimpaired, place a stigma upon the authors of the article . . .

"The command of the section to the State Governments to maintain proscribed bounds, and to Congress to enforce obedience to the command, is imperative. The excesses apprehended were invasions of the personal rights of individuals under color of authority . . ."

After arguing that the state's police power did not authorize the creation of monopolies, and that Louisiana had done so in contravention thereto, he said: "If the right of a man to choose and prosecute a lawful industry reaches to the rank of a personal privilege, and his hopes and expectations either of happiness or of profit shall be classed as property, then the Fourteenth Amendment to the Constitution stamps with nullity the act of the legislature of Louisiana . . ." The relationship of every national citizen to his state had been changed by that Amendment, he emphasized; the Amendment says to the state: "That this citizen of ours must not be disturbed in his privileges and immunities, or in his life, liberty or property . . ."

Campbell's argument made such a profound impression on the bench that it greatly influenced the thrust of the majority and minority opinions rendered by the Court. Black and Carpenter denied that the Louisiana Law violated the 13th and 14th Amendments. The granting of exclusive privileges by a state government as in the instant case, when properly safeguarded, as this was, for the health and comfort of the people of the community, was merely a police regulation, within the power of the state legislature and not within the realm of federal intervention. If Campbell's construction of the Amendments were accepted by the Court, it would wreak havoc with the economic systems of the states. Laws imposing license fees on certain employment, laws limiting the manufacture or sale of liquor, "all existing laws regulating and fixing the hours of labor, and prohibiting the employment of children, women and men in any particular occupations or places for more than a certain number of hours per day" would become invalid. Such a result would "bring within the jurisdiction of the [Supreme] Court all questions relating to any of these kindred subjects, and deprive the legislatures and state courts of the several states from regulating and settling their internal affairs."

WHEN THE OPINION OF THE COURT was delivered by Mr. Justice Miller on April 14, 1873, Judges Clifford, Davis, Strong and Hunt concurring, the courtroom was practically empty. A Washington correspondent noted that the case "has as yet attracted little attention outside of legal circles, although the Judges of the Court regarded the case as the most important which has been before them since the Dred Scott decision. The opinion of Mr. Justice Miller is held by the Bar to be exceedingly able, while passages in it were regarded as striking examples of judicial eloquence."

Miller's opinion in *The Slaughter-House Cases* is considered to be one of his best, and he always referred to it in terms of pride. He was the ablest and most progressive member of the Court and a staunch Republican. Chief Justice Chase admitted that Miller was "beyond question the dominant personality . . . upon the bench." Born in Kentucky in 1816 he had moved to Iowa because he was against slavery. As a youth he studied medicine and practiced for ten years in a country hamlet. Discovering that he had a natural aptitude for law, he read law between sick visits for two years. He was thirty years old, and the father of two children when he abandoned medicine for law. Strong and capable, with a tremendous capacity for work, he quickly became such an outstanding member of the Bar that he was appointed just sixteen years later, in 1862, to the Supreme Court. Miller's self-education in law was reflected in his weak legal scholarship. He was recognized as "a man of wisdom rather than of knowledge." The story is told of a lawyer arguing a case before the Supreme Court, in which he used the words "Dominus Litis." Miller interrupted him by asking with a tone of annoyance "And what is Dominus Litis?" "Why sir," stammered the lawyer, "it is . . ." and he explained the meaning. "Well why did you not say so," was Miller's gruff reply, "instead of coming in here with Latin, or whatever it is, for I think the English sounds better than that."

Miller recognized the importance of the decision to the nation and pointed out how grave a problem had been presented to the Supreme Court in that it was being called upon for the first time to give construction to the 13th and 14th Amendments.

"No question so far-reaching and pervading in their consequences, so profoundly interesting to the people of this country, and so important in their bearing upon the relations of the United States and the several states to each other, and to the citizens of the states, and of the United States, have been before this court during the official life of any of its present members."

Miller, although a strong Republican, put a much more limited interpretation upon the Thirteenth and Fourteenth Amendments, than had been anticipated. Miller's reason for this approach was based on his purpose not only to protect Negro rights but also to uphold state police powers against the attacks of business and industry he could envision in the future.

After historically examining the causes which led to the adoption of these amendments he established that their pervading purpose was "the freedom of the slave race, the security and firm establishment of that freedom, and the protection of the newly-made freeman and citizen from the oppressions of those who had formerly exercised unlimited dominion over him . . ."

"We do not say that no one else but the Negro can share in this protection . . . If . . . rights are assailed by the states which properly and necessarily fall within the protection of those articles, that protection will apply though the party interested may not be of African descent."

Finding that the use of the word "servitude" was intended to prevent all forms of involuntary servitude and was not applicable to the instant case, Miller also held that the police power of the state of Louisiana give validity to the act establishing the monopoly. Although it is difficult to define the scope and limitations of police power by reason of its very nature, certainly, "the regulation of the place and manner of conducting the slaughtering of animals and the business of butchering within a city, and the inspection of the animals to be killed for meat, and of the meat afterwards, are among the most necessary and frequent exercises of this power."

MILLER THEN CONSIDERED WHETHER the language of the Fourteenth Amendment prohibiting any abridgment of "the privileges and immunities of citizens of the United States" was applicable to the case before the Court. Rejecting the assumption of Campbell that there was no distinction between citizenship of the United States and the citizenship of a state and the privileges and immunities granted by the 14th Amendment were the same, Miller held that "the distinction between citizenship of the United States and the citizenship of a state is clearly recognized and established by the first section of the Fourteenth Amendment" for the next paragraph of the same section speaks only of privileges and immunities of citizens of the United States, and does not speak of those of citizens of the several States."

"If, then," he contended, "there is a difference between the privileges and immunities belonging to a citizen of the United States as such, and those belonging to the citizens of the State as such, the latter must rest for their security and protection where they have heretofore rested; for they are not embraced by this paragraph of the amendment . . . With the exception of [a few express limitations which the Federal Constitution imposed upon the States — such, for instance as the prohibitions against ex post facto laws, bills of attainder, and laws impairing the obligation of contracts] . . . the entire domain of the privileges and immunities of citizens of the states . . . lay within the constitutional and legislative power of the states, and without that of the Federal Government."

Having thus distinguished between the rights of a citizen of the United States and of a citizen of a State he then questioned the nationalistic principles espoused by Campbell. "Was it the purpose of the Fourteenth Amendment, by the simple declaration that no state should make or enforce any law which shall abridge the privileges and immunities of *Citizens of the United States,* to transfer the security and protection of all the civil rights . . . from the states to the Federal Government? And where it is declared that Congress shall have the power to enforce that article, was it intended to bring within the power of Congress the entire domain of civil rights heretofore belonging exclusively to the states? . . ." The purpose of the Fourteenth Amendment was not to bring within the federal jurisdiction "the entire domain of civil rights heretofore belonging to the States." If this had been its design the Supreme Court would become "a perpetual censor upon all legislation of the states on the civil rights of their own citizens with authority to nullify such as it did not approve as consistent with these rights, as they existed at the time of the adoption of this amendment. . . ." This was asking too much of the Court. The effect would be "to fetter and degrade the State governments by subjecting them to the control of Congress, in the exercise of powers heretofore universally conceded to them . . . and [would] radically change the whole theory of the relations of the state and Federal governments to each other and of both of these governments to the people . . . We are convinced that no such results were intended by the Congress which proposed these amendments nor by the legislatures of the states which ratified them."

WHAT THEN WERE THE PRIVILEGES and immunities of a citizen of the United States? Here, Miller recognized that he was treading on thin ice — for to this day, it is not certain what "privileges and immunities of citizens of the United States" were meant to be covered when the phrase was composed and he judiciously avoided the issue. Indicating that he considered the right to come to the seat of government and to assert any claim he may have upon that government, as well as the right of free access to its seaports and to demand the protection of the Federal Government over his life, liberty and property when on the high seas or within the jurisdiction of a foreign government, as illustrations of the privileges of citizens of the United States, he added: "We may hold ourselves excused from defining the privileges and immunities of citizens of the United States which no state can abridge, until some case involving those privileges may make it necessary to do so." Certainly the rights asserted by Campbell to have been abridged by the Louisiana Statute did not come within the scope of the first section of the Fourteenth Amendment, as they belonged to the class of "fundamental rights" which still pertained exclusively to state citizenship.

On the issues of "due process" and "equal protection" raised by Campbell, Miller paid scant attention. Looking to the judicial interpretation of the Fifth Amendment and to similar clauses on "due process" in the state constitutions he casually stated: "It is sufficient to say that under no construction of that provision that we have ever seen, or that we deem admissible, can the restraint imposed by the State of Louisiana . . . be held to be a deprivation of property within the meaning of that provision."

Ruling on the applicability of the "equal protection" clause to the butchers' appeal, Miller made a prophesy which subsequent events disproved. Referring to his historical analysis of the amendments, he concluded that their pervading purpose was to protect the civil rights of Negroes. If the states did not conform their laws to its requirements, then, by the fifth section of the 14th Amendment, Congress was authorized to enforce it by suitable legislation. "We doubt very much whether any action of a state not directed by way of discrimination against the Negroes as a class or on account of their race, will ever be held to come within the purview of this provision. It is so clearly a provision for that race and that emergency, that a strong case would be necessary for its application to any other."

However, Miller never again asserted that the purpose of the Fourteenth Amendment was only to protect Negro rights. In an impressive argument held in the Supreme Court in December, 1882 on *San Mateo County v. Southern Pacific Railroad Co.*, in which the Fourteenth Amendment was invoked to prevent discriminatory assessment of railroad property by California, Mr. Sanderson, counsel for the Railroad entered into the following illuminating colloquy with Judge Miller.

Miller: "As we decided in the *Slaughter-House Cases.* . . . 'And so, if other rights are assailed by the States which properly and necessarily fall within the protection of these articles, that protection will apply, though the party interested must not be of African descent.'"

Sanderson: "I am glad to hear that, your honor."

Miller: "I do not know that anybody in this Court — I have never heard it said in this Court or by any Judge of it — that these articles were supposed to be limited to the Negro race."

Sanderson: "But there is a notion out among the people, and our friends on the other side have cited several cases for the purpose of showing that it was the intention of this Court to give to this provision of the Constitution as restricted and limited application as possible."

Miller: "The purpose of the general discussion in *The Slaughter-House Cases* on the subject was nothing more than the common declaration that when you come to construe any act of Congress, any statute, any Constitution, any legislative decree you must consider the thing, the evil which was to be remedied in order to understand fully what the purpose of the remedial act was."

HAVING DISPOSED OF THE ISSUES of state police power, of involuntary servitudes, abridgement of the privileges and immunities clause, deprivations of property without due process of law and denial of equal protection, in favor of the defendants in error, Miller affirmed the judgments of the Supreme Court of Louisiana.

Associate Justice Stephen J. Field, adopting Campbell's argument, vehemently dissented in an opinion which was concurred in by Chief Justice Chase and Justices Swayne and Bradley. Swayne and Bradley also filed dissenting opinions of their own. Although Field was a Democrat, and entirely out of sympathy with the reconstruction plan imposed on the South by the Republican-controlled Congress, he still maintained that the privileges and immunities clause of the Fourteenth Amendment authorized the Federal Government to protect the "inalienable rights" of its citizens. As the right to enter or conduct a trade was a "privilege" of a citizen and one of his "immunities" was the right to be free of state-created monopolies, the plaintiffs were entitled to federal protection under the Fourteenth Amendment. Swisher has properly noted that although Miller's interpretation of the clause "has in large part remained the law of the land until the present day, it was in the dissenting opinions that the trend of the near future was more accurately forecast." Those opinions stressed the postwar amendments, and particularly the Fourteenth Amendment, as protecting civil rights generally, without reference to state-federal distinctions; and due process of law was an important source of that protection. Field insisted that the issues involved were "of the gravest importance" to the country at large as well as the parties, as it pertained to "nothing less than the question whether the recent amendments . . . protect the citizens of the United States against the deprivation of their common rights by state legislation." The Fourteenth Amendment "inhibits any legislation which confers special and exclusive privileges like those under consideration. The Amendment was adopted . . . to place the common rights of the American citizens under the protection of the National Government." As a result of Miller's construction of the 14th Amendment it had become a "vain and idle enactment, which accomplished nothing and most unnecessarily excited Congress and the people on its passage. With privileges and immunities thus designated no state could ever have interfered by its laws, and no new constitutional provision was required to inhibit such interference."

Bradley energetically added that the "due process" clause protected the plaintiffs in error, as well as the privileges and immunities clause. "A law which prohibits a large class of citizens from adopting a lawful employment . . . does deprive them of liberty as well as property, without due process of law . . . also deprives [them] of the equal protection of the laws." Swayne held similarly, "The construction adopted by the majority . . . is . . . much too narrow. It defeats, by a limitation not anticipated, the intent of those by whom the instrument was proved . . . To the extent of that limitation it turns, as it were, what was meant for bread into a stone."

When word of the *Slaughter-House* decision became
known, the reaction of the Radical Reconstructionists was
one of dismay and complete frustration. All their hopes
and plans for a strong nationalistic government achieving
equality for the Negro by federal protection of their civil
rights, which were so intimately interwoven with the passage of the 13th, 14th and 15th Amendments, were now
confronted by a new barrier. How could this have happened? What had gone wrong? These questions were
particularly raised by irate members of Congress who had
helped draft the amendments and who claimed to be cognizant of the legislative intent at the time. Senator George
S. Boutwell wrote that the Supreme Court had "erred in
holding that there were two classes of rights, National and
State." Senator George F. Edmunds complained, "there is
no word in [the Fourteenth Amendment] that did not
undergo the completest scrutiny. There is no word in it
that was not scanned, and intended to mean the full and
beneficial thing it seems to mean. There was no discussion
omitted; there was no conceivable posture of affairs to the
people who had it in hand which was not considered. And
yet it was found upon the first time to enforce its first
clause . . . that the Court, by a division of five to four,
radically differed in respect both to the intention of the
framers and the construction of the language used by
them."

Democrats in the West joined the Republicans in
vehemently denouncing the decision as they feared the
effect of State-created monopolies. "We are astonished by
this opinion of the court," editorialized the *Cincinnati
Enquirer.* "It gives a legal sanction to the consummation of
an outrage on individual rights that is almost unparal-
leled. . . ."

On the other hand, there were others who, objecting
to the centralizing tendency of the government since the
Civil War, concluded that the thrust of the decision was
advantageous to the political structure of the Republic.
Actually, they had dreaded that the Amendments would
alter the relationship between the States and the Federal

Government at the expense of state sovereignty, and therefore hailed the decision as preserving the framework of government established by the Framers of the Constitution. Then again, they noted, the Supreme Court had not sanctioned monopolies, but had instead ruled that the control of state monopolies was a matter for the States rather than for the Federal government. The *New York Times* said the decision was "calculated to throw the immense moral force of the Court on the side of rational and careful interpretation of the rights of the States and those of the Union." The *New York Tribune* noted that it "set up a barrier against new attempts to take to the National Government the adjustment of questions legitimately belonging to State Tribunals and Legislatures." The *Boston Advertiser* added that if the Court had arrived at a contrary decision, it "would constitute this Court a perpetual censor upon all State legislation concerning the rights of its citizens." Even John Campbell, many years later, admitted that it was "probably best for the country that the case so turned out."

Judge Moody summed up its historical importance in 1908 in *Twining* v. *N.J.*, "Criticism of the case," he noted, "has never entirely ceased, nor has it ever received universal assent by members of this Court. Undoubtedly, it gave much less effect to the Fourteenth Amendment than some of the public men active in framing it intended, and disappointed many others. On the other hand, if the views of the minority had prevailed, it is easy to see how far the authority and independence of the States would have been diminished by subjecting all their legislative and judicial acts to correction by the legislature and review by the judicial branch of the government."

Professor William W. Crosskey, in his highly controversial but distinguished book, *Politics and the Constitution in the History of the United States*, strongly criticizes the ruling in *Barron* v. *Baltimore* that the first eight amendments to the United States Constitution did not apply to the states. Categorizing the opinion as "incorrectly decided" he concludes that except for the First Amendment, which specifically applies to Congress, and the Appeals Clause of the Seventh Amendment, the framers of the Constitution intended the first eight amendments to be applicable not only to the federal government, but to the states as well. The Dred Scott Case ruling that Negroes could not be citizens of the United States, meant that they were not entitled to any of the "privileges or immunities" provided by the Constitution. The 14th Amendment overruled the Dred Scott Case with reference to the federal government, but by reason of *Barron v. Baltimore*, the states could continue to infringe on the rights of the newly emancipated Negroes without interference from federal courts. Crosskey asserts, however, that the Privileges and Immunities Clause of the 14th Amendment was also intended to overrule *Barron v. Baltimore*, as well as Dred Scott and hence bound the states to refrain from abridging the rights of all citizens as set forth in the Bill of Rights. He also maintains that the Equal Protection Clause of the 14th Amendment corrected the Interstate Privileges and Immunities Clause in Article 4 of the Constitution so that each state is required to accord citizens of another state the same privileges enjoyed by its own—but as individuals rather than as a group, which was the situation before the 14th Amendment. Thus, the purpose of the Equal Protection Clause is to deny to the states the power to create inequities amongst its own citizens. The Privileges and Immunities Clause of the 14th Amendment also incorporated the Fifth Amendment provision that no person may be deprived of life, liberty or property without due process of law, thus making this prohibition applicable to the states as well as the federal government and in favor of "any person" whether he be a citizen or not. To Crosskey, the true test of "dueness" is the propriety of procedure. That is whether the procedure involved is unconstitutional, or fair and reasonable, or unsupported by common law precedents.

CROSSKEY'S THEORIES HAVE BEEN severely criticized and vehemently defended. Certainly they do not reflect the doctrines now held by the Supreme Court.

To this day, Miller's interpretation of the "Privileges

and Immunities" clause is followed by the Supreme Court, tautological as it may appear. The Court has been consistent in denying that the guarantees in the Federal Bill of Rights are applicable to the states by reason of the clause. Mr. Justice Black made a valiant effort in his dissenting opinion in *Adamson* v. *California,* to establish that the purpose of the 14th Amendment was to enfold the Federal Bill of Rights, but the majority of the Court still remains unconvinced.

The situation was changed dramatically, however, with reference to the "due process" clause. By invoking the "due process" clause, the Court has opened the door to the application of specifics of the Federal Bill of Rights to the states. Those guarantees, in the words of Justice Cardozo, "have been taken out from the earlier articles of the Federal Bill of Rights and brought within the Fourteenth Amendment by a process of absorption . . . [which] has had its source in the belief that neither liberty nor justice would exist if they were sacrificed."

In answering the question: How many of the specifics of the Bill of Rights have been held to be absorbed by the "due process" clause of the Fourteenth Amendment, Mr. Justice Brennan has concluded that all the protections of the First Amendment now extend to the exercise of state power. Another is the requirement of the Fifth Amendment that "just compensation" must be paid by the states for private property taken for the public use. This principle was used with telling effect and persistently invoked by lawyers representing business and industry against the efforts of the states to regulate economic enterprise. The Field-Bradley dissents, reflecting the views of Campbell and the concept of laissez-faire, gradually became accepted by the Court and were applied to safeguard property rights. Then again an accused charged with a serious criminal offense is entitled to "the assistance of counsel for his defense" as set forth in the Sixth Amendment, at all stages of the proceeding. It is still uncertain whether *Gideon v. Wainright* which removed the distinction between a capital and non-capital crime for an indigent defendant, applies to right to counsel in petty misdemeanors and "violations". The due process clause has also been applied to the Fourth Amendment's guarantees "against unreasonable searches and seizures" by state officials. Thus, a state conviction arising out of evidence illegally obtained would be unconstitutional.

Rejected by the Court has been the right to trial by jury in civil cases (7th Amendment) and, by dictum, in non-capital cases (6th Amendment). Pointing out that many of the states effectively enforce the counterparts in state constitutions of the specifics of the Bill of Rights, Mr. Justice Brennan still finds it necessary to record with regret the abuses by state officials in the administration of justice. Only the absorption of more specifics of the Bill of Rights by the "due process" clause can "further increase respect for our federalism."

THE CONCEPT OF THE EQUAL PROTECTION clause of the Fourteenth Amendment has also undergone remarkable changes despite Miller's extreme doubt "that any action of a State not directed by way of discrimination against the Negroes as a class, or on account of their race, will ever be held to come within [its] purview." Not only did Miller himself later recant, but the Court, in deciding cases involving economic interests and the authority of the States to classify businesses in order to regulate and tax them, actually held that the clause was applicable to these cases and to corporations as well as individuals. Equal protection, to meet constitutional requirements, provides that when a standard is applied, it must be done without discrimination. In this respect it differs from "due process," which insists on minimum Constitutional standards. Although the equal protection cases decided by the Court up to World War II were concerned mainly with government action discriminating or interfering with economic interests rather than civil rights, they now pertain almost exclusively to the latter. By using the equal protection clause to test legislative and administrative classifications, the Court, by a process of assimilation, has closely related it to the concept of due process. Only recently, the landmark case of *Baker v. Carr* held that state legislative malapportionment could constitute a violation of the Equal Protection Clause of the 14th Amendment.

It is obvious today that if Campbell's argument had been accepted, the Court would have eventually been overwhelmed by the great number of civil rights cases brought before it for protection from state action. "Moreover," as Pritchett notes, "it would have left the Court small room to maneuver, to feel its way toward self-chosen goals within the limits of the politically possible." While on the one hand Miller seemed to be closing the door on the constitutional check of state abridgment of civil rights, actually he "made it possible for the American constitutional system to evolve, as it always has, by slow 'Burkean' accretions rather than by a single great mutation; and he left the court free to define as it had in the past, its own role in the national polity."

Five Knights and the King

*Habeas Corpus and
Liberty of the Person*

"ON MONDAY, THE JUDGES sat in Westminster Hall to persuade the people to pay subsidies; but there arose a great tumultuous shout amongst them: 'A parliament! a parliament! else no subsidies!' The levying of the subsidies verbally granted in parliament, being propounded to the subsidyman in Westminster, all of them saving some thirty among five thousand (and they all the king's servants) cried: 'a parliament! a parliament!'"

This entry in a letter written in 1626 by Joseph Mede, the noted biblical scholar, reveals one of the most dramatic confrontations in the constitutional history of England. By the time it was resolved, the greatest of human rights had been secured for Englishmen—the liberty of the person. Yet, strangely enough, the very mechanism which was to achieve this result, the Writ of Habeas Corpus, originally was used to imprison people!

The accession of Charles I in 1625 did not improve the strained relations that had existed between the Crown and Parliament. Lacking confidence in Charles, and especially in his minister, the Duke of Buckingham, the Commons refused to grant him all the funds he demanded to conduct his ill-fated intrigues against France. Impatient and arrogant, Charles suddenly dissolved the Parliament.

Charles was now confronted with a dilemma. To govern without the concurrence of Parliament meant he had to devise a plan to raise funds. He decided to issue letters of privy seal to the Lord Lieutenants of the counties which directed them to list the names of persons of means and how much money these people could afford to loan to the Crown. Some were assessed £20, some £15 and others £10. Commissioners and Lords of the Council were appointed to visit the counties to expedite the collection of this forced loan. All those who refused or delayed payment were ordered to appear before the Council. If they persisted in this course they were then committed to prison. Sir Randolf Crew, the Lord Chief Justice, believing this procedure to be unconstitutional, refused to cooperate. He was removed by Charles and replaced by Sir Nicholas Hyde.

It was clear to all that these forced loans would never be repaid, despite Charles' promise to do so in eighteen months. In a sense, therefore, Charles was arbitrarily taxing the people of England. There was much opposition to the loan, as Mede's letter tells it. If the King needed funds he should call a parliament! Guided by the Duke of Buckingham, Charles refused to change his policy.

Of the many who were imprisoned for refusal to contribute, five decided to challenge the King's authority. Their case, known as *Darnel's Case* or *The Five Knights' Case*, decided in 1627, immediately became a landmark in English constitutional history. Challenging the King's prerogative, they opened up that most sensitive of legal problems—the immunity of the English subject to arbitrary imprisonment. They also clarified for the first time the role of the Writ of Habeas Corpus in English Constitutional Law, a role which had intrigued the greatest legal authorities in England from the time of Magna Carta.

Sir Thomas Darnel and four other knights were imprisoned in the Fleet Prison under a warrant signed by the King's Attorney-General for refusing to contribute their share of the loan. Through their counsel, they moved the justices of the King's Bench to grant them a writ of Habeas Corpus *cum causa* directed to the Warden of the Fleet, to show cause why they were being detained. In his return the warden justified their imprisonment on the ground that they were "committed by the special command of his majesty," assigning no other cause.

THE LEGAL ARGUMENT BEFORE the King's Bench was marked by the great ability of the eminent lawyers who participated: Sir Robert Heath, Attorney-General for the Crown, and Noye, Selden, Bramston, Calthorpe and others for the prisoners.

In order to appreciate the legal problem presented to the court, the history of the Writ of Habeas Corpus must be understood. In the early medieval period the liberty of Englishmen was protected by the following writs:

De Homine Replegiando — Using the principles of replevin, (a form of action at common law to recover personal property illegally taken) a person unlawfully imprisoned could sue out out this writ to replevy a man in prison, just as he would with chattels unlawfully distrained. The main purpose of this writ was to direct a sheriff to release a prisoner on bail who was detained in violation of the law.

Mainprize — The purpose of this writ was similar to the writ *de homine replegiando* except that the person released provided mainprize or sureties rather than bail. Mainpernors were only sureties for the appearance of the prisoner and technically he was therefore not in prison. In the former writ, the prisoner on bail was considered still in the custody of the gaoler.

These writs were not used much after the medieval period, and as Holdsworth shows were not too significant, for they were not applicable when a person was imprisoned by the King's command.

De Odio et Atia — When a man was appealed of homicide, the former two writs could not be used to obtain his freedom, and the writ *de Odio et Atia* was devised. It directed the taking of an inquest to determine whether the prisoner was appealed "from hatred and malice." It is to be remembered that appeal of homicide was sued out by a private person, usually a close relative of the deceased, formally accusing a suspect of the crime committed after he had been acquitted by a jury, and hatred and malice could easily be the reasons for appealing a former determination of acquittal. If the inquest found that hatred and malice were not the cause for the appeal the prisoner remained in prison, if otherwise, he was released on bail.

All these writs were more or less cumbersome, and survived mainly because the crown earned needed revenue by charging fees for granting them. Eventually they died out through disuse. By the 17th century, lawyers looked to the Writ of Habeas Corpus to protect an Englishman's liberty.

The present form of the Writ of Habeas Corpus can be traced back to the reign of Edward I. Although there were several types of this writ, the one which finally evolved into modern dress was the Writ of *Habeas Corpus ad subjiciendum*. In its earliest period the writ was merely procedural. By the late medieval period it began to assume a new role.

THE HISTORIAN, JENKS, knowledgably notes that, "the more one studies the ancient writs of Habeas Corpus, the clearer grows the conviction, that whatever may have been its ultimate use, the writ of Habeas Corpus was originally intended not to get people out of prison, *but to put them in it.*" Oddly enough, this appears to be so when we note that originally under the name of *Capias*, or arrest on mesne process, (intermediate process between the original and final process) the Writ of Habeas Corpus was used to expedite the bringing of a personal action. After the summons had been served, a *capias ad respondendum* was issued ordering the Sheriff to have the body of the defendant before the Court on an appointed day. Other forms of the writ were also used with the purpose of bringing the body of a litigant before the court under different circumstances. Pollack and Maitland state that the Habeas Corpus, in its form of a *Capias*, was known in English law as early as the late 13th century.

The Writ of *Habeas Corpus subjiciendum* was issued in the early medieval period on occasion to order a Sheriff or a private person to produce a person in his custody. Originally too, it was used to summon a jury to serve in a case. It began to take on more importance by reason of a curious development in the English court system. The common law courts recognized the writ as an excellent vehicle for enlarging their jurisdiction. An action brought in a local and franchise court, and later in rival central courts such as the Chancery, the Council and Star Chamber and the Admiralty, could be transferred to the Common Law Courts by means of this writ, thus expanding their jurisdiction at the expense of their rivals. By the 15th century, the King's Bench (a common law court) would issue a Writ of Habeas Corpus to accompany a writ of certiorari, thus insuring not only that a proceeding in an inferior or rival court would be transferred to its jurisdiction, for review, but also that the parties to the action would be brought in as well. They also used it to accompany Writs of Privilege. The Writ of Privilege was a peculiarly characteristic medieval writ which was used to protect an official of one tribunal from detention by another. Thus when he was sued in another court, he would claim the privilege of release to attend to the business of his own court. If this could be established a Writ of Habeas Corpus was sent to the detaining court requesting that tribunal through its proper officer to "have the body of" (the privileged person) "before us" (on a day certain) "together with the cause of his detention". By the 16th century, the common law courts were using the writ, known then as the Writ of *Habeas Corpus ad Subjiciendum et Recipiendum*, quite liberally in their contest for supremacy over other courts. By this means they released many prisoners sentenced by the Admiralty, Court of Requests and the Court of High Commission. This practice became even more marked when Sir Edward Coke was appointed Lord Chief Justice, for he was a spirited defender of the supremacy of the Common Law Courts. It is also to be noted that by the time of Coke, the writ had been used so extensively that it was acknowledged as an independent writ and did not have to depend on the issuance of a writ of certiorari or privilege to be effective.

DURING THE 17TH CENTURY, the common law judges issued Writs of Habeas Corpus to release prisoners committed by order of the Crown, on the theory that the arrests were illegal unless they conformed to due process as specified in Magna Carta, the common law, and statutes enacted by Parliament. Of course, the King refused to accept any limitation on his prerogative to make arrests and actually during the Tudor period the Crown made many which were not challenged because the safety of the nation required them. Holdsworth notes that in the fight that ensued over the power of the King and his Council to imprison, the common law courts accepted the version that such imprisonment was contrary to the common law. They therefore seized this situation as an opportunity to enlarge their jurisdictional powers and as they had previously done in their battle with rival courts, they issued the Writ of Habeas Corpus to contest the legality of these commitments. By reason of these cases the Writ of Habeas Corpus began to be looked upon as the best means of securing freedom from unlawful imprisonment by the Crown. Holdsworth adds, "It is not surprising, therefore that when the contest with the prerogative began in the [17th century] it at once took its place as the great constitutional weapon for the protection of the liberty of the subject—and after the Great Rebellion it assumed this position without question."

It was for these reasons that Darnel and the other four knights decided to challenge the King's prerogative by means of the Writ of Habeas Corpus. Counsel for the prisoners demanded the release and discharge of the prisoners on the theory that the 29th section of Magna Carta provided that "no free man shall be taken or imprisoned unless by lawful judgment of his peers, or the law of the land," and by the statute 25 Edward III which provided that "no one shall be taken by petition or suggestions to the King or his counsel, unless it be (i.e. but only) by indictment or presentment, or by writ original at the common law." In other words, the King and the Privy Council had to show some legal cause for which a person was committed to prison.

Sir Robert Heath, the Attorney-General replied to the arguments of counsel "in a speech of considerable ability."

"This committment" he said, "is not in a legal and ordinary way, but by the special command of our Lord, the King, which implies not only the fact done, but so extraordinarily done, that it is notoriously his majesty's immediate act, and he wills that it should be so. Shall we make inquiries whether his commands are lawful? Who shall call in question the justice of the King's action? Is he to be called upon to give an account of them?" Thus he argued "the King can do no wrong."

The judges decided in favor of the Crown. Lord Chief Justice Hyde pronounced the judgment of the Court. He held that when the King "specially commanded" the arrest of a person, this was sufficient. "That if a man be committed by the commandment of the King, he is not to be delivered by a Habeas Corpus in this court, for we know not the cause of the commitment." The prisoners were then remanded to jail.

IT WAS OBVIOUS THAT THIS decision abrogated the effect of the Magna Carta and the many statutes that had been enacted to protect the personal liberties of Englishmen. In the words of the noted historian, Hallam, these statutes "had become a dead letter, since the insertion of four words in a warrant (per speciale mandatum regis), which might become matter of form, would control their remedial efficacy. And this wound was the more deadly in that the notorious cause of these gentlemen's imprisonment was their withstanding an illegal exaction of money. Everything that distinguished our constitutional laws, all that rendered the name of England valuable was at stake in this issue."

Rather than being overwhelmed by the decision, the will of the people stiffened. Despite tremendous pressures exerted on them by the Crown, many refused to cooperate. Poor men were forced to serve as soldiers; rich men were imprisoned; householders were forced to billet troops. When Buckingham's foreign intrigues failed again, Charles desperately in need of money called another Parliament in March, 1628. Prior thereto, however,

Charles, for political reasons, released all persons who had been imprisoned for failure to lend him money. Seventy-six were thus liberated—and of this number, twenty-seven were elected to the new Parliament. With these members present—and the *Five Knights' Case* to reflect on—it can well be understood why this session of Parliament became one of the most important in English constitutional history. When it covened the storm burst. The Commons refused to pass on Charles' demands for funds until their grievances had been redressed.

The decision in the *Five Knights' Case* was the first grievance considered in the House. Commitment by the King without legal cause was the focal point of attack. Sir Edward Coke, the venerable former Lord Chief Justice, rose to carry the battle to the King's supporters.

"This draught of the judgment," he said, "will sting us, *quia causa fuit ostentata* (because no reason has been shown)—'being committed by the command of the King, therefore he must not be bailed.' What is this but to declare upon record, that any subject committed by such an absolute command may be detained in prison for ever? What doth this tend to but the utter subversion of the choice, liberty, and right belonging to every free-born subject in this kingdom. A parliament brings judges, officers, and all men into good order."

After much heated debate, in which some of the best legal minds of England participated, the Commons and the Lords agreed to confer upon "some ancient fundamental liberties of the Kingdom." As it was recognized that statutory limitations on the King's prerogative would not carry the House of Lords, Coke suggested that the Parliament proceed by a Petition of Right. There was no precedent for redressing public grievances by the Petition of Right; yet Parliament decided to be guided by the great jurist. Coke drafted the Petition, itemizing the abuses the Kingdom had endured, such as the forced loan and billeting of troops.

Then he recited "that contrary to the Great Charter and the good laws and statutes of the realm . . . divers of Your Subjects have of late been imprisoned without any cause shewed; and when for their deliverance they were brought before your Justices by your Majesty's Writs of *Habeas Corpus ad Subjiciendum* . . . and their keepers commanded to certify the causes of their detainer, no cause was certified, but that they were detained by your Majesty's Special Command, signified by the Lords of Your Privy Council, and yet were returned back to several Prisons, without being charged with anything to which they might make answer according to the law." The Petition of Right then proposed "that no freeman in any such manner as is before mentioned be imprisoned or detained."

THE KING FOUGHT BACK strongly through his Attorney-General and Speaker of the House. Heath, the Attorney-General, spoke for two days! The history of the liberty of the subject and the *Writ of Habeas Corpus* was thoroughly considered. Parliament, however, remained adamant and refused to budge. Finally, the King gave an evasive reply generally agreeing to confirm the Magna Carta, but without more, only assuring the Parliament that he would act properly in the future. After much heated debate on whether this reply was sufficient, Coke again carried the day when he exclaimed, "Was ever a verbal declaration of the King *Verbum Regis* (the word of the king)? Did ever Parliament rely on messages? The King's answer is very gracious, but we have to look to the law of the realm. I put no diffidence in his Majesty, but the King must speak by record; and in particulars, not in generals . . . messages of love have no lasting endurance on Parliament. Let us put up a Petition of Right. Not that I distrust the King, but that I cannot take his trust save in a parliamentary way."

The Parliament remained firm. The King through his Minister, Buckingham, made another evasive answer:

"The King willeth that right be done according to the laws and customs of the realm; and that the statutes be put in due execution, that his subjects may have no cause to complain of any wrongs or oppressions contrary to their just rights and liberties, to the preservation where of he holds himself in conscience as well as obliged as of his own prerogative."

These generalities caused considerable anger in Parliament. Coke arose again and denounced Buckingham so severely that Charles realized he could forestall the Parliament no longer. Wishing to avoid the impeachment of Buckingham, the King went to the House of Lords on June 7, 1627, where the Commons had been summoned. With Charles sitting on his throne, the Lord-Keeper presented the Petition of Rights and said:

"May it please your most excellent majesty, the Lords Spiritual and Temporal, and Commons in Parliament assembled, taking into consideration that the good intelligence between your majesty and your people doth much depend upon your Majesty's answer unto their Petition of Right formerly presented; and with unanimous consent do now become most humble suitors unto your Majesty, that you would be graciously pleased to give a clear and satisfactory answer thereunto in full Parliament."

Charles replied:

"The answer I have already given you was made with so good deliberation, and approved by the judgments of so many wise men, that I could not have imagined but it should have given you full satisfaction; but to avoid all ambiguous interpretations, and to shew you that there is no doubleness in my meaning, I am willing to please you as well in words as in substance; read your Petition, and you shall have an answer that I am sure please you."

The Petition was then read, following which the King ordered the clerk to give royal assent in its usual form and he announced, "Soit droit fait comme il est desiré." And thus the famous Petition of Right known as the second Magna Carta became enrolled in the statute books.

The Journal of the Parliament records that "when these words were spoken, the commons gave a great and joyful applause, and his Majesty rose and departed." Lord Campbell adds that "in the evening there were bonfires all over London and the whole nation was thrown in a transport of joy." The Commons were so exalted by this turn of events that they immediately voted the funds the King desired. But the final victory had still not been achieved. In essence the Petition of Right was merely a declaration of policy. The big question was how to enforce and effectuate it. Much more still had to be accomplished.

BEFORE CHARLES GAVE HIS ASSENT to the Petition he directed his Lord Chief Justice and Lord High Chancellor to answer the following question: "Whether, if the King grant the Commons Petition, he doth not thereby exclude himself from committing or restraining a subject for anytime or cause whatsoever without showing a cause?"

The Judges' reply gave Charles reason to believe that he could avoid the effect of the Petition.

"Every law," they stated, "after it is made, hath its exposition, and so this petition and answer must have an exposition as the case in the nature thereof shall require to stand with justice: which is to be left to the courts of justice to determine, which cannot particularly be discovered until such case shall happen. And although the petition be granted, there is no fear of conclusion as is intimated in the question."

Thus Charles believed that despite the Petition of Right, the law had not been changed to his detriment. And soon thereafter, he had an opportunity to test his belief.

Parliament refusing once again to cooperate, Charles decided to rule without it. He dissolved Parliament and immediately thereafter arrested the leading opponents of his program—men such as John Selden and Sir John Eliot. This arrest produced the *Six Members Case*, decided in 1629, in which the Court held that they could not be released in habeas corpus as they had been committed by the King's "special command" for "notable contempts against the King and his government" and "for stirring up sedition against him." In fact, this was a setback for the Petition of Right, but the members of Parliament bided their time. When the Long Parliament was called in 1640, this question was the first order of business. Legislation was enacted abolishing the Star Chamber and providing that the *Writ of Habeas Corpus* was to be granted to test the legality of commitments by command or warrant of the King or Privy Council. The Court on the return was required to decide within three days whether the detention was lawful.

It was not until Charles II's reign that the *Writ of Habeas Corpus* took on the stature it now enjoys as a constitutional bulwark against tyranny. Several procedural defects reduced the efficacy of the *Writ*, and Charles II capitalized on these defects. Judicial tenure was insecure, hence judges were loath to displease the King. When a *Writ of Habeas Corpus* was applied for to the Chancellor or the Court of King's Bench, they claimed the writ could only be issued during the legal term. As they were on vacation more than half the year, persons committed by royal command could languish in jail for long periods before a return could be made. Then again, these people were often committed to remote islands in order to frustrate their attempts to procure a writ. After a while it became more feasible to bribe a courtier in order to secure release than to apply for the writ.

PARLIAMENT TRIED FOR MANY years to enact legislation to meet this situation, but failed after some very close balloting — especially in the House of Lords.

Finally, in 1679, as a result of Lord Clarendon's arbitrary proceedings and the *Jenke's Case* decided in 1676, in which a man committed by the King could get neither bail nor trial as the Chancery was on vacation, the famous Habeas Corpus Act of 1679 was enacted. An amusing anecdote related by Bishop Burnett tells how the bill was passed in the House of Lords. He claims it was carried by an "odd artifice." "Lord Grey and Lord Norris were named to be the tellers. Lord Norris being a man subject to vapours was not at all times attentive to what he was doing: so a very fat Lord coming in, Lord Grey counted him for ten, as a jest at first, but seeing Lord Norris had not observed that, he went on with his misreckoning of ten for one: so it was reported to the House and declared that they who were for the bill were the majority, though it indeed went on the other side: and by this means the bill passed!"

The Habeas Corpus Act of 1679 is essentially a procedure act. It created no personal rights of freedom as such. But it made the *Writ of Habeas Corpus ad Subjiciendum,* as Holdsworth expressed it, "the most effective weapon devised for the protection of the liberty of the subject — by providing both for a speedy judicial inquiry into the justice of any imprisonment on a criminal charge and for a speedy trial of prisoners remanded to await trial." The act also provided that a judge delaying habeas corpus would forfeit £500 to the party aggrieved. This was a huge sum for those days and was incorporated in the law because the judges who would offend in these matters often were of high rank and wealth and the sanction imposed for non-compliance had to be sufficient to dissuade them.

The story of the *Writ of Habeas Corpus* is a long one. It does not stop with the Habeas Corpus Act of 1679. Several defects were to be cured. For example, the 1679 Act only pertained to persons detained on criminal charges. Could persons illegally detained in private custody, such as infants and lunatics, seek release by the Writ of Habeas Corpus? The cases were not too clear. In 1771, a Negro slave by the name of Somerset, was released from his bondage by Lord Mansfield, on a *Writ of Habeas Corpus.* His detention was illegal in England, declared Lord Mansfield, as slavery was "odious" to the laws of England. Similarly in 1810, Zachary Macauly used the *Writ of Habeas Corpus* to determine whether an alien woman known as the Hottentot Venus, who was being exhibited throughout England, was doing so against her will and under duress. The *Writ of Habeas Corpus* was strengthened in England by the Act of 1816 which provided for the issuance of the Writ for persons other than criminals (except imprisoned debtors and those in contempt of Court) whose personal liberties had been restrained.

By the time of Blackstone, the *Writ of Habeas Corpus* was held in such high esteem, that he referred to it in his *Commentaries* as the "most celebrated writ in the English law" and as "The great and efficacious writ, in all manner of illegal confinement." Samuel Johnson told Boswell proudly that "The habeas corpus is the single advantage our government has over that of other countries."

IN THE UNITED STATES the Petition of Right and *Darnel's Case* are reflected in the provision in the Sixth Amendment to the United States Constitution which reads that: "In all criminal prosecutions, the accused shall enjoy the right . . . to be informed of the nature and cause of the accusation. . . ."

The historic and famous *Writ of Habeas Corpus* has also become closely identified with American law. The Habeas Corpus Act of 1679 was actually adopted by some of the colonies prior to the Declaration of Independence in 1776. The American colonists thought so highly of the writ as a bulwark of personal liberty, that after the Revolution, it was incorporated into the Constitution itself. Article 1, Section 9 of the Constitution provides that: "The Privilege of the Writ of Habeas Corpus shall not be suspended, unless when in cases of rebellion or invasion the public safety may require it." During the Civil War, the question arose whether the President or the Congress could suspend the writ in the great case of *Ex Parte Merryman.* President Lincoln insisted that he had such right, although Chief Justice Taney denied it. As the Congress subsequently ratified Lincoln's action by law, this question still remains unresolved.

The English common law pertaining to the *Writ of Habeas Corpus* has been generally applied by the courts in the United States. The Judiciary Act of 1789 expressly empowered federal judges to issue the writ. In 1867, Congress enacted a law providing broadly that the federal courts should "have power to grant writs of habeas corpus in all cases where any person may be restrained of his or her liberty in violation of the Constitution or of any treaty or law of the United States." Even a "next friend" could apply for the writ. In its present form, a federal court may issue the writ "for the purpose of an inquiry into the cause of restraint of liberty" provided that it "shall in no case extend to a prisoner in a jail unless where he is in custody under or by color of the authority of the U.S. . . . or is in custody for an act done or omitted in pursuance of a law of the U.S. . . . or is in custody in violation of the Constitution or a law or treaty of the U.S." As the statute is silent on the definition and use of the *Writ of Habeas Corpus*, Mr. Justice Stone has stated that: "recourse must be had to the common law, from which the term was drawn, and the decisions of the Supreme Court interpreting and applying the common law principles which define its use when authorized by the statute." Stone added that the use of the *Writ of Habeas Corpus* "was defined and regulated by the Habeas Corpus Act of 1679. This legislation and the decisions of the English courts interpreting it have been accepted by [The Supreme Court] as authoritative guides in defining the principles which control the use of the Writ in the Federal Court."

In Habeas Corpus proceedings the Supreme Court has consistently refused to review "questions which do not concern the lawfulness of the detention." Therefore the writ may not be used to convert an "erroneous judgment of crime" but "may be resorted to only where the judgment is void because the Court was without jurisdiction to render it."

The 1867 Act affected the Administration of Justice in the states in that it provided for a petition for Habeas Corpus to be issued in a federal court whenever the detention violated the Constitution, laws or treaties of the United States. This permitted the federal courts to review state criminal proceedings by issuing the writ where the judgment of the state court was considered to be void. The federal courts, however, have refused to issue the writ where it appears that the purpose of the application is merely to attack collaterally the state judgment as in a certiorari proceeding or by way of review of errors. In the sense that the federal courts have become appellate courts reviewing state court decision by means of the writ of Habeas Corpus, they have been severely criticized as interfering with the administration of state criminal law.

The Supreme Court in *Mooney v. Halahan* held in

1935 that the states must provide in their courts, post-conviction corrective review of claims of violation of constitutional rights to the extent enforced by the federal courts in habeas corpus proceedings through the due process clause of the 14th Amendment. As a result, many states have expanded the scope of Habeas Corpus as a remedy for violations of constitutional rights.

In *U.S. ex rel La Near v. La Vallee*, the United States Court of Appeals for the 2nd Circuit held that since New York provides no remedy for a multiple felony offender accused of a prior felony conviction in another jurisdiction to question the validity of that conviction although such conviction may be utilized in sentencing him to additional punishment, the multiple felony offender may resort to a collateral attack by means of habeas corpus in the federal courts. As a result the Attorney General of the State was required to litigate the question of the validity of out-of-state convictions, many of which were had many years prior thereto. This created excessive difficulty and expense. To remedy this situation the state enacted a Multiple Felony Offenders law in 1964, which gives those accused of prior felony conviction the right to attack the validity of those convictions at the time they become so accused.

By reason of the great effectiveness of the *Writ of Habeas Corpus*, the Federal district courts are flooded with a great number of worthless applications for its issuance. Out of 4,849 federal-question habeas corpus cases disposed of in the district courts during the period from 1946 through 1954, the petitioners were successful in only 77 or 1.6% of the cases.

It has been said that for all practical purposes the Habeas Corpus Act is worth a hundred articles guaranteeing constitutional liberty. Dicey, the great constitutional authority, has summed it up aptly. "There is no difficulty, and there is often very little gain, in declaring the existence of a right to personal freedom. The true difficulty is to secure its enforcement. The Habeas Corpus Acts have achieved this end, and have therefore done for the liberty of Englishmen more than could have been achieved by any declaration of rights."

Vera Effigies Viri clariſſ: EDOARDI COKE.
Equitis aurati nuper Capitalis Iuſticiarij
ad Placita ·coram Rege tenenda aſsignati

Wm SPIGGOT *under pressure, in* NEWGATE, *for not pleading to his Indictment.*

Peine Forte et Dure

Giles Corey was a wizzard strong,
 A stubborn wretch was he,
And fitt was he to hang on high
 Upon ye Locust Tree.
So when before ye magistrates
 For tryall he did come,
He would not true confession make
 But was completely dumbe.
"Giles Corey," said the magistrate,
 "Whast thou here to pleade
To those who now accuse thy soul
 Of crimes and horrid deed."
Giles Corey he sayed not a word,
 No single word spoke he.
"Giles Corey," sayeth the magistrate,
 "We'll press it out of thee."
They got them then a good wide board
 They layde it on his breast,
They loaded it with heavy stones
 And hard upon him prest.
"More weight," now sayd the wretched
  man,
 "More weight," again he cried.
And he did not confession make
 But wickedly he dyed.

THIS ANONYMOUS OLD POEM written shortly after the death of Giles Corey in 1692 was inspired by his Salem trial and execution for witchcraft. Corey has the dubious distinction of being the only person in America who ever suffered the ancient English penalty of *peine forte et dure*, or pressing to death, for refusal to plead to an indictment.

Cotton Mather, standing at Giles Corey's grave in the Potters Field was moved to exclaim:

"O sight most horrible! In a land like this spangled with Churches Evangelical inwrapped in our Salvations, must we seek in mouldering statute books of English court, some old forgotten law, to do such a deed?"

In his condemnation of the practice of the *peine forte et dure*, Cotton Mather echoed the puzzlement and indignation which have been expressed of this awesome torture for centuries. "The whole law of England presents no more characteristic incident than this," wrote Sir James Stephens in 1883. "It exemplifies the extreme scrupulosity of its founders, their occasional and rather capricious indifference to the infliction of pain, the power and tradition and practice to vary even the plain meaning of a statute, and the astonishing tenacity of legal forms . . ."

How did this barbarous punishment ever become legally accepted in England, a land where abhorrence of torture has been characteristic of justice from its very inception? Although the explanation·is perhaps mainly of historical interest, it is of importance also in understanding one aspect of pleading in criminal cases today.

IN EARLY TIMES, AN INDICTED person on arraignment was required by custom to raise his hand and be identified. Thereafter the indictment was read to him and he was questioned as follows by the clerk of the court:

"How say you, are you guilty or not guilty?" At this point the defendant could plead "Guilty" or "Not Guilty."

Upon the plea of "Not guilty," the clerk would reply "Culprit, how will you be tried?" The prisoner was then required to answer "By God and my country."

Blackstone's explanation for the use of the word

"culprit" is enlightening. "When the prisoner hath thus pleaded not guilty, *non culpabilis*, or *nient culpable*, which was formerly used to be abbreviated upon the minutes thus '*non* (or *nient*) *cul.*,' the clerk of the assize or the clerk of the arraigns, on behalf of the crown replies, that the prisoner is guilty, and that he is ready to prove him so. This is done by two monosyllables in the same spirit of abbreviation, '*cul. prît*,' which signified first, that the prisoner is guilty *(cul., culpable, or culpabilis)*, and then that the King is ready to prove him so, *(prît praeso sum, or paratus verificare.)* This is, therefore, a replication on behalf of the King *vivo voce* at the bar, which was formerly the course in all pleadings, as well in civil as in criminal causes. . . . By this replication the King and the prisoner are therefore, at issue . . ."

The phrase "*By God* AND *my country*," which the defendant was required to utter verbatim has had a fascinating history. Barrington, writing in 1766, observed that originally the defendant's answer must have been "*By God* OR *my country*." An understanding of the historical development of this declaration reveals the soundness of his keen analysis

In 1215 persons suspected of crimes or felonies were denounced by the *jury of presentment* or grand jury. This did not mean, however, that the person so denounced was either entitled or required to submit to a jury trial to prove his innocence. He could exonerate himself also by submitting to the "ordeals" or by compurgation.

The ordeal was an ancient superstitious mode of trial. The trial by ordeal was by fire or water. When tried by the ordeal of fire, the accused either walked barefoot over burning hot ploughstones or carried burning irons in his hands. In the ordeal by water, the suspect would be thrown into a river or lake, and if the body floated to the surface, it was a sign that he had been rejected and hence was guilty. Another method was to put the accused's hand into scalding hot water. If he survived this test, as in the ordeal by fire, it was a sign of God, attesting to his innocence.

In compurgation, the accused would swear, before a judge, under the most solemn and sacred circumstances that he was innocent of the charge levied against him. After thus purging himself upon oath, he would then call upon some of his neighbors, called compurgators, who swore that they believed him on his oath. No one could testify on the other side. If the compurgators did not agree to make the oath, he was put to the ordeal. Modern character witnesses, in a sense, are descended from this ancient practice.

THESE OLDER METHODS of proof were permitted although the judges preferred the trial by petit jury. Writing at the time, Glanville describes the trial by petit jury as an "inquest by the country," and adds that the person so submitting to the petit jury is considered as referring his case to the "*patria*" — or to the country. But there was one added feature to the trial by petit jury which was peculiarly different from our current practice.

To be tried by inquest or petit jury in preference to the ordeal was considered at the time to be an unusual privilege. In fact, to obtain such a right, it was necessary to pay a fee to the King. Hence it can be seen that a defendant in a criminal case had a choice to determine his innocence — the inquest or the older form of ordeal. When the officer of the court thus questioned the defendant "Culprit, how will you be tried?" the defendant could choose between the ordeal (by God) or the inquest (my country). It would seem, too, that if the prisoner was not entitled to a jury trial, he had to plead necessarily "by God" and submit to the ordeal. By the same token, if he had paid the fee for a jury trial, he could plead "by my country."

Ordeals were for all purposes abolished in 1215 when Innocent III in the Fourth Lateran Council ordered clergy to refrain from granting them religious sanction. Without this sanction they could not be used as a legal means of trial. This development created an unusual problem, the solution of which has confounded English historians for centuries. It must be understood that the defendant purchasing a license to be tried by a jury agreed to accept its verdict. When resort to the ordeal was denied to the defendant after 1215, the only means of trial remaining was by petit jury. Suppose the defendant refused to accept trial by jury? The judges strongly believed that a man could not be sentenced to death merely on the charge of the grand jury. There had to be the formality of some kind of trial. As the defendant had lost access to the ordeal, and as he could not be tried traditionally by the petit jury without his approval, the judges were confronted with a dilemma. They were concerned that technically the defendant was being deprived of his right to be tried by ordeal unless he renounced it, for the courts had substituted in its place the trial by jury. He could only renounce it by submitting to the jury!

What was to be done to a man who refused to be tried by the petit jury under these circumstances? The situation was further complicated by the importance given to the phrase "By God and my country." If the prisoner pleaded "Not Guilty" he could not be tried by the jury unless he declared his willingness to be tried "By God and my country." Even if he refused to say part of it, as by omitting "By God" or "by my country," he was considered as standing mute.

This situation resulted in one of the most extraordinary developments in the history of English law. When a man stood mute, a jury was sworn to determine whether he stood "mute of malice" or "mute by the visitation of God." In the latter case the trial was allowed to proceed. When he was found to stand "mute by malice" he was adjudged to be guilty in cases involving treason or misdemeanors. If he thus stood mute in felony cases, however, to compel him to accept trial by jury he was condemned to a horrible torture — the *peine forte et dure*.

It has been said that the *peine forte et dure* "is a most remarkable example of judge-made law," as no statutory authority can be found for the manner in which it was applied. It first appears in the Statute of Westminster I, c.12, enacted in 1275, which reads:

"Notorious felons, openly of ill-fame, who will not put themselves on inquests for felonies with which they are charged before the justices at the King's suit, shall be put in strong and hard imprisonment *(en le prison forte et dure)* as refusing the common law of the land." Thus originally *peine forte et dure* was *prison forte et dure.*

ACCORDING TO BARRINGTON, this meant that the prisoner who refused to plead was to be starved till he died, but not tortured; and he quotes in proof of it a pardon granted in the reign of Edward III to Cecilia, wife of John de Rygeway, indicted for the murder of her husband, who "pro eo quod se tenuit mutam," was put "in actâ prisonâ" and there lived without eating or drinking for forty days, which was regarded as a miracle. Starvation was employed for this purpose until the reign of Henry IV, when references to the practice of pressing to death for standing mute first appear. The purpose of the *peine forte et dure* was to expedite the administration of justice, for obviously an itinerant assize judge could not wait for a defendant to plead if he preferred to starve to death over a period of time. Before pressing was resorted to, the practice was instituted of tying the defendant's thumbs with whipcord until the extreme pain forced him to plead.

The punishment of pressing reached its most horrible form in the reign of Elizabeth. It was applied by order of the judge, who usually warned the prisoner three times of the dire results which would ensue from his silence. The consequences of standing mute were so terrible, that time was given to the accused to reflect on his decision. Often his friends and relatives would also entreat him to reconsider. When the prisoner persisted in his course the *Judgment of Penance* was pronounced. Note that by that time the word "peine" or penance had been substituted for "prison"—all accomplished by judicial fiat. "*Staundeforde, in Les Plees del Coron*" recites the awesome judgment:

"That you be taken back to prison whence you came, to a low dungeon into which no light can enter; that you be laid on your back on the bare floor, with a cloth around your loins, but elsewhere naked; that there be set upon your body a weight of iron as great as you can bear and greater; that you have no substance, save on the first day, three morsels of the coarsest bread, on the second day three draughts of stagnant water from the pool nearest to the prison door, on the third day again three morsels of bread as before, and such bread and such water alternately from day to day until you die." Later a sharp stone was placed under the back of the unfortunate man to hasten his death.

The practice of standing mute was not uncommon. Many cases appear in the records. Radzinowicz notes that during the ten successive years of the reign of James I (1607–1616), thirty-two persons of whom three were women died by the *peine forte et dure* for declining to confess or plead to indictments for crimes committed in Middlesex. The Newgate prison had a place called the Press Yard, so named because many criminals had been pressed to death there. Why then did prisoners stand mute or refuse to plead?

IT MUST BE REMEMBERED that in those days the real property of a person found guilty of felony was forfeited on the theory of corruption of blood. If the defendant could avoid being formally adjudged guilty by refusing to plead, he could preserve his lands for his heirs. That was one of the reasons for Giles Corey's refusal to plead to his indictment. His personal property, however, could be seized. Actually, what could an innocent person do, when falsely accused of felony? His only protection lay in challenging the jurors — many of whom had been members of the grand jury which had accused him. The number of his challenges, however, was limited and therefore only silence and submission to the *peine dure et forte* could protect his heirs.

Blackstone comments that the judgment of *peine forte et dure* was "a monument of the savage rapacity with which the lordly tyrants of feudal antiquity hunted after escheats and forfeiture, since no one would ever have been tempted to undergo such a horrid alternative . . . Therefore his lingering punishment was probably introduced in order to extort a plea; without which it was held that no judgment of death could be given, and so the lord lost his escheat."

Other reasons for submitting to the punishment are recorded. Some prisoners stood mute in order to avoid the spectacle of a public execution which would bring shame to their families. In 1721, Nathaniel Hawes, a highwayman, refused to plead because a handsome suit of clothes had been taken from him, and he was determined not to be publicly exhibited on the way to the gallows in a shabby suit. After bearing a weight of 250 pounds for about seven minutes, he gave in, and was thereafter tried and duly executed.

A bizarre case of pressing occurred in 1659. A Major Strangewayes, indicted for the murder of his brother-in-law, refused to plead and was sentenced to be pressed. The weights placed on his breast were too light to cause his immediate death, but his suffering was intense. Some of his Cavalier friends, noting his distress, jumped on the weights and he expired in about ten minutes. The question has been asked "were they guilty of murder?

The judgment of *peine forte et dure* remained in force until the year 1772, when it was decreed that in cases of felony or piracy, standing mute was to be considered equivalent to a conviction of the crime charged. In 1777, Frances Mercier, stood mute, upon arraignment at Old Bailey. A jury was impanelled by the sheriff, and in finding that Mercier stood mute fraudulently, wilfully and obstinately and not by Act of God, the court passed sentence of death on him. A final change was made in 1827. The new law directed the court to enter the plea of "Not Guilty" for prisoners refusing to plead. In the United States the rule is similar. Thus section 342 of the New York Code of Criminal Procedure reads: "If the defendant refuses to answer an indictment by demurrer or plea, a plea of not guilty must be entered."

Bracton, writing in the early thirteenth century, recommended that silence on the part of a person indicted for felony should be considered a confession of guilt. It took more than five hundred years for the English to advance as far as his enlightened view and then another half-century to find a more civilized solution to this vexing problem.

Trial
of
William Penn

*A Landmark
in the Development
of the Jury System*

T HE TRIAL OF WILLIAM PENN in Old Bailey during the
first five days of September, 1670, brings to mind a
murder trial which took place during the pioneer days in a
Western mining town. Strangly, the defendant was not in
court as the evidence was presented to the jury. After
retiring, the jury returned a verdict of "Not Guilty." The
judge, noted for his arbitrary decisions and apparently
displeased, suggested to the jury that it reconsider its verdict. Seeing the light, the jury quickly returned a verdict of "Guilty." "Ah, that's better," the judge announced
with a smile of satisfaction. "You see, we hanged the prisoner this morning!"

William Penn, the fabled founder of Pennsylvania,
fared little better. His trial, one of the most dramatic in the
annals of Anglo-American law, reflects a fascinating development in the history of trial by jury. It has been described as "an outstanding battle in [the] struggle for un-
trampled justice and the rights of accused persons."

The significance of the Penn trial which was later
resolved in the case of Bushell, a member of his jury, is
better understood by appreciating the historic role of the
jury in the English system of justice.

Near the end of the 12th century the function of the jury was to extract from inhabitants of the neighborhood the true answer (or *verdict*) to a question presented to them. These neighbors were sworn (*jurata*) to disclose the truth as they personally knew it. In this respect therefore, the jury's role then was quite different from that of its modern counterpart, for today a juror with an independent knowledge of the facts of the case would be disqualified from serving. It is important to note that the jury then determined the law as well as the facts. The integrity of the jury was enforced by the very severe *writ of attainder.* Once the verdict was proven wrong in any respect the jury could be attainted, resulting in cancellation of civil rights and loss of property. Of course, the verdict was set aside as well. Under these circumstances, juries became loath to decide questions of law fearing the dire effects of the *writ of attainder.* The custom therefore arose for the jury to bring in a special verdict on the facts alone. This practice was particularly true in civil cases. The judges, however, were more insistent in criminal cases, demanding a verdict from the jury on the law, as well. Questions of law involved in criminal cases, they argued, were not so complicated or difficult as to excuse jurors from assuming their responsibility. Judges used many methods to force a jury to do their will. A jury could be locked up, without water, food, heat, tobacco, or light, until it returned a unanimous verdict, or one the judge directed. The judge could also make it quite clear that the jurors would be fined if they brought in a contrary or corrupt verdict.

Bushell's Case, arising from the trial of William Penn, is considered a landmark in the development of the jury system. There it was finally decided in 1670 that a jury in a criminal case could legally return a general verdict of "Not Guilty," despite the contrary direction of the judge. Since then, juries have disregarded the recommendations of the presiding judge without fear, although in civil cases a jury's verdict may still be set aside as contrary to the evidence. Incidentally, it has been cleverly suggested that the reason a jury's verdict may be set aside in a civil case is because "the law impolitely describes (such a verdict) as one which a reasonable man could not find."

PENN AND A SMALL GROUP of Quakers held a meeting in Grace Church Street, London, in 1670, after being shut out of their meeting house by government soldiers. The meeting was thus held because the "Conventicle Act," declared unlawful any meetings for worship other than those of the Church of England. William Mead and Penn were indicted for illegally disturbing the King's peace "by preaching to an unlawful assembly and causing a great concourse and tumult." The court ordered the jury to find them guilty, for, said the court, if the jury found the Quakers had met

---

THE
Peoples {Ancient and Juſt} Liberties

ASSERTED,

IN THE

TRYAL

OF

William Penn, and *William Mead,*

At the Seſſions held at the *Old-Baily* in *London,* the firſt, third, fourth and fifth of *Sept.* 70. againſt the moſt Arbitrary procedure of that Court.

Iſa. 10. 1, 2. *Wo unto them that Decree Unrighteous Decrees, and write grievouſneſs, which they have preſcribed ; to turn away the Needy from Judgment, and to take away the right from the Poor, &c.*
Pſal. 94. 20. *Shall the Throne of Iniquity have fellowſhip with thee, which frameth miſchief by a Law.*

Sic volo, ſic jubeo, ſtat pro ratione voluntas.

Old-Baily, 1ſt. 3d. 4th, 5th of *Sept.* 1670.

Printed in the Year, 1670,

at all, then the very meeting by itself was unlawful and, therefore, it followed as a matter of course that the peace was disturbed. The jury, however, though it found that the Quakers had met, refused to find that the law had been violated.

Penn at the time was only 26 years old. Accused persons in criminal actions were not then allowed counsel to represent them, and he had to conduct his own defense. As we read the transcript of the trial, the youthful Penn's confidence, logic, and legal acumen must be admired. The trial is a dramatic example of the cavalier methods employed at the time by judges. As Penn and the jury and especially Bushell, courageously and independently asserted their rights as Englishmen in defying the orders of the very powerful trial judges, it is difficult not to be stirred by what transpired. The reasoning and the moving incidents are as modern in display as any trial can offer today. This jury which refused to change its verdict, despite threats of starvation and imprisonment, was not an elite group but consisted of twelve ordinary middle-class men, selected at random from the jury rolls of the city of London.

The ten judges who heard the case were a formidable bench for they included the Lord Mayor, Starling, the Recorder, Sir John Howel, and other representatives of the Government who were very partisanly concerned in enforcing the Conventicle Act. Hardly an impartial court!

Although the Court was duty bound to protect the interests of prisoners, Penn and Mead were teased, bullied, and questioned unfairly. Penn, however, maintained his poise at all times. An interesting by-play occurred when Penn was directed to plead to the indictment.

"I affirm I have broken no law," he said, ". . . and to the end that the Bench, the jury, myself, and those who hear us may have a more direct understanding of the procedure, I desire you would let me know by what law it is you prosecute me, and on what law you ground your indictment?"

The Recorder replied, "Upon the common law."

Penn saucily demanded, "Where is that common law?"

The Recorder replied angrily, "You must not think that I am able to sum up so many years and ever so may adjudged cases which we call common law, to satisfy your curiosity."

Penn pressed on. "The answer I am sure is very short of my question, for if it be common it should not be so very hard to produce."

The Recorder by this time had become quite exasperated. "Sir, will you plead the indictment?" he queried.

Penn, however, continued in the same vein. "Shall I plead to an indictment that has no foundation in law? If it contain that law you say I have broken, why should you decline to produce it, since it will be impossible for the jury to determine, or agree to bring in their verdict, who have not the law produced by which they should measure the truth of the indictment."

THIS EXCHANGE CONTINUED FOR a while and soon the whole bench began to heckle and bully Penn. Finally the Recorder blared out: "You are an impertinent fellow. Will you teach the court what law is? It is *lex non scripta*. That which many have studied thirty or forty years to know, would you have me tell you in a moment?"

Penn replied calmly, "Certainly, if the common law be so hard to be understood it is far from being very common; but if the Lord Coke in his *Institutes* be of any weight he tells us that 'common law is common right, and common right is the great charter privileges confirmed by 9 Henry III, c.29; by 25 Edward I, c.1; and by 2 Edward III, c.8.'"

After a while the Recorder, completely frustrated, cried out to the soldiers: "Take him away! Put him into the bale dock." The bale dock was a locked cage recessed below the floor level, located at the very end of the courtroom, where recalcitrant prisoners were secured during a trial. As Penn was pushed into the bale dock, he continued to address the court and jury until he could neither see nor be seen.

Thus the trial continued and at its conclusion the jury

agreed upon its verdict and returned to the jury box. The following then ensued:

"How say you?" questioned the clerk of the court, "Is William Penn guilty of the matter whereof he stands indicted in manner and form or not guilty?"

The Foreman replied, "Guilty of speaking in Grace Church Street."

The Recorder intervened. "You had as good say nothing."

The Lord Mayor added, "Was it not an unlawful assembly? You mean he was speaking to a tumult of people there?"

The Foreman then explained that the jury could not agree on that. At this point the court polled each juror separately, directing them to find an unlawful assembly. Bushell and three others refused to so find. As they persevered in this manner, the Recorder and other members of the Bench attempted to bully them, threatening them with punishment and using profane language. At one point the Recorder expressed his admiration for the Spanish Inquisition and the Mayor threatened to cut Bushell's throat as soon as he could.

FINALLY THE RECORDER BLUSTERED: "The Law of England will not allow you to depart till you have given in your verdict."

The Foreman refused to be shaken. "We have given in our verdict, we can give in no other."

The Recorder, however, refused to accept the verdict. "Gentlemen, you have not given in your verdict. You had as good say nothing as what you had said. Therefore, go and consider it once more."

After retiring again, the jury returned and gave the same verdict. By this time the judges on the bench had become highly incensed.

The Recorder spoke up angrily. "Gentlemen, you shall not be dismissed till you bring in a verdict which the court will accept. You shall be locked up, without meat, drink, fire and tobacco. You shall not think thus to abuse the court. We will have a verdict by the help of God or you shall starve for it."

Penn jumped up indignantly: "My jury, who are my judges, ought not to be thus menaced. Their verdict should be free—not forced," he cried out.

"Stop that fellow's mouth, or put him out of Court," hotly replied the Recorder speaking to the Guards.

Penn continued to argue however: "The agreement of twelve men is a verdict in law, and such a one being given by the jury, I require the clerk of the peace to record it—as he will answer at his peril. And, if, after this, the jury bring in another verdict contrary to this, I affirm they are perjured men."

At this point, while Penn was still talking, the soldiers started to push the jury back to the juryroom—then occurred a most inspiring and dramatic incident. Turning to the jury, Penn called out:

"Ye are Englishmen, mind your privilege, give not away your right!"

And the jury, while being dragged out of the Courtroom, replied as one, "Nor will we ever do it."

It was courage and inspiration of this sort upon which our civil rights are based today.

THE JURY PERSISTED IN ITS course for two days and nights, refusing to bring in a different verdict, although kept without food, water and heat. Finally the court ended the trial abruptly, fining them each forty marks and committing them to imprisonment until they paid their fines.

Bushell and the other jurors obtained a writ of habeas corpus from the Court of Common Pleas. Releasing them from their imprisonment, Chief Justice Sir John Vaughan, speaking for the court stated: ". . . for if it be demanded, what is the fact? The Judge cannot answer it: if it be asked, what is the law in the case, the Jury can not answer it." Although the judgment was later reversed on appeal because the Court of Common Pleas did not have jurisdiction in criminal matters, *Bushell's Case,* as it became known, established the right of trial juries to decide cases according to their convictions. *Bushell's Case*, in the words of Raymond Moley "stands in the history of criminal procedure as decisive in regard to the proper function and right of the jury [and] ended a long struggle between jury and judge in English Jurisprudence." From that time on juries really became the triers of the facts in trials.

Penn later published his version of the trial, in what is now a bibliographic gem. He entitled it *"The Peoples' Ancient and Just Liberties Asserted in the Tryal of William Penn and William Mead . . . Against the Most Arbitrary Procedure of that Court . . ."* It was republished in 1919.

It may be said without exaggeration that the Penn trial and *Bushell's Case* gave a new meaning to the institution we know as the jury system. It has also been suggested that the finding in *Bushell's Case* made the jury a living power in the state on a par with the executive branch in the person of the King and the legislative branch embodied in the Commons.

Andrew Hamilton, one of the foremost attorneys in the colonies, used the case with telling effect as a precedent in Peter Zenger's trial in 1735 in New York. Zenger was accused of publishing a libel in his newspaper defaming the Governor General of the Province of New York. Though the court ruled that the truth of the libel could not be set up as a defense, Hamilton insisted, based on the Bushell case, that it was for the jury to determine whether Zenger's comments were true, for after all the jury was the judge of both the law and the facts.

"The rights of the jury," he said, "to find such a verdict as they in their conscience do think is agreeable to their evidence, is supported by the authority of Bushell's case beyond any doubt. . . . It appears by the same case, that though the discreet and lawful assistance of the judge, by way of advice to the jury, may be useful, yet that advice or direction ought always to be upon supposition, and not positive and upon coercion."

The jury followed his advice and acquitted Zenger, thus establishing freedom of the press for us today.

Peter Zenger's Trial

Cornerstone
of the Liberty
of the Press

"ON TUESDAY LAST, His Excellency William Cosby, Esq., Governour of this Province, arrived at Sandy Hook in his Majesty's Ship Seaford, Capt. Long, Commander, in seven weeks from Great Britain, and landed here about 10 o'clock, in the evening, and was received at the Waterside by several Gentlemen, who attended him to the Fort. The next Day between the hours of 11 & 12 his Excellency walked to the City Hall, (A Company of Halbertiers & a Troop of Horse marching before, and the Gentleman and Merchants of this City following, the streets being lin'd on each side with the Militia) where his Commission was published, and then his Excellency returned (attended as before) to the Fort. The Militia then drew up on the Parade and saluted him with three Volies."

As the people of the Province of New York read this account of the warm welcome given to King George II's personal representative in the *Boston Weekly News Letter* of August, 1732, they scarcely envisioned that soon thereafter they would be engaged with Governor Cosby in one of the most dramatic political power struggles witnessed in his Majesty's North American colonies. Nor for that matter did they suspect that, out of the struggle would evolve a climatic cause célébre of such importance, it would indelibly inpress on the law the inalienable right of freedom of the press.

Governor Cosby was ill-equipped to fill his sensitive position. He owed his appointment not to merit but to the Earl of Halifax, his brother-in-law, who was closely associated with Newcastle, the Prime Minister. Governor Cosby has been described as "boisterous and irritable, having little understanding and no sense of decorum." A man of limited education, he believed firmly in the power of superior force. Haughty, pompous, and avaricious, his main purpose in coming to the new world was to amass as large a fortune as possible, for he was sorely in debt.

The people of New York wanted nothing better than to be friendly with Governor Cosby. As personal representative of the King, the Governor was practically omnipotent, and they knew full well that their personal welfare was very much dependent on his policies. Yet inexorably, as in a Greek tragedy, a power struggle began. Then suddenly the sensational *Zenger Trial* burst upon the public. And it all began with a most unusual sequence of events.

When Governor John Montgomerie died on July 1, 1731, Rip Van Dam as Senior Member of the Council, became its president and assumed the position of acting Governor until the new Governor arrived. Van Dam was voted a full Governor's salary by the Council as well as the perquisites of the office. Governor Cosby was appointed in January, 1732, but did not arrive in New York until August 1, 1732. By authority of a royal order he had brought from England, he demanded that Van Dam restore to him one-half of his salary and fees from the time of his appointment until his arrival. Cosby could not have selected a worse victim. Even by the standards of his own day Van Dam was considered to be a "stubborn Dutchman." He was a prominent merchant and leader of the Popular Party and no one was going to impose his will on him! Van Dam replied that he would be pleased to submit to the demand provided Cosby accounted to him for half the fees he had collected in England as perquisites of the office. Rumor had it that in the six months Cosby had received £6,047, whereas Van Dam had collected but £1,925. Van Dam refused to budge from his position and Cosby decided to bring suit.

BUT COSBY HAD A PECULIAR legal problem to solve. The Supreme Court lacked equity jurisdiction and he could not sue in chancery, because he was Chancellor himself, and thick skinned as he was, he could not pursue such an unlawful course! On the other hand, an action at common law would involve a jury trial and under the circumstances, he knew that the local jury would sympathize with Van Dam.

Arbitrarily misusing his authority, he arranged by ordinance for the judges of the Supreme Court to hear cases as Barons of the Exchequer. Having thus bestowed equity jurisdiction on them, he directed Richard Bradley, the Attorney General, to bring an action against Van Dam in the King's name. Cosby instituted this suit even though advised that the General Assembly by resolution had condemned the creation of a court of equity without its consent.

Van Dam was represented in Court by two of the leading attorneys in the Province, James Alexander and William Smith. Alexander had formerly been Attorney General and was in the forefront of every public spirited cause. He later became one of the founders of the American Philosophical Society. Alexander and Smith objected to the jurisdiction of the Court, and Chief Justice Lewis Morris agreed with them, issuing a long, scathing opinion which concluded:

"And as I take it the giving of a new Jurisdiction in Equity by Letters Patent to an old Court, that never had such Jurisdiction before, or Errecting a new Court of Equity by Letters Patent or Ordinance of the Governor and Council, without Assent of the Legislature, are equally unlawful, and not a sufficient warrant to justify this court to proceed in a course of Equity. And therefore, by the

Grace of God, I, as Chief Justice of this Province, shall not pay any Obedience to them in that Point." He then ostentatiously left the bench.

Infuriated by the Chief Justice's action, Cosby demanded a copy of the opinion and indicated his doubt of the Chief Justice's integrity. But Morris was one of the most distinguished men in the colonies. Wealthy, aristocratic, highly intelligent, and bold, he was a political power in his own right. His two grandsons Gouverneur Morris and Lewis Morris later were to take leading roles in the Revolution. Refusing to be awed by Governor Cosby, he replied in characteristic style:

"As to my integrity, I have given you no occasion to call it in Question. I have been in this office almost twenty years, my Hands were never foul'd with a Bribe; nor am I conscious to myself that Power or Poverty hath been able to induce me to be partial in the Favour of either of them. And as I have no Reason to expect any favour from you, so am I neither afraid nor ashamed to stand the test of the strictest inquiry you can make concerning my conduct. I have served the Public faithfully and honestly, according to the best of my Knowledge; and I dare and do appeale to them for my Justification."

HERE WAS A DEFIANCE COSBY refused to brook. He summarily dismissed Morris from the bench, not even obtaining the consent of the Council, and appointed James DeLancey as Chief Justice and Frederick Philipse as second justice, leaving the third position vacant. The Court as reconstituted then decided that it had jurisdiction and ordered the trial to proceed.

The people were horrified by this action. If the Governor could treat the most important members of the community so cavalierly, what could he do later to lesser lights who opposed him. Van Dam exploded: "We are Tenants at Will to Governors, and exposed to be fleeced by them from time to time at their Pleasure." Morris, Alexander, Smith, and others decided to express their opposition through the Popular Party and more specifically to expose the activities of Governor Cosby so that public indignation could be aroused. There was only one newspaper in the Colony, published by William Bradford under the name of the *New York Gazette,* and its editorial policy was completely dominated by Governor Cosby and his Court party. Obviously, another paper had to be founded for this purpose. The solution appeared in the form of John Peter Zenger, a German printer, who had emigrated to this country in his youth, had served an apprenticeship under William Bradford, and who was barely eking out a living. He was persuaded by the Popular Party leaders to join them in publishing an opposition newspaper, although he was not particularly interested in politics at the time.

The first issue of Zenger's *New York Weekly Journal* appeared on November 5, 1733 and it immediately attained the importance its sponsors planned for it. Folio in size, and four pages in length, it contained many grammatical errors, reflecting Zenger's limited knowledge of English. But Zenger did not write the articles. They were written by such stalwarts as James Alexander, William Smith, Lewis Morris and Cadwallader Colden, as well as others. Vincent Buranelli has described Zenger's *Journal* as the *"first political independent* ever published on this continent. The men behind it created a journalistic category new to American experience when they deliberately decided to make a continuing open battle with Governor Cosby the rationale of their editorial policy. . . . Here was something original for this side of the ocean, an experiment in journalism as critical as ever was attempted by any member of our fourth estate; and successful, for the *Journal* lived and throve and became the ancestor of the great American political organs of modern times."

The *Journal* became so popular that some of its issues were republished as many as three times. Articles were well written and the continuing attack on Cosby's conduct began to take their toll on him. A theme that kept recurring throughout the various issues centered on "Liberty of the Press," as if Zenger and his editorial staff were anticipating Cosby's next move. The issue of November 12, 1733, for example, featured this thought: "The liberty of the press is a subject of the greatest importance, and in which every individual is as much concerned as he is in any other part of liberty."

Aware that the vigorous tirades against him and his cohorts in the *Journal* were undermining his rule, Cosby finally counter-attacked. The only name associated with the *Journal* of course, was Zenger's. Cosby knew the men who actually were editing the paper and that Zenger was merely the printer, but he could not proceed against them as only the publisher of a libel could be held responsible. After vainly attempting to persuade the Grand Jury, through Chief Justice DeLancey, to indict Zenger for seditious libel, he arranged for Zenger to be arrested on Sunday November 17, 1734 on warrant of the Council. The warrant read:

"It is ordered that the Sherriff for the City of *New York,* do forthwith take and apprehend *John Peter Zenger,* for printing and publishing several seditious Libels, dispersed throughout his Journals or News Papers, entitled, *The New-York Weekly Journal, containing the freshest Advices, foreign and domestick;* as having in them many things tending to raise Factions and Tumults, among the People of This Province, inflamming their Minds with contempt of His Majesty's Government, and greatly disturbing the Peace thereof, and upon his taking the said *John Peter Zenger, to commit him to the Prison or common Gaol of Said City and County.*"

GRAVE DOUBT WAS EXPRESSED as to the legality of this action, for the Council also sat as a court for the correction of errors and appeals. The situation was aggravated by the fact that the warrant merely expressed the opinion of the Council and was not based on a hearing in which Zenger's evidence could be interposed.

James Alexander and William Smith appeared for Zenger and demanded reasonable bail. Instead DeLancey set bail at so high a figure that Zenger remained in prison until his trial on August 4, 1735. The *Journal* appeared every Monday as usual, however, as Zenger, from his cell, advised his wife how to carry on.

Public bitterness increased at this turn of events. The *Journal* skillfully played on the populace's sympathy. Anticipating the trial, it meticulously advised prospective jurors on their rights in cases involving seditious libel. For the law of seditious libel, as it was then construed, favored Governor Cosby's position, and it was obvious to the leaders of the Popular Party, that DeLancey, a good common law judge, would make every effort to enforce it at the trial. Only the jury could possibly thwart the Government's position, and in order to understand this feature of the trial, it is important to understand the then existing law of seditious libel.

The invention of printing had created many problems in England for it greatly expedited the circulation of information and concepts which could be detrimental to the government in power. Severe censorship became the rule, enforced first by the Church and later by the Court of Star Chamber during the reign of Elizabeth. The Star Chamber decided both the law and the facts of each case, and violators of the law were punished summarily. Prosecutions for political libels and seditious words appear frequently in the state trials of the period. No relief ensued after the Star Chamber was abolished in 1641, for Parliament carried on with the same stringent rules. Under the Licensing Act of 1663, the Crown assumed control of the Press, closely censoring its activities, and upon the expiration of this act in 1695, the law of libel became the only restraint on the printed word.

The law of seditious libel, however, at the time merely carried on the tradition of the old licensing acts, for the King's Bench in the 18th century adopted the doctrines of the Court of Star Chamber. Stephens, in his *History of the Criminal Law in England* defines seditious libel in the 18th century as "written censure upon public men for their conduct as such, or upon the law, or upon the institutions of the country." This was the definition on which the Star Chamber acted invariably, and which was adopted after the Restoration by the Court of King's Bench. Truth was no defense. Blackstone stated, "It is immaterial with respect to the essence of a libel, whether it be true or false, since the provocation, not the falsity, is the thing punished criminally." In fact the courts held that "the greater the truth, the greater the libel." The crime consisted merely in the publication of such a defamatory comment; not even the writer's motive was considered.

THE JURY PLAYED AN ODD role in these trials. It was required to find only a special verdict pertaining to the fact of publication and that the words of the libel were actually used in the sense complained of in the indictment. After the jury found the defendant guilty in this respect, the judge then decided as a question of law, on a motion in arrest of judgment by the defendant, whether the writing was a seditious libel. But the jury also had the legal power to render a general verdict both on the facts and the law as in a murder trial. It had no moral right to do so, but whether it would render a general verdict contrary to the direction of the presiding justice was another matter.

Stephens comments that the practical enforcement of this doctrine was wholly inconsistent with any serious public discussion of political affairs, and so long as it was recognized as the law of the land all such discussion existed only on sufferance. This situation prevailed in the colonies as well, and the leaders of the opposition recognized it as the crux of the *Zenger Trial*.

Alexander and Smith filed objections to the Commission of DeLancey and Philipse in that their tenures were subject to the will of the Governor rather than during good behavior. Persisting in their course, even though warned by the Chief Justice, they were held in contempt and disbarred. This was indeed an unusual and arbitrary action. It was done deliberately, however, to remove from Zenger's defense the most brilliant attorneys in the Province, and the ones most likely to succeed.

John Chambers, who was assigned by the Court to defend Zenger, entered a plea of not guilty. Chambers had recently started to practice, and Richard Bradley, the Attorney General was confident of victory. After all—the law was clear—truth was no defense and the judges decided as a matter of law whether the words published constituted a libel. The jury had to find necessarily that Zenger had published the *Journal* and it would be over in short order.

The trial opened August 4, 1735, before DeLancey and Philipse in the City Hall, then located at Nassau and Wall Streets. (George Washington was later sworn in there as first President of the United States.) The room was packed with many of Zenger's friends and partisans. It was obvious to DeLancey that any attempt on his part to browbeat the jury or Zenger's counsel would be met with ill-favor by the crowd. Unknown to both Chambers and the prosecution, a political society called the "Sons of Liberty" had retained an additional attorney to defend Zenger. The jury having been selected, Chambers arose and argued on the nature of libel. Then the Attorney General started his case. At this point, a venerable, old gentleman arose from the crowd and after identifying himself as Mr. Hamilton of the Philadelphia Bar, said:

"May it Please your Honour; I am concerned in this cause on the part of Mr. Zenger the defendant." As he strode forth to the bench a gasp arose, not only from the closely packed spectators but from the Attorney General and DeLancy as well. For the man who had thus spoken was Andrew Hamilton—leader of the Philadelphia Bar, and considered the most eminent practitioner of his time in the colonies. The secret of his retainer had been well kept. DeLancey, unprepared for this turn of events, and awed by the importance of the man before him, grudgingly permitted him to continue.

Hamilton was close to eighty years old when he appeared in the *Zenger Case*. He had established a handsome practice and his reputation as a lawyer was second to none. He had represented William Penn's interests in Pennsylvania and in England. A contemporary letter brings out a feature of his character that probably was influential in his decision to defend Zenger. "He is a very able lawyer, very faithful to his client, and has generally refused to be concerned for any Plaintiff who appeared not to have Justice on his side. . . ." He is noted, too, for his role in building Independence Hall in Philadelphia. Hamilton appeared in practically every important case in Pennsylvania, and he was the special adviser to several of the Provincial Governors on political and financial matters.

Hamilton had been well briefed by Alexander and Smith on the law, and particularly on the hostility to be expected from the court. The law was definitely against him—but he shrewdly had decided that the members of the jury detested its effect and would probably seek a solution favorable to Zenger, if one could only be offered them. And that was exactly what Hamilton planned to do. His course had to be bold and daring. He had to take the prosecution by storm!

Instead of allowing the Attorney General to prove the publication of the libel in the *Journal*, he candidly admitted it:

". . . I cannot think it proper for me, without doing violence to my own Principles, to deny the publication of a Complaint, which I think is the Right of every free born Subject to make, when the Matters so published can be supported with Truth; and therefore I'll save Mr. Attorney the trouble of examining his Witnesses to that point; and I do, for my Client, confess, that he both printed and published the two News Papers set forth in the Information; and I hope in so doing he has committed no crime!"

AFTER DISMISSING THE WITNESSES, the Attorney General tried to bring the case to immediate conclusion. Addressing himself to DeLancey he said:

"Indeed sir, as Mr. Hamilton has confessed the Printing and Publishing these Libels, I think the Jury must find a verdict for the King: for supposing they were true, the Law says that they are not the less libellous for that; nay indeed the Law says, their being true is an Aggravation of the Crime."

Hamilton quickly replied:

"Not so neither, Mr. Attorney, there are two words to that Bargain. I hope it is not our bare Printing and Publishing a Paper, that will make it a Libel. You will have something more to do, before you make my client a Libeller; for the Words themselves must be libellous, that is *false, scandalous,* and *seditious,* or else we are not guilty."

The Attorney General replied setting forth the traditional construction of the Law of Libel and the authorities for his conclusions.

Hamilton fought back:

"May it please your Honour," he continued, "I cannot agree with Mr. Attorney: For tho' I freely acknowledge, that there are such things as Libels, yet I must insist at the same time, that what my client is charged with is not a Libel; and I observed just now, that Mr. Attorney in defining a Libel, made use of the Words, *scandalous, seditious,* and *tend to disquiet the People;* but, whether with Design or not I will not say, he ommitted the word *False.*

Bradley replied: "I think I did not omit the *False;* But it has been said already, that it may be a Libel, not withstanding it may be true.

But Hamilton pressed his point: "In this I must still differ with Mr. Attorney. . . . This word *false* must have some meaning, or else how came it there? . . . No, the falsehood makes the scandal, and both make the Libel." Then he threw down the gauntlet "And to shew the Court that I am in good Earnest, and to save the court's time, and Mr. Attorney's trouble, I will agree, that if he can prove the Facts charged upon us, to be false, I'll own them to be scandalous, seditious, and a Libel. So the Work seems now to be pretty much shortened, and Mr. Attorney has now only to prove the words *false,* in order to make us *Guilty.*"

When Bradley protested that a negative could not be proved, Hamilton offered to carry the burden of proof.

At this point, DeLancey, recognizing the effect Hamilton was making on the jury, intervened.

"You cannot be admitted, Mr. Hamilton," he exploded, "to give the truth of a Libel in Evidence. A Libel is not to be justified; for it is nevertheless a Libel that is true."

Hamilton calmly, but firmly, continued: "I am sorry the Court has so soon resolved upon that Piece of Law; I expected first to have been heard to the point. I have not in all my Reading met with an authority that says, we cannot be admitted to give the truth in Evidence, upon an information for a Libel."

After an extended argument in which DeLancey and Bradley participated and in which Hamilton cited every precedent in his favor especially emphasizing the *Seven Bishops' Case*, it began to appear that Hamilton was carrying the day with the Jury. Certainly the partisan onlookers, noted with delight every point he made. One of his arguments was received most favorably by the onlookers although at first they must have been taken aback by it.

"What strange doctrine is it," he said "to press everything for law here which is so in England? I believe we should not think it a favour, at present at least, to establish this practice."

Hamilton refused to accept the Court's ruling that the facts could not be proved, hitting back hard at every opportunity. Finally in exasperation DeLancey exclaimed:

"Mr. Hamilton, the Court have delivered their opinion, and we expect you will use us with good Manners; you are not to be permitted to argue against the opinion of the Court."

Hamilton was stubborn too. "With submission, I have seen the Practice in very great courts, and never heard it deemed unmannerly to . . ."

The Chief Justice however, insisted on his way and Hamilton necessarily had to comply: "I will say no more at this point: the Court, I see is against us on this point; and that I hope, I may be allowed to say."

DeLancey relented: "Use the court with good manners, and you shall be allowed all the Liberty you can reasonably desire."

And now the case was ready to go to the Jury!

Hamilton looked closely at each member of the Jury and began his summation slowly:

"Then Gentlemen of the Jury, it is to you we must now appeal, for Witness, to the Truth of the Facts we have offered, and are denied the Liberty to prove; and let it not seem strange, that I apply myself to you in this Manner, I am warranted so to do, both by Law and Reason. The last supposes you to be summoned, *out of the Neighborhood* the Fact is alleged to be committed, and the Reason of your being taken out of the Neighborhood is, *because you are supposed to have the best knowledge of the fact that is to be tried.*" (It will be recalled that in those days the jury was drawn from people of the neighborhood actually cognizant of the facts in dispute at the trial). Hamilton continued that the jury consisting of lawful and honest citizens of New York, knew the truth of the Zenger matter "and therefore in your justice lies our safety."

Hamilton then argued that the Jury had the right to determine both the law and the facts in a seditious libel case. That the jury "*must understand* the words in the Information to be *scandalous,* that is to say *false.* . . ."

"NO, MR. HAMILTON," DELANCEY intervened. "The Jury may find that *Zenger* printed and published those Papers, and leave it to the Court to judge whether they are libellous; you know this is very common; it is in the Nature of a special verdict, where the Jury leave the Matter of Law to the Court."

Hamilton refused to accept this doctrine: "I know, may it please your Honour, the Jury may do so; but I do likewise know they may do otherwise. I know they have the Right beyond all Dispute, to determine both the Law and the Fact, and where they do not doubt of the Law, they ought to do so. This practice of leaving it to the Judgment of the Court, *whether the Words are libellous or not,* in Effect renders Juries useless, to say no worse in many cases. . . ." (Hamilton was right, for juries could historically render general verdicts applying the law to the facts. It was the fear of attaint that made them prefer to render special verdicts only. In criminal cases, however, the general verdict was a common occurrence.)

Hamilton continued with a long and impressive speech in which he reviewed the great cases of the past. In proving the right of the Jury to judge both the facts and the law, he quoted with effect from *Bushel's Case*, where the jury trying William Penn for disturbing the peace refused to follow the direction of the Judge in the giving of its verdict. There, the Court supported the right of the jury "to find such a Verdict as they in their conscience do think is agreeable to their Evidence." And the jury there in finding the law and the fact proved "that Jurymen are to see with their own Eyes, to hear with their own ears, and to make use of their own Consciences, and Understandings in judging of the Lives, Liberties or Estates of their fellow subjects!"

He rose to forensic eloquence in his closing peroration and in a sense was most prophetic.

"You see I labour under the weight of many years, and am born down with great Infirmities of Body; yet Old and Weak as I am, I should think it my Duty, if required, to go to the utmost Part of the Land, where my Service could be of any Use in assisting to quench the Flame of Prosecutions upon Informations set on Foot by the Government, to deprive a People of the Right of Remonstrating, and complaining too, of the arbitrary attempts of Men in Power. . . .

"But to conclude: The Question before the Court and you, Gentlemen of the Jury, is not of small nor private concern, it is not the cause of a poor Printer, nor of New-York alone, which you are now trying: No! It may in its consequence, affect every Freeman that lives under a British Government on the main of America, It is the best Cause. It is the cause of Liberty, and I make no Doubt but your upright conduct, this Day, will not only entitle you to the Love and Esteem of your Fellow Citizens; but every man who prefers Freedom to a Life of Slavery will bless and honour You, as Men who have Baffled the attempt of Tyranny; and by an impartial and uncorrupt Verdict, have laid a noble Foundation for securing to ourselves, our Posterity, and our Neighbours, that to which Nature and the Laws of our Country have given us a Right, — the Liberty — both of exposing and opposing arbitrary Power, in these Parts of the World, at least, by speaking and writing truth."

IT WAS CLEAR TO ALL that Hamilton had finally swayed the Jury to his way of thinking. The Attorney General spoke briefly and DeLancey charged the Jury to leave the question of law to him.

The Jury retired and quickly returned with a verdict of Not Guilty. Zenger later wrote "Upon which there were three huzzas in the Hall which was crowded with people, and the next Day I was discharged from my Imprisonment."

So completely had Hamilton dominated the trial that his fearlessness carried over to others. When DeLancey rebuked the crowd for its cheers, Captain Norris, son-in-law of Lewis Morris stepped forward and exclaimed "Cheers were customary on such occasions, and especially on the occasion of the trial of the Bishop of London."

Hamilton was dined and feted by the people of New York and returned to his home with great honors. The report of the trial was widely published throughout the colonies and in England. It became the common topic of conversation in all the coffee houses, and was commented on by the leaders of the Bar. "If it is not law it is better than law, it ought to be law and will always be law wherever justice prevails," said one of them.

Zenger was later made public printer and died in 1746. Hamilton retired from public life in 1739 and died in 1741. His obituary written by Benjamin Franklin concludes, "He steadily maintained the cause of Liberty. . . ." As for Cosby, the trial broke his spirit. He never collected his share of Van Dam's fees, and he died shortly thereafter.

It is interesting to note, it was not until the *Fox Libel Acts* of 1792 that a jury was authorized to render a general verdict of guilty upon the whole matter put in issue in a libel action. And it was not until 1843, in *Lord Campbell's Act*, that on a criminal prosecution for a defamatory libel the defendant was entitled to plead the truth of the matters charged.

In the United States, the first Amendment to the Constitution, appeared to set aside the common law of seditious libel. It therefore came as an unwelcome surprise to the American people when Congress enacted the Sedition Act of 1798. Strangely enough, this law, which punished false, scandalous and malicious writings against the President or members of Congress, allowed truth to be interposed as a defense and permitted a jury to find a general verdict.

Over the years, the determination of criminality in libel actions in the states have been entrusted to the jury by statute, as well as admitting truth as a defense. In 1805, for example, New York passed a statute similar to the *Fox Libel Act* adding truth as a defense. The New York State Constitution, since 1821, provides similarly. In New York today, under the provisions of the Penal Law, in cases involving criminal libel, the jury may not only render a general verdict on the law and the facts, but may also disregard the court's instruction on the law. Of course, the judge may still direct an acquittal or set aside a conviction.

Since 1925, the protections of the first Amendment have been applied to the States as well as the Federal government on the theory that the Fourteenth amendment has absorbed them.

The Zenger trial turned out to be the cornerstone of the liberty of the press in this country. It provided a defense to arbitrary power and established the right of critical comment on the activities of public officials.

Gouverneur Morris, grandson of Lewis Morris, recognizing how much his generation owed to the trial later said: "The trial of Zenger in 1735 was the germ of American Freedom, the morning star of that liberty which subsequently revolutionized America. . . ."

Writs of Assistance

Of Smugglers

and the

Fourth Amendment

"**O**TIS WAS A FLAME OF FIRE! *With a promptitude of clas-sical allusions, a depth of research, a rapid summary of historical events and dates, a profusion of legal authori-ties, a prophetic glance of his eye into futurity, and a tor-rent of impetuous eloquence, he hurried away everything before him. . . . Then and there was the first scene of the first act of opposition to the arbitrary claims of Great Britain.* Then and there the child Independence was born."

This memorable description of an epochal argument, written by John Adams fifty-seven years after he had heard it, marked a celebrated milestone in the annals of Anglo-American jurisprudence. It also revealed how one of the basic cornerstones of American Constitutional lib-erty came to be laid. Today there is a prevailing tendency to hold that the Fourth Amendment to the United States Constitution, outlawing "unreasonable searches and sei-zures," was principally evoked by the history surrounding the Otis appeal in the famous case of the *"Writs of Assist-ance,"* or *Paxton's Case* in February 1761. Yet, the events leading to Otis's fiery rhetoric arose out of circumstances so characteristic of eighteenth century America that they can only be fully understood in the context of the political and economic history of the period. Mr. Justice Frankfurter has aptly stated: "The provenance of the Fourth Amendment bears on its scope." Mr. Justice Story said earlier that the Fourth Amendment "is little more than the affirmance of a great constitutional doctrine of the Common Law."

Robert Carr, in explaining why the American people wanted specific individual guarantees written into the Federal Constitution, commented that they "looked to the experience of the past, and reflecting upon the evils of the preceding ages, concluded that the threat of arbitrary, tyrannical government was very serious. Bills of rights are, for the most part, reactions against evils of the past rather than promises for the future."

To THE FOUNDERS OF OUR FORM of government, the ancient maxim that "a man's house is his castle" had been indelibly impressed on their memories by reason of centuries of English governmental abuse. Still fresh in their minds was the obnoxious British practice of issuing "writs of assistance" to revenue officers which gave them blanket authority to search anywhere for contraband goods smuggled into the colonies in violation of the English Trade Laws. This Americans had objected to vehemently and had opposed vigorously. Above all, however, they remembered James Otis's argument in the *Paxton Case* and the events that occurred in England shortly thereafter.

Early in 1761, the people of the Province of Massachusetts Bay were in a state of turmoil. A victorious Great Britain, flushed with the conquest of Canada, had decided to come to grips with the American colonies and seriously enforce the notorious laws of trade and navigation. Designed to protect England's own industries and commerce, in accordance with mercantilist principles, the trade laws provided that all colonial owned cargoes had first to be brought to an English port, before they could be sold elsewhere. Of particular significance was the *Molasses Act of*

1733, which put a prohibitive tariff on every gallon of molasses and sugar brought from the non-British West Indies to North America. England's purpose here was to discourage colonial trade with the French West Indies and to promote the economy of the British West Indies. But this law was so detrimental to the American colonies that it was observed more in the breach than in the enforcement. The importation of molasses and sugar from the French West Indies supplied the very life's blood of colonial trade; to be deprived of it meant economic disaster.

New England converted the molasses to rum, which merchants then exported to Africa in exchange for cargoes of slaves and gold dust. These were in turn exchanged for more sugar in the West Indies.

Although the British realized that they were losing considerably by this triangular trade, the *Molasses Act* was considered so unfair, even in England, that it was weakly enforced. Indeed, had the Colonists complied with the *Molasses Act,* the entire molasses production of the British West Indies would have supplied only one-eighth of their annual requirements. Then again, British West Indies prices were almost double that of the French because of the heavy exportation duties levied by the British.

A favorable balance of trade permitted the Colonists to liquidate their indebtedness to British merchants, develop their own natural resources, and provide for their merchant marine. Illicit trade was also carried on by the Colonists with Holland, Hamburg and France. Legal cargoes were shipped there from New England. On the return trip, however, the colonial merchantmen carrying cargoes of dry goods, wines, gun powder and tea circumvented the English ports in order to avoid the payment of the heavy duties imposed by British law.

SMUGGLING AND BRIBERY of royal officials became an accepted practice in the conduct of Colonial trade. A contemporary newspaper accused the customs collectors "of shutting their eyes or at least opening them no further than their own private interest required." Yet public opinion boldly sanctioned this corruption, for it was bringing prosperity to the provinces and wealth to many merchant families. One commentator has seriously concluded that if the *Molasses Act* had been strictly enforced from the time of its enactment the American Revolution might well have occurred thirty years sooner.

Like a bolt from the blue, on August 23, 1760, the British Home Government sent a circular dispatch to colonial officials ordering that the *Molasses Act of 1733* be strictly enforced. During the war with France, the colonists had traded with the French in America, reaping great profits thereby, and had actually supplied them so well with provisions that the war had been prolonged. The English were very much aware of this illicit and unpatriotic trade and, as a war measure, increased their efforts to suppress it. Moderately successful in curtailing it, the English government determined that once the war was over and the good will of the colonists and their legislatures were no longer needed, a real attempt would be made to force the colonists to sustain their burden of maintaining the British colonial system. Why, they reasoned, should the provincials enjoy affluence and luxury at the expense of the mother country which had invested millions of pounds in the development of the colonies? The Americans had been loath to share the financial burden of the war—had even traded with the enemy, and they should be made to pay for it. In England, the public debt amounted to £18 per person; in the colonies it was only 18 shillings. This situation had to be corrected, and the best way to do so was to carry into effect the acts of trade.

The news that the *Molasses Act* was to be enforced "caused greater alarm in this country than the taking of Fort William Henry did in 1757," wrote Governor Bernard from Boston. In a sense, the British had shown poor political judgment in failing to insist from the beginning on compliance with the trade laws, for a certain respectability had come to be attached to smuggling over the years. Many colonists firmly believed that the Home Government's attitude towards smuggling reflected legal acceptance of the practice. Suddenly, without warning, it had become illegal, notwithstanding, in the words of John Adams, "There never had been a time when [the laws of trade] would have been or could have been obeyed." Boston merchants publicly bewailed their plight and predicted that the trade of Massachusetts Province would be reduced to a trickle "sacrificed to the West Indian Planters" and that there would be no other alternative to taking up farming and homespun. Similar protestations came from the other colonies. Even more important than the loss of trade, however, was the machinery established by the government for the administration of the trade laws—for if properly executed, aggressions on the colonists' freedom were inevitable.

GENERAL AUTHORITY FOR THE conduct of the colonists was lodged in the Board of Trade and Plantations in England, which was answerable to the Privy Council. The Lords of Trade delegated the administration of the Laws of Trade and Navigation to the Governors of the several provinces, who in turn supervised their enforcement by the naval officer, the collector of customs, the surveyor-general, the collectors and the surveyors and searchers for each port. When it became obvious that juries in the ordinary colonial courts of record would not convict violators of the trade laws, no matter how clear the evidence was against them, separate admiralty courts were established to try these cases without juries.

The customs officials, however, were confronted with another obstacle—the sympathy felt by the public for the law breakers. How could they detect and ferret out smugglers and their contraband goods when they were hidden by their neighbors and informers suffered the wrath of an incensed populace? Ordinary search warrants served little purpose under these circumstances, as they could only be issued on information and for specific goods in specified places. To be effective, the contraband had to be searched for in hidden places and seized without warning, before it could be removed by an alerted owner. The only solution was the use of a catchall device known as a "Writ of Assistance." Hence the Order in Council which was directed to Governor Bernard of Massachusetts authorized the customs officers to apply to the Superior Court of Judicature of the province for such writs. This is what stirred up the hornets' nest!

"Writs of Assistance" were derived from the ancient "Writs of Aid" which were normally addressed to the sheriff from the Court of Exchequer. General in form, the *Writ of Assistance* authorized officers of the customs and their deputies and assistants "in the daytime to enter and go into any house, shop, cellar, warehouse or room, or other place, and, in case of resistance, to break open doors, chests, trunks, and other packages, to seize and from thence to bring any kind of goods or merchandise whatsoever, prohibited and uncustomed, and to put and secure the same in his Majesty's warehouse." Ships anchored in or near the post could also be similarly entered at night. The *Writ* received its name from the fact that it ordered all officers and subjects of the King to assist in its execution; disobedience was punishable as contempt of court.

The *Writ* was particularly vicious in that it was so general and arbitrary. No special writ of search, issued on sworn testimony that the smuggled goods were concealed in a definite place, was needed. The *Writ* was not returnable to the court after execution but rather continued in effect indefinitely, until the demise of the reigning monarch and for six months thereafter, as a license to search and seize uncustomed goods anywhere. The official in possession of the writ therefore had absolute and unlimited discretion in its execution.

In England although special warrants upon complaints under oath, stating the crime and specifying the name of the accused, were technically the only legal warrants upon which a person could be arrested, a practice had arisen from the time of Charles II of issuing general warrants in the enforcement of the seditious libel laws and in regulation of the press. These general warrants authorized government officials to take into custody persons unknown who could possibly be the authors, printers and publishers of the obscene or seditious libels particularly specified in the warrant. Thus these general warrants authorized the apprehension of all persons suspected, without naming or describing any person in particular. When these acts expired, in 1694, they were re-enacted in every new reign, and were still in effect in 1760.

OFFENSIVE AS THE GENERAL warrants were, the *Writs of Assistance* were more so. The general warrants at least applied to a specific case of libel and therefore were restricted as to persons and time. The *Writ of Assistance*, however, was a permanent writ, effective during the lifetime of the King, generally applicable to anyone under suspicion and therefore even more dangerous in the hands of an unscrupulous official.

The indignation of the colonists was reflected by Lord Chatham in his eloquent speech on general warrants, when he said they infringed upon "The immunity of an English home where the wind might blow through every cranny but the King's writ could not enter. . . . The poorest man may, in his cottage, bid defiance to all the forces of the Crown. It may be frail; its roof may shake. The wind may blow through it, the storm may enter; the rain may enter; but the King of England may not enter; all his force dares not cross the threshold of the ruined tenement."

A law enacted during the reign of William III directed that custom house officials be given the same aid and assistance in the administration of the trade laws by the colonial courts as was required by law to be rendered in England by the Court of Exchequer. Governor Hutchinson noted in his *History of Massachusetts Bay* that although *Writs of Assistance* were not used for more than half a century in the colonies, "the collectors and superior officers of the customs, merely by the authority derived from their commission, had possibly entered warehouses, and even dwelling houses, upon information that contraband goods were concealed in them. The people grew uneasy under the expense of this assumed authority, and some stood upon their defence against such entries, whilst others were bringing their actions in the law against the officers, for past illegal entries, in attempts to enter." Shirley, while Governor of the Province, had, in his capacity as a civil magistrate, authorized the issuance of *Writs of Assistance* in 1755 to customs officers, but the legality of this action was challenged by the merchants so effectively that he became more cautious and referred the officers to the Superior Court for their warrants. From that time on, the writs had been issued by the Superior Court in the same manner as the Court of Exchequer in England. As a result informers were encouraged by offers of bounty to disclose the location of uncustomed goods, and several seizures of contraband were made. On the whole, the situation was still tolerable, however, and despite the state of irritation manifested by the public, only minor protests were made.

The decision of the Home Government to enforce the trade laws, however, dramatically changed the situation. The issuance of *Writs of Assistance* in Shirley's time, though perhaps unconscionable, was still understandable, since the immediate purpose was to prevent trading with the enemy. But now the government was committed to destroying the "illicit" trade of the provinces completely; a program so drastic in its implications that a general state of alarm seized the mercantile community. The crisis came to a head with the death of George II on October 25, 1760, for according to the law the validity of all *Writs of Assistance* issued by the Superior Court in his name expired six months after his death.

SMOLDERING WITH RESENTMENT, the merchants consulted on how to prevent the issuance of new writs. Their dismay became even more pronounced when royal officers, armed with *Writs of Assistance*, increased their activities and began to seize illicit cargoes on a grand scale. In the summer of 1760, a highly valuable shipment from Holland, worth over £10,000, was confiscated. Indignation knew no bounds — especially when merchants considered that the obnoxious trade laws were not being enforced equally throughout the colonies. Rhode Island, for example, where smuggling was rampant, was not subjected to such treatment, and illegal trading flourished there at the expense of the Boston merchants. There was no doubt about it. They had to be relieved of the *Writs of Assistance!*

Their opportunity to contest them came shortly thereafter. In November, 1760, Charles Paxton, head of the customs in Boston, directed a Mr. Cockle, one of his deputies in Salem, to petition the Superior Court of Massachusetts for *Writs of Assistance,* in the name of the new King, George III. Highly indignant, sixty-three shipping merchants banded together to resist the issuance of the writ. Prior thereto they had requested an interview with Stephen Sewall, then Chief Justice of the Superior Court. Greatly respected for his integrity, ability and moderation, Sewall listened conscientiously to their plea. Only the Court of Exchequer in England could issue such writs, they argued. By what authority did the Superior Court of Massachusetts assume similar jurisdiction? This was a novel question which had never been presented to the court before; and Sewall, learned in the law, expressed doubts of his own. True the law directed the colonial courts to give to revenue officers all such aid as was given to officers by Courts in England. But did the Superior Court's jurisdiction correspond to that of the Court of Exchequer? Perhaps the Superior Court did not have such authority and the writs were tainted with illegality! Unfortunately for the merchants, Sewall had died on September 11, 1760, and Governor Bernard had appointed the Lieutenant Governor, Thomas Hutchinson, as his successor. Inasmuch as the application had been petitioned by the Crown, and the Boston merchants had petitioned for a hearing thereon, it was set down for argument for the next term of court, to be held in February, 1761, at Boston.

Hutchinson's appointment caused consternation in Massachusetts. A merchant of considerable wealth, of marked ability, and commanding appearance, he was still not a lawyer, and as he candidly admits in his diary, it was

250

James Otis arguing against the Writs of Assistance

From a painting by Robert H. Reid.
By permission of the Commonwealth of Massachusetts Art Commission.

"an eyesore to some of the Bar that he was not bred to the law." As an avowed King's man who had been well repaid for his loyalty to the Crown, he was quite unpopular. In addition to being Chief Justice, he continued to serve as Lieutenant-Governor, a member of the Council and Judge of Probate. Members of his immediate family also occupied lucrative office in the government, and it was apparent that the interests of the Crown would be well-served by the new Chief Justice. Political circles were aware that Governor Bernard's predecessor in office had promised the first vacancy on the bench to Colonel James Otis, a leader of the Bar and a man of great influence in the community, who would have been better disposed to the merchants' cause. The purpose in denying Otis was clear enough to exacerbate public anxiety and opposition.

BOTH THE GOVERNMENT and the merchants prepared for a bitter and decisive legal struggle. The merchants retained James Otis, son of Colonel Otis, to represent them, and rumor had it that he accepted the case in order to avenge the slight to his father; "that he would set the province in flames, if he perished by the fire." Actually this was quite untrue, for Otis at 36 years of age, although a firebrand, was an ardent patriot and had a reputation for brilliance at the Bar. He had been Advocate General of Admiralty with a lucrative income, and he had resigned from that office rather than represent the Crown on behalf of what he believed to be an illegal and tyrannical writ.

The merchants also retained Oxenbridge Thacher, 41 years of age, another ardent patriot, whose reputation at the Bar at the time was even more distinguished than Otis's. A scholar of great learning and ability, Thacher was a member of one of the finest families of the province, and his reputation for moderation and good sense was such that the Crown feared him more than it did Otis. Both refused to accept the large fees which the merchants had offered. "In such a cause, I despise all fees," Otis exclaimed.

Jeremiah Gridley, a veteran of the Bar under whom both Otis and Thacher had studied law, appeared on behalf of the Crown as Attorney General. Noted for his learning, ingenuity and dignity, he was a worthy opponent and a lawyer to be respected.

The memorable trial of *"Paxton's Case"* was held in the Old State House in Boston on February 24, 1761. It was a cold and damp day and the five judges of the Superior Court, Benjamin Lynde, John Cushing, Chambers Russell, and Peter Oliver sat in the Council Chamber near a great fire, Chief Justice Thomas Hutchinson, presiding. All the barristers-at-law of Boston and Middlesex County were present as well. Chairs had been brought in for the sixty-three merchants who were opposing the issuance of the Writ, and all realized that a historic event was taking place. An air of expectancy and subdued disquiet permeated the handsome room.

Unfortunately, no contemporary account of the argument is available today. But seated at the table with the wigged and gowned barristers was a young man, just 26 years old, who later was to become the second President of the United States, John Adams. Adams had obtained special permission to attend as an observer, and what he noted that day he recorded in a famous letter fifty-seven years later to William Tudor, Otis's biographer.

"That Council Chamber," he wrote, "was as respectable an apartment as the House of Commons or the House of Lords in Great Britain, in proportion, or that in the State House in Philadelphia, in which the Declaration of Independence was signed, in 1776. In this Chamber, round a great fire, were seated five Judges with Lieutenant-Governor Hutchinson at their head, as Chief Justice, all arrayed in their new, fresh, rich robes of scarlet English broadcloth; in their large cambric bands, and immense judicial wigs. In this Chamber were seated at a long table all the barristers at law of Boston, and of the neighboring County of Middlesex, in gowns, bands, and tie wigs. They were not seated on ivory chairs, but their dress was more solemn and more pompous than that of the Roman Senate, when the Gauls broke in upon them . . . Two portraits, at

more than full length, of King Charles the Second and of
King James the Second, in splendid golden frames, were
hung up on the most conspicuous sides of the apartment. If
my young eyes or old memory have not deceived me,
these were as fine pictures as I ever saw; the colors of the
royal ermines and long flowing robes were the most glow-
ing, the figures the most noble and graceful, the features
the most distinct and characteristic, far superior to those of
the King and Queen of France in the Senate Chambers of
Congress—these were worthy of the pencils of Rubens
and Van Dyke. There was no painter in England capable
of them at that time. They had been sent over without
frames in Governor Pownall's time but he was no admirer
of Charles or James. The pictures were stowed away in a
garret, among rubbish, till Governor Bernard came, who
had them cleaned, superbly framed, and placed in Council
for the admiration and imitation of all men—no doubt with
the advice and concurrence of Hutchinson and all his
nebula of stars and satellites. One circumstance more,
Samuel Adams and John Adams had been admitted barristers of the term. John was the youngest; he should be
painted looking like a short thick archbishop of Canterbury, seated at the table with a pen in his hand, lost in
admiration, now and then minuting those poor notes . . ."

IT WAS APPARENT TO ALL that Hutchinson and Governor
Bernard in setting the stage and scenery for the trial had
attempted to awe the provincials, and to subdue whatever
thoughts of independence flickered in their minds, by
reflecting in the room all the majesty, pomp and circumstance of the omnipotent British Government. The effect
was indeed brilliant and impressive. But they had not
reckoned with James Otis!

The tension in the old Council Chamber was almost
unbearable when Jeremiah Gridley stepped forward to
open the case for the Crown. That Chamber as Hosmer
has so well said, "has been the theatre of as many great
events probably as any one spot in America, but this one
in February, 1761, was perhaps the most important of all."
Gridley was a superb advocate, a recognized leader of the

Massachusetts Bar. He "argued", Adams said, "with his characteristic learning, ingenuity, and dignity." Gridley admitted that the "common privileges of Englishmen are taken away" by the *Writ of Assistance,* but it was justified by "the necessity of the case and the benefit of the revenue". It was just as necessary as the distraint of goods and chattels by a local officer in the recovery of taxes. Actually it was less inconsistent with English rights and liberties. "Necessity authorizes both."

As to the question whether the Superior Court of Massachusetts was authorized to exercise the functions of the Court of Exchequer in England, he noted that certain acts of Parliament in the reigns of Charles II and William and Mary had given revenue officers in the colonies power similar to those in England and hence they could call upon the Superior Court for *Writs of Assistance,* just as the English officials applied to the Court of Exchequer. He also quoted a provincial law enacted by the General Court in 1699, which gave to the Superior Court the jurisdiction of the English Courts of Exchequer, King's Bench and Common Pleas:

"By Act of Parliament they [the custom officers] are entitled to like assistants; now how can they have like assistants, if the Court cannot grant them it; and how can the court grant them like assistants if they cannot grant this Writ. Pity it would be, they should have like Right, and not like Remedy. The law abhors Right without Remedy. But the General Court has given this Court authority to grant it, and so has every other Plantation Court given their Superior Court." Although the common law did not sanction general writs, Parliament was not subject to the control of the common law, and an act of Parliament could not be declared repugnant and unconstitutional by reason of its conflict therewith. "If it is law in England," he calmly emphasized "it is law here; it is extended to this country by Act of Parliament." Bowing to the Court, he sat down. Hutchinson nodded approvingly, quite satisfied that Gridley's technical argument was unimpeachable. The merchants stirred uneasily.

Then Thacher stood up. Hopefully his countrymen turned their attention to him as he bowed to the judges. Thacher argued "with the softness of manners, the ingenuity and cool reasoning, which were remarkable in his amiable character." There was "but one" proper Writ of Assistance, and that was the one issued by the King's Court of Exchequer. "No other can grant it . . . and . . . no other officers but such as constitute that Court can grant it . . . This Court is not such one." There were diversities between the provincial Superior Court of Judicature and the King's Court of Exchequer, and the Statutes referred to by Gridley "did not give the Authority." The Custom-House officers in England were officers of the Court of Exchequer and hence answerable to that Court for misconduct. This was not so in the colonies. When he had concluded, there was an uncomfortable feeling in the room that much more had to be said. Thacher's argument was not sufficient, although he had spoken well. Two basic questions still had to be determined. Were the writs unconstitutional, and could Parliamentary acts be overruled in the colonies?

NOW IT WAS UP TO OTIS. A contemporary pictured him as "a plump, round-faced, smooth-skinned, short-necked, eagle-eyed politician." But for John Adams "Otis was a flame of fire!" And as Catherine Bowen has vividly observed: "There was violence in him and magnetism; the room felt it instantly. He was almost frightening; one had the feeling he might do or say something monstrous. His head was thrust forward on its short neck; he stood before the judges a moment, then began to walk up and down as he talked."

Otis spoke for more than five hours. Instead of concentrating on the legal questions involved, he applied the main thrust of his argument to the rights of the colonists as Englishmen. To Otis the most important principle before the Court was whether it should enforce an act of Parliament which violated a fundamental right of Englishmen. By stressing this aspect of his argument, Otis enlarged the concept of the dispute, arousing the passions of the people and "breathed into this nation the breath of life."

"I will to my dying day," Otis wrathfully threatened, "oppose with all the powers and faculties God has given me, all such instruments of slavery on the one hand, and villainy on the other, as this *Writ of Assistance* is. I am determined to sacrifice estate, ease, health, applause, and even life, to the sacred calls of my country, in opposition to a kind of power, the exercise of which cost one King his head and another his throne." These were ominous words, and the spectators were stirred by their implications.

Otis acknowledged that special writs directed to special officers to search specific places were legal, but he fervidly declaimed, the *Writs of Assistance* appeared to him to be "the worse instrument of arbitrary power, the most destructive of English liberty and the fundamental principles of law, that ever was found in an English law book." It was a weapon "that places the liberty of every man in the hands of every petty officer."

"If the King of Great Britain in person, at the head of 20,000 men, were encamped on Boston Common, with all his navy on our coast, he would not be able to execute these laws. They would be resisted or eluded." Then boldly continuing, he added, "One of the most essential branches of English liberty is the freedom of one's house. A man's house is his castle; and whilst he is quiet, he is as well guarded as a prince in his castle. This writ, if it should be declared legal, would totally annihilate this privilege. Custom-house officers may enter our houses when they please; we are commanded to permit their entry. Their menial servants may enter and whether they break through malice, or revenge, no man, no court, can inquire . . . "what a scene," he protested, "does this open! Every man, prompted by revenge, ill-humor, or wantonness to inspect the inside of his neighbor's house may apt a writ of assistance. Others will ask it from self-defense; one arbitrary exertion will provoke another until society is involved in tumult and blood."

Otis was still not done, however. Raising his voice in support of guarantees of civil liberties as a matter of natural right rather than statutory sanction he cited Coke's classic statement in *Dr. Bonham's Case,* to prove the illegality of the *Writs of Assistance.* "No act of Parliament," he thundered, "can establish such a writ; even though made in the very language of the petition, it would be a nullity. An act of Parliament against the Constitution is void. An Act against natural equity is void. The . . . courts must pass such acts into disuse." Here indeed was a sobering thought which struck a responsive chord in those who heard him. Professor Schwartz agrees with Professor Corwin that then and there American Constitutional Law was born, for Otis according to Justice Gray, "denied that [Parliament] was the final arbiter of the justice and constitutionality of its own acts; and . . . contended that the validity of statutes must be judged by the courts of justice; and thus foreshadowed the principle of American Constitutional Law, that it is the duty of the judiciary to declare unconstitutional statutes void." Otis also made a powerful protest against the tyranny of taxation without representation.

AT THE CLOSE OF HIS PLEA, "Every man of a crowded audience," Adams later related, "appeared to me to go away, as I did, ready to take arms against Writs of Assistance. Then and there was the first scene of the first Act of Opposition to the arbitrary claims of Great Britain. Then and there the child Independence was born. In fifteen years, namely in 1776, he grew up to manhood, and declared himself free." For now there was something to fight for—the basic rights of Englishmen. Adams summed it up well when he declared that from that time he could never read "any section of the acts of trade without a curse." Thatcher and Otis had not spoken in vain. "They had electrified the people, and scattered the seeds which soon germinated in the spirit of combined resistance against the encroachments of unlawful power."

It is not without interest to note that Gridley was full of

pride for his former pupils, Thacher and Otis. He later wrote "I raised up two young eagles [and] they pecked out both my eyes."

Had the judges decided the case immediately after the arguments, the majority of them would have been against the writs; but Hutchinson, seeking the favor of the Crown, "prevailed on his brethren to continue the cause till the next term." This gave him an opportunity to write to England and "inquire what is the practice at home, and what the grounds are that underlie this practice."

After a second argument in November, the Superior Court, under the influence of Hutchinson, gave judgment in favor of the writs and in December, the first of the new writs was issued to Charles Paxton. (Paxton, incidentally, became one of the most unpopular men in Boston as a result.) Hutchinson gave as his reason the reply he had received from William Bollan, an agent for Massachusetts in England, that the Court of Exchequer issued general writs as a matter of course, without affidavit or court order, upon application by the Commissioners of the Customs.

The validity of General Warrants in England, however, was not that clear. For several years later, England itself was rocked by the *Wilkes Case* and *Entick v. Carrington* which judicially condemned enforcement through general warrants. The *Entick Case* was later enshrined by the Supreme Court of the United States in *Boyd v. U. S.*, as "one of the landmarks of English liberty." In the *Entick Case*, Lord Camden held that the general warrant for the seizure of papers was contrary to the common law, despite its many years of acceptance by the courts, and could not be justified on the grounds that it was "necessary for the ends of government to lodge such a power with a state officer." Recognizing that there was no justification for the abuse of the search and seizure power in suppressing seditious libel even if it be considered true that "men ought not to be allowed to have such evil instruments in their keeping," he added: "If [permitted], I am afraid that all the inconveniences of a general seizure will follow upon a right allowed to seize a part. The search in such cases will be general, and every house will fall under the power of a secretary of state to be rummaged before proper conviction."

In the *John Wilkes Case,* Lord Camden decided that the general warrants used against Wilkes for his publication of issue No. 45 of the *North Briton,* which authorized the arrest of unnamed persons connected with the alleged libel and seizure of their papers, amounted to a "discretionary power given to messengers (agents of the Secretary of State) to search wherever their suspicions may chance to fall." "If such a power is truly invested in a Secretary of State, and he can delegate this power," he said, "it certainly may affect the persons and property of every man in this kingdom and is totally subversive of the liberty of the subject." Wilkes recovered £1000 in damages from Wood, the Under-Secretary of State who had supervised the seizure of the property. "Wilkes and Liberty" were acclaimed all over England and even in the American colonies, and he became a popular hero.

And in *Leach v. Money,* the King's Bench adjudged these general warrants to be illegal and void for uncertainty. The judges held that it was illegal to arrest a person not guilty of the offense named in the warrant. Persons so arrested could sue the messenger for wrongful arrest. Leach claimed and was awarded £400 damages. As a result, the general warrant lost its value to the government, as it subjected the Secretary of State and his assistants to a suit for damages unless it resulted in the arrest of the actual author printer or publisher of the libel. Although general warrants were thus condemned in England, general *Writs of Assistance* continued to be issued until 1817, when an order of the Board of Customs practically put an end to the practice by denying the issuance of the writ to any officer "unless he should previously make oath before a magistrate of his belief and grounds of belief that smuggled goods were lodged in a certain house." Certainly this was a vindication of Otis's position in the *Paxton Case.*

OTIS'S DEFENSE OF PRIVACY made such a lasting impression on the people of Massachusetts that it was incorporated in the Massachusetts Constitution of 1780:

"XIV — Every subject has a right to be secure from all unreasonable searches and seizures of his person, his houses, his papers, and all his possessions. [Warrants therefore have to be supported by affidavit, the suspect identified, and the property to be seized specified] . . . and no warrant ought to be issued but in cases, and with the formalities prescribed by the laws."

Virginia provided similarly in Article X of the Constitution of 1776, although its scope was not as general.

Thus it was that when Madison in 1791 gave thought to amending the Constitution of the United States by adding the Bill of Rights, "this history," as Justice Brennan expressed it, "was part of the intellectual matrix within which our own constitutional fabric was shaped." The Fourth Amendment grew out of the experiences of the colonists with the writs of assistance and their reaction to Otis's masterful address, and also remembered were the English landmark cases of *Wilkes* and *Entick v. Carrington* and *Leach v. Money*. We perceive from this history the rationale of the Fourth Amendment.

> *"The right of the people to be secure in their persons, houses, papers, and effects against unreasonable searches and seizures, shall not be violated, and no warrants shall issue, but upon probable cause, supported by oath or affirmation, and particularly describing the place to be searched, and the persons or things to be seized."*

The apprehension felt by the American people with regard to the exercise of oppressive and unreasonable power by the English Crown is reflected not only in the Fourth Amendment, but also in every state constitution of the United States. In fact, in many state constitutions the precise language of the Fourth Amendment is used; in others, the import of the clause is similar.

The Fourth Amendment prohibits such searches and seizures as are "unreasonable" in the light of what was deemed unreasonable when it was adopted. As such, it applies to governmental action only and not private acts of individuals. In the words of Justice Frankfurter dissenting in *Harris v. U. S.*, "the plain import of [this history] is that searches are 'unreasonable' unless authorized by a warrant, and a warrant hedged about by adequate safeguards . . . The 'reason' by which search and seizure is to be tested is the 'reason' that was written out of historic experience in the Fourth Amendment."

It should not be overlooked, of course, that peace officers may forcibly break into a building without a warrant to arrest a suspected criminal. As "incident" to a lawful arrest, incriminating papers or other articles related to the crime may be seized at the time. The Supreme Court, however, has attempted to impose general limitations on such action.

THE FOURTH AMENDMENT is silent on the legal admissibility of papers and other articles procured as a result of an unreasonable or, for that matter, reasonable search or seizure. Strangely enough, it was not until 1886 that the Supreme Court of the U. S. for the first time, in *Boyd v. U. S.*, comprehensively examined the scope of the Fourth Amendment. There the plantiff in error, under protest, was required by an act of Congress to produce invoices to imported goods, which were later used by the government as evidence against him of defrauding the customs. The compulsory production of the invoice, Justice Bradley held, amounted to an unreasonable search and seizure. Although there was no forcible entry into a man's house and seizure of property, still the Fourth Amendment had been violated. "A compulsory production of a man's private papers to establish a criminal charge against him or to forfeit his property is within the scope of the Fourth Amendment in all cases in which a search and seizure would be . . ." The Court also held that the Fourth Amendment's unreasonable search and seizure clause, was related to the Fifth Amendment's self-incriminating clause. "We have been unable to perceive," Justice Bradley said, "that seizure of a man's private books and papers to be used in evidence against him is substantially different from compelling him to be witness against himself." Although highly criticized, it would appear that the Supreme Court is presently following this Bradley ruling.

A troublesome situation with which the Supreme Court has been contending pertains to the admissibility of evidence obtained as a result of an unlawful search and seizure. In *Weeks v. U. S.*, the Court excluded such evidence in federal prosecutions. In *Mapp v. Ohio*, the intimate relationship between the Fourth and Fifth Amendment was underscored as running "almost into each other", and the Court applied the exclusionary rule against the states as well as the Federal Government. The Court thus held that "the exclusionary rule is an essential part of both the Fourth and Fourteenth Amendments."

Many interesting legal problems have arisen out of the *Mapp* decision. Did it mean in the words of Justice Cardozo, that "the criminal is to go free because the constable has blundered?" Justice Clark in the *Mapp Case* had to acknowledge that "the criminal goes free, if he must," but he hastened to emphasize, "it is the law that sets him free." Another disturbing result of the *Mapp Case* relates to the fate of prisoners convicted by reason of illegally obtained evidence. Should they be released? Should they be retried? The courts have held to date that where an appeal was still pending from the original conviction, the *Mapp* rule would be applied retroactively. They have drawn the line, however, where final judgment has been rendered, and they have denied retroactive application.

The immunities of the American people against unreasonable searches and seizures "affect the very essence of Constitutional liberty and security." This is the debt we owe to the "boldness" of Wilkes, the "wisdom" of Lord Camden and the fearless eloquence of James Otis.

Ashford

v.

Thornton

The Last Trial by Battle

O N NOVEMBER 17, 1817, a cold Monday morning, it was
obvious that something was "brewing" in Westminster
Hall in London. A large crowd had collected and the air
was filled with rumors and speculations. As counsel forced
their way in the Court of King's Bench, the onlookers
impatiently waited for the defendant. Suddenly a shout
arose — "There he is!" – "The bloody murderer!" – "Now
you won't get away this time!" – "They'll hang you sure!"

The butt of this demonstration, who had just appeared
escorted by a tipstaff, was Abraham Thornton. He had
been acquitted shortly before at Warwick assizes for the
rape and wilful murder of Mary Ashford. The interest
excited by the trial had spread throughout England. Mary
Ashford had been young and pretty, although apparently
not as innocent as claimed. Thornton was about 25 years
of age — "very lusty and a builder and bricklayer." Despite
the public anger aroused by the event, the jury deliber-
ated only a few minutes and then returned a verdict of
"Not Guilty."

The verdict had been greeted by great surprise and
disappointment. Newspapers took up the cause adding to
the public resentment. As one newspaper expressed it:

"The *Law* may acquit the offender but thank God it is the *Law* only." It was generally felt that something had to be done to make the "guilty culprit" accountable for his dastardly act.

As the newspapers graphically described the sordid details, interested civic leaders probed into the law.

Although it was the year 1817 and the principle, that no man was to be put into jeopardy of his life more than once for the same imputation of guilt, was the law of the land, some one came across a statute enacted in 1488 which apparently was still in effect at that late year. It provided that if one arraigned for murder was acquitted after a trial, ". . . the wife or next heir to him so slain as shall required, may take and have their appeal of the same death and murder within the year and day after the same felony and murder done, against the said person so arraigned and acquit . . . so that by this statute, *autrefois acquit* upon an indictment of murder is no bar of appeal for the same death."

This was indeed an unusual legal situation. The reasons for it were explained by historians of the law by pointing out that since the Norman period there had been three modes of trial in criminal cases, namely, trial by ordeal, trial by battle and trial by jury. Trial by battle had originally been classified as one of the ordeals, along with trial by fire and trial by water, but it later took on added significance. Actually its orgins could be traced back to the Germanic tribes and it had been introduced into England by the Normans. It soon became an ordinary means of settling disputes in the King's Court. Closely related to trial by battle was the appeal or accusation by a private person that a felony had been committed by another. The appeal was made before the coroner by the appellor (or plaintiff) who had to establish his accusation with great particularity. The appellee (or defendant) would then be allowed the opportunity to plead to the accusation or to resolve the matter by battle between the parties. In appeals of murder, the indictment was tried first, and on acquittal, the appeal could be taken.

WHEN A PARTY OFFERED BATTLE, either he or a paid professional champion, publicly swore under oath that he believed his cause to be true as to his own knowledge, and that he was prepared to defend with his body the truth of what he alleged. The other party could similarly obtain a champion, and both champions would fight from dawn to dusk according to a strict code of procedure. If the Court of Chivalry were trying the issue the parties would fight with spear and sword and in armour. If otherwise, they would fight with staves and leather shields. If by the time the stars appeared the appellee was defeated, he was hanged on the spot. If however, he successfully defended himself until then, or he conquered the appellor, he was acquitted of the appeal.

Trial by battle, however, had been exceedingly costly, and gradually it had been superseded by the trial by jury. Trial by battle had become practically obsolete by the end of the thirteenth century and it had been rarely used thereafter. In fact it had almost become forgotten when it had suddenly been revived in 1571 and later in 1638, but in both these cases, an actual battle had not taken place. Thereafter, although it had never been abolished it had relapsed once again into desuetude. Similarly, appeals of murder, which had been so closely related to trial by battle, had never been abolished although almost completely forgotten by the early nineteenth century.

When all this was made clear, in light of the statute which permitted the next heir of the victim to take an appeal of murder, the question arose, why should not an appeal be brought by the deceased's heir-at-law, her elder brother, William Ashford? Ashford was a farm laborer, young and illiterate, and after some persuasion he finally was induced to bring an "appeal."

Now the public excitement arose to fever pitch. Everyone discussed the implications of the "appeal." It became widely known that in cases of murder after an acquittal upon a trial on the prosecution of the crown in the event an appeal was brought and the appellee found guilty by the second jury, contrary to the first, the appellee had to suffer death. This result the public hoped for and anticipated.

Once again Abraham Thornton was taken into custody by virtue of a warrant issued to the High Sheriff of the County of Warwick, on a count of appeal at the instance of William Ashford.

AS THE PUBLIC REJOICED at this action the attorneys for Thornton diligently delved into the law books. They went all the way back studying a large part of the book of *Bracton, de Corona*, and the first book of *Britton*, and they brought up something interesting. Word spread that a most unique event was to take place in the Court of the King's Bench during the trial of *Ashford v. Thornton* – and hence the reason for the crowd that eventful day. What would the appellee's lawyers do now to prevent the brutal Thornton from receiving his just punishment? The crowd did not wait in vain.

Lord Ellenborough, the Chief Justice, called the court to order. The appellee was placed at the bar and the clerk read out the appellant's count (equivalent to an indictment) charging Thornton with the sister's murder. Then looking directly at Thornton he asked: "Are you guilty or not guilty of the said felony and murder whereof you stand so appealed?"

There was an intense, expectant silence in the court room as all eyes turned towards Thornton. Thornton, wearing a "new black coat, drab-coloured breeches and gaiters" giving the "appearance of a respectable-looking farmer" was the personification of confidence. He apparently relished his trump card which he was now prepared to play. His counsel handed him a slip of paper and Thornton replied, reading from it: "Not guilty, and I am ready to defend the same with my body" and thereupon he threw a gauntlet upon the floor of the court. Trial by battle – this was something new in the year of our Lord 1817!

The air of excitement in the court became even more intense. What would the appellant do now? Turning to the appellant and his counsel, the Lord Chief Justice inquired:

> **Horrible Rape and Murder !!**
>
> THE
>
> **AFFECTING CASE**
>
> OF
>
> # MARY ASHFORD,
>
> *A beautiful young Virgin,*
>
> Who was diabolically Ravished, Murdered, and thrown into a Pit, as she was returning from a Dance;
>
> INCLUDING THE
>
> # TRIAL
>
> OF
>
> # ABRAHAM THORNTON,
>
> FOR THE
>
> **Wilful Murder**
>
> OF THE SAID MARY ASHFORD;
>
> WITH THE WHOLE OF
>
> *The Evidence, Charge to the Jury, &c.*

"What have you to say?" The appellant stood dumb. He was of "poor physique and of a timid disposition" and he obviously did not look forward to a battle to the death with husky and powerful Thornton. His counsel replied:

"My Lord, I did not expect that at this time of day this sort of demand would have been made. The Trial by Battle is an obsolete practice . . . and it is hard to believe that in these enlightened days the person who has murdered the sister should be allowed to prove his innocence by seeking to murder the brother as well."

"Nay," his Lordship cut in, "it is the law of England, we must not call it murder."

THEN ENSUED A GREAT LEGAL ARGUMENT, in which the famed Mr. Joseph Chitty was called upon to frame a counter plea to the answer. Then there was a replication and additional affidavits, while Thornton was kept in confinement in the Marshalsea, that ancient prison.

Final hearing was held on April 16, 1818, when Lord Ellenborough delivered judgment. The appellee had a right to his "trial by battel." This was the court's judgment even though only three examples of wager of battle in appeals of murder appeared to be on record in the law reports, the last being in 1638, and actually not fought. *(Claxton v. Lilburn.)* Ashford, of course, was not prepared to fight to the death to establish the guilt of Thornton, and hence did not pick up the gauntlet. The result was that no further judgment was given and the action was ended by Thornton's arraignment on the appeal, to which he pleaded *autrefois acquit.* The final judgment of the court was then rendered "that defendant be discharged from this appeal and that he be allowed to go forth without bail."

There was much general dissatisfaction with the entire situation and it finally resulted in the passage of a statute which recited that "appeals of murder, treason, felony, and other offences and the manner of proceeding therein, have been found to be oppressive; and the trial by battle in any suit is a mode of trial unfit to be used; and it is expedient that the same should be wholly abolished."

It is not without interest to recall the comment, on the second reading of this law in the House of Lords, of Lord Eldon, noted for his extreme conservatism as Chancellor. He said: "It was a great absurdity that a man who had been acquitted by the unanimous opinion of a jury should again be put in jeopardy of his life, provided any person, standing in a certain degree of relationship to the deceased, thought proper to proceed against him by civil suit. . . . It was indeed surprising that such a law should have continued a part of our system which in other respects, came so near to perfection."

Benefit
of
Clergy

Reading Tests
and Penal Reform

A NGLO-AMERICAN LAW HAS HAD more than its share of
odd institutions, and one of the most curious features
of such institutions has been their tendency to lead to good
results. Benefit of clergy is a prime example of this phe-
nomenon.

In the *Year Books of Edward II* (1313–14), the case of
Thomas of Sarre is reported. Thomas was indicted for
poisoning his father. When the accused "was asked how
he would acquit himself, and he said that he was a clerk,
but that saving his clergy, he put himself on the country
(that is reserving to himself the right to plead the benefit of
clergy, he agreed to a jury trial). The Ordinary handed
him the Book and he read two verses therein.

"*Spigurnel, J.* Will you hold by your clergy or go to the
jury? You must make your election of one or the other, for
you cannot have both. And he put himself upon the country, that is to say, upon the hundred wherein the facts
alleged against him happened, and they acquitted him."

In the aftermath of the Boston Massacre of 1770, Captain Preston and his squad of British soldiers, who had
fired on the Americans, were forced to surrender to the

civil authorities of Boston. They were indicted on several counts by the Grand Jury for Suffolk County. After a trial during which they were brilliantly and courageously defended by John Adams and Josiah Quincy, Jr., they were all acquitted of murder. Two of the defendants, however, Matthew Killroy and Hugh Montgomery were found guilty of manslaughter. The reporter of the trial then noted:

> "Killroy and Montgomery prayed the benefit of clergy, which was allowed them, and thereupon they were each of them burnt in the hand, in open court, and discharged."

These two cases, almost 500 years apart, illustrate one of the least known and strangest developments of Anglo-American law — the privilege of benefit of clergy. Although now obsolete, it was once considered the last hope of English criminals. In fact, it actually meant the difference between life and death!

Jerome Hall, writing in *Theft, Law and Society*, says: "So important was this privilege that an analysis of it is essential for an undertanding of contemporary law administration. For benefit of clergy developed a number of practices which sharply accentuated what was and still remains the distinctive administrative problem, namely the ways in which we depart from rules to arrive at entirely different results from those prescribed . . ."

Benefit of clergy is one of the oldest legal institutions recorded in the annals of Christendom. Its influence on medieval criminal law was so pronounced that the later development of English criminal law till the 19th Century was colored by its effect. In the end, as Holdsworth states, it became "a clumsy set of rules which operated in favour of all criminals to mitigate in certain cases the severity of the criminal law." Stephen adds: "hardly any branch of the law was so technical and so full of legal quibbles."

Privilegium clericale, or privilege by clergy, received full recognition in 12th Century England by reason of Thomas Becket's martyrdom. The titanic struggle between Henry II and Becket involved the authority of the secular courts over members of the clergy. Becket insisted in contradiction to Henry, that the King's Courts were incompetent to judge criminous clergy or clerks—that by tradition only the ecclesiastical courts had jurisdiction over them. Henry II became very unpopular by ordering the murder of Becket. To preserve his throne, he finally capitulated, surrendering jurisdiction over the clergy to the ecclesiastical courts.

IN ITS ORIGIN, THEREFORE, benefit of clergy as a rule of common law meant the privilege or right of members of the clergy to be tried for their misdeeds by ecclesiastical courts only. A clerk charged in the King's Court with commission of a felony could plead his clergy and be turned over to the Bishop's Ordinary (or representative) for trial in the Bishop's Court. However, the term *clericus* or "clerk" included a great number of persons in the so-called minor orders, in addition to those in Holy Orders, and therefore encompassed a considerable number of Englishmen.

Writing in the Thirteenth Century, Bracton gave the following account of the privilege:

"When a clerk of whatever order or dignity is taken for the death of a man or any other crime, and imprisoned, and an application is made for him in the Court Christian by the Ordinary . . . The prisoner must be immediately delivered up without making any inquisition. He must not, however, be set at liberty and allowed to wander about the country, but is to be safely kept either in the Bishop's prison, or in the King's prison if the Ordinary wishes, till he has duly purged himself from the accusation laid upon him, or has failed to purge himself, for which he ought to be degraded."

Benefit of clergy was quickly recognized as a great privilege. It was most advantageous to the accused because the church courts did not impose a sentence of capital punishment or a "judgment of blood," as it was known. The situation in the secular courts was vividly different. At common law, homicide (murder and manslaughter), rape, burglary, arson, theft and mayhem were held to be felonies. Death was the punishment imposed for all these felonies, and as originally they were all subject to the benefit of clergy, criminals attempted every device to be recognized as a clerk.

The benefit was valuable, too, owing to the simple manner of obtaining acquittal in an ecclesiastical court by the process of purgation. The trial was held before the bishop or his deputy and a jury of twelve clerks. The accused would first swear to his own innocence and then he would call upon twelve compurgators who swore they believed the accused spoke the truth. The only witnesses permitted to testify were those called by the accused. Generally, the jury would bring in a verdict of acquittal. On the rare occasion when a clerk was found guilty, he could purge himself by penance or a mild prison sentence, for the bishops were loath to undergo the expense of supporting a prisoner for a longer period of incarceration. Thus by the 16th Century ecclesiastical purgation was recognized as a farce. Sir Henry Hobart, in his Reports, commenting on this process of purgation, bitterly complained in *Searle v. Williams*:

"The perjuries indeed were sundry: one in the witnesses and compurgators; another in the jury, compounded of clerks and laymen. And of the third, the Judge himself, was not clear, all turning the solemn trial of truth by oath, into a ceremonious and formal lye."

This attitude, together with estrangement of church and state in the 16th Century, brought about the abolition of purgation in 1516; furthermore, the ceremony of turning clergy over to the bishop's Ordinary was discontinued. In its place, the lay judges were authorized to imprison for a year those persons entitled to clergy but not actually in holy orders.

FROM THE TWELFTH CENTURY ON, the scope of benefit of clergy slowly was changed by statutory restrictment, so that from century to century its effect varied.

First it was enacted by the Statute of Westminister (1275) that the Bishop's Ordinary could not claim the criminous clerk until he was indicted. By the reign of Henry

VI (1422–61) the claim of clergy could not be made until the clerk had actually been convicted in the King's Court. The King and the accused had much to gain by this practice. The King could claim the goods and chattels of the convicted clerk by forfeiture before surrendering him to the church officials. On the other hand, the clerk had an opportunity to prove his innocence before undergoing the ecclesiastical trial.

In 1350, the *statute pro clero* dramatically created a new class of persons entitled to the claim of clergy, for it enacted that "all manner of clerks, as well secular as religious, which shall from henceforth be convict before the secular justices . . . shall from henceforth freely have and enjoy the privilege of Holy Church." This was construed by the King's judges to mean that *anyone who knew how to read*, whether or not he had "*habitum et tonsuraum clericalem*" (clerical dress and tonsure) could claim benefit of clergy. Commenting on this development, Sir James Stephens wrote:

"The result of this was to bring about for a great length of time a state of things which must have reduced the administration of justice to a sort of farce. Till 1487 anyone who knew how to read might commit murder as often as he pleased, with no other result than that of being delivered to the ordinary to make his purgation. That this should have been the law for several centuries seems hardly credible but there is no doubt that it was."

Despite changes in the law, vestiges of the clerical origin of the benefit of clergy remained. This became apparent when women claimed the privilege. Formerly only nuns in holy orders were entitled to it. The King's judges, attempting to be logical in its extension, started with the premise that women could not be ordained as clerks and, hence, decided that only nuns could claim the privilege. This was most unfortunate for many female criminals, and it was not until the 17th Century that they were placed on a par with their "brothers-in-crime."

Another interesting trace of the old ecclesiastical influence was the refusal of the courts to grant benefit of clergy to a "bigamus." The church refused to accept in holy orders any man who had married a widow or had been married to two different women at different times. This, incidentally, is quite different from our current concept of bigamy. Thus, the "bigamus" was classed in the same position as women and he, too, was excluded until clergy were allowed to "bigami" in the 16th Century.

Several other important changes took place. For one, it was decreed towards the end of the 15th Century, that unless a person was actually in holy orders, he would be denied benefit of clergy more than once — something similar to allowing a dog one bite! But how would such a person be identified in an era when information about court proceedings was barely known in the county concerned

Dodd delin.   *White sculp.*

Mode of punishment by BRANDING, *or burning on the* HAND, *at the New Sessions House.*

and rarely known in the other counties of England? This was a simple matter to Englishmen of the period! One needed only to brand the person convicted of clergible felony with the letter "M" on his thumb for murder, and "T" for theft.

LATER, PEERS OF THE REALM, even though unable to read, were granted the privilege of a "clerk convict," which absolved them from burning in the hand, loss of inheritance, or corruption of blood. The necessity for reading was abolished in the 18th Century, and instead of branding, persons guilty of clergible larcencies could be transported to the colonies.

As the claim for benefit of clergy was extended to those persons who could read aside from those in holy orders, statutes were enacted excluding many crimes from the privilege. With these exclusionary statutes, crimes which had theretofore been considered clergible, became nonclergible and thus subject once again to the old common law punishment of death. Some of these were: high treason, petty treason, piracy, murder, arson, burglary, housebreaking and putting in fear, highway robbery, horse stealing, stealing from the person above the value of a shilling, rape, abduction with intent to marry, and stealing clothes off the racks. The number of crimes that were made nonclergible was increased in the 18th century. Blackstone was of the opinion that in his time at least 160 felonies had been declared by statute to be without benefit of clergy.

Of course, the poor character who couldn't read at all was in a dreadful state. For, in addition to the felonies indicated, he would suffer death for conviction of manslaughter, robbery, and theft of any nature above the value of a shilling. Hence every conceivable effort was made by the illiterate to take advantage of the reading test. In the 14th Century very few persons outside the church were sufficiently educated to read the Latin manuscript written by scribes. The situation changed radically, however, with the invention of printing, and the publication of books in the vernacular. But still there were many unable to read.

Sir Thomas Smith in his classic, *Commonwealth of England*, published in 1565, described the manner of administering the reading test. The curious ceremony took place after the defendant had been found guilty by the jury. At this stage the judge would ask the convicted felon whether he had anything to say (a practice which has continued to our day in criminal trials). This was the opportunity to pray the benefit of clergy.

"The bishop must send one with authority under his seal, to be a judge in that matter at every gaol delivery. If the condemned man demandeth to be admitted to his book, the judge commonly giveth him a Psalter and turneth to what place he will. The prisoner readeth so well as he can. (God knoweth sometimes very slenderly.) Then he, the Judge, asketh of the bishop's commissary (also known as ordinary) '*Legit ut clericus?*' The commissary must say *legit* or *non legit* for these be words formal. If he say *legit*, the judge proceedeth no further to sentence of death; if he say *non*, the Judge forthwith proceedeth to judgment."

After a period of time, the privilege was exercised quite mechanically. With the publication of the King James Version, "the clergy," as the copy of the Gospels kept in court for this purpose was officially known, was invariably opened to the Fifty-First Psalm. The opening words, "*Miserere mei Deus . . . .*," "Have mercy upon me, God, according to thy loving kindness . . ." came to be known as the "neck-verse," obviously a verse to save one's neck! English dramatists alluded to the "neck-verse" in their works. In *The True Chronicle History of King Leir*, which was produced in 1594, and was the inspiration for Shakespeare's *King Lear* several years later, Gonorill, eldest daughter of King Lear, requests to see a letter a messenger is bearing from the King. The messenger replies:

> "Madame, I hope your grace will stand betweene me and my neck-verse, if I be call'd in question for opening the King's letters."

ILLITERATE CRIMINALS AFTER conviction used all conceivable devices to take advantage of the benefit of clergy. If possible, they would recite the Fifty-First Psalm from memory or stumble over the words incomprehensibly. There is a case recorded in 1383 of a vicar of Round Church in Canterbury who was tried "for that by the license of the jailer there, he had instructed in reading one William Gore, an approver, who at the time of his apprehension was unlearned." It all depended on the Ordinary, and the invariable answer to the judge's question was "*legit*."

By the 18th Century, in the event the culprit was allowed the benefit of clergy, the customary sentence was imposed of branding M or T on the brawn of the left thumb, a year in prison, or transportation of seven years to the the colonies, usually America, and later Australia.

Government officials finally realized that the claim of clergy and the reading test had become a farce and actually were obstructing the proper administration of criminal justice. Parliament, therefore, enacted a law in 1707 eliminating the reading test and granting benefit of clergy to all who were eligible. This meant that a first offender, whether male or female, convicted of a clergible crime such as manslaughter or theft, would be branded and sentenced to one year imprisonment. Of course, a second offender would automatically suffer death as his punishment.

After benefit of clergy was made applicable to all Englishmen, Parliament embarked on a statutory program of limiting in great detail the offenses for which it could be requested. New felonies were created by statute which were declared to be nonclergible. By the reign of George IV, an authority noted that "all felonies except petty larceny and mayhem were theoretically punishable with death."

So severe did the criminal law become by reason of these enactments, that both the people and the judges revolted, avoiding whenever possible imposing the punishment of death in cases which aroused their sympathy. These cases were usually those which had theretofore been considered clergible.

Judges accomplished this by pardoning the convicted felon on condition he accept transportation to the colonies. A ritual soon became established for this humanitarian purpose. After conviction of a nonclergible felony, the felon was asked by the judge or his clerk whether he had anything to say before sentence was imposed. At this point, they "fell upon their knees and prayed their clergy." The judges would then sentence them to transporatation for seven years or fourteen years, or to whipping and imprisonment for a year depending on the magnitude of the crime. Judges would also deliberately avoid the application of a criminal statute by strict interpretation of its meaning.

Juries helped by placing fictitious values on stolen property to bring the offense into a category just below that prescribed in the nonclergible statutes (one shilling). Both judges and prosecutors accepted these deliberate misstatements to the extent that capital punishment in this period was almost nullified in nonclergible felonies. Juries and judges decided, for example, that a five-pound note was worth less than a shilling, or that a colt was not a horse, or a heifer a cow.

BENEFIT OF CLERGY WAS ABOLISHED in England in 1827 by an act which was designed to improve the administration of justice in criminal cases. The act, however, failed to abolish the privilege equivalent to benefit of clergy which had been extended to Peers in the 15th Century. This was realized in 1841 when Lord Cardigan was tried for killing a man in a duel. The editor who reported the trial indicates in a note that Lord Cardigan planned to claim the benefit in the event of a conviction. Shortly thereafter, this last remnant of the long history of benefit of clergy was repealed by law.

The privilege played an important role in the history of America. Twelve of the colonies recognized it as a rule of law, and we have seen its application in the trial of the British soldiers for the Boston Massacre in 1770. Incidentally, this was the last instance of its use in Massachusetts, where it was abolished shortly after the Revolution. The First Congress of the United States enacted in 1790 that "the benefit of clergy shall not be used or allowed upon conviction of any crime for which the punishment is death." By a strange quirk, this was picked up by the Revisers of the Code and it can still be found in Section 5329 of the Revised Statutes of 1873 as a general and permanent law of the United States.

The states followed suit. In 1796, for example the Virginia House of Delegates passed a penal reform law which stated in part:

"That all claims to dispensation from punishment by benefit of clergy shall be and are hereby forever abolished; and every person connected of any felony heretofore deemed clergyable shall undergo imprisonment at hard labor and solitary confinement in the said goal and penitentiary house for any time not less than six months and not more than two years."

More than seventy-three years elapsed thereafter before benefit of clergy was removed from the law books of all the states. Most of the cases recorded took place in the south. Benefit of clergy was particularly granted to slaves so that their masters could preserve their property. Flogging was substituted for capital punishment when slaves were involved. North Carolina abolished it in 1854 and South Carolina fifteen years later.

Of course, benefit of clergy subtly influenced America in an entirely different manner. It helped to populate and improve its wide expanses, for a great many English criminals were transported to America as part of the pardon granted by judges, substituting deportation for capital punishment.

Benefit of clergy served a useful purpose while it flourished, for it made tolerable the barbarism of the substantive law which had prevailed over the centuries. By the beginning of the 19th Century, however, it served even a more worthy end. For the realization of its former scope and effectiveness encouraged judges and juries to circumvent the law and allow minor criminals to avoid the death penalty. This state of affairs acted as a catalytic agent in speeding the process of reforming the law of punishment. English officials realized that the law would have to be humanized before it would be enforced by the people. One hundred sixty capital offenses, and even more, were just too much for the citizenry to stomach.

In 1810, Sir Samuel Romilly said, "There is probably no other country in the world in which so many and so great a variety of human actions are punishable with loss of life as in England." In 1819, Sir Thomas Buxton set the number of capital offences at 223. The great reform bills finally took cognizance of the public dissatisfaction, and in a process of statutory attrition Parliament by 1861 had reduced the number of capital offenses to four: treason, murder, piracy with violence, and setting fire to dock yards and arsenals. This influence was felt in America, too, and as the states adopted modern penal codes and established penitentiaries with a schedule of civilized and humane punishments, statutes, were enacted abrogating benefit of clergy there.

Thus the severity of the criminal law, strangely enough, was modified in accordance with enlightened theories of penology, by use of the archaic privilege of benefit of clergy. Blackstone, writing in the 1760's believed that the state of benefit of clergy in his day had been gloriously solved by the law makers of England.

THE WISDOM OF THE ENGLISH legislature," he wrote in the Fourth book of his Commentaries, had "in the course of a long and laborious process, extracted by a noble alchemy rich medicines out of poisonous ingredients; and converted by gradual mutations what was at first an unreasonable exemption . . . into a merciful mitigation of the general law, with respect to capital punishment."

A little premature, perhaps, but Blackstone would have been right if he had lived in the 19th Century and made the statement then!

Impeachment
of
Justice Chase

*Jeffersonian Assault
on Independence
of the Judiciary*

"**YOU MUST HAVE HEARD** of the extraordinary charge of Chase to the Grand Jury at Baltimore. Ought this seditious and official attack on the principles of our Constitution and on the proceedings of a State go unpunished, and to whom so pointedly as yourself will the public look for the necessary measures? I ask these questions for your consideration; for myself, it is better that I should not interfere."

This caustic and denunciatory letter, written by President Thomas Jefferson to Congressman Joseph Nicholson in 1804, presaged one of the most striking episodes of Jefferson's first administration and ultimately made an enduring contribution to American constitutional law. The question it finally settled went far beyond the interests of the individuals involved. The very independence of the federal judiciary was concerned. Had the issue been resolved another way, our form of government might have been quite different from what it is today.

Samuel Chase, the "torch that lighted up the Revolutionary flame" in Maryland, was born in 1741. He later became a signer of the Declaration of Independence and

Chief Justice of Maryland, and was appointed by President Washington to the Supreme Court of the United States in 1796. John Quincy Adams considered Chase "one of the men whose life, conduct, and opinion had been of the most extensive influence upon the Constitution of this country . . ." Known in colonial Maryland as "the Maryland Demosthenes" he was vigorously eloquent and imposing in stature. Despite his great ability as a judge, his absolute integrity, and his fearless patriotism, he had a side to his character which was most unfortunate. To his contemporaries he was overbearing, obstinate, and prejudiced. He was also described as an "arrogant old peacock, bilious, egotistical and violent. Habitually he violated not merely the proprieties, but the common decencies of his position." But his greatest fault as far as Jefferson was concerned was his ardent support of Federalist principles. To understand and to appreciate the significance of this comment, the state of the nation in 1804 must be considered.

When the Federalists realized that the election of Jefferson in 1800 marked the close of their days of power, they sought to entrench themselves in the judiciary by enacting the Judiciary Law of Feb. 13, 1801. This statute rearranged the judicial districts and established federal circuit courts as intermediate courts of appeal, separate in their membership from that of the Supreme Court. The new arrangement relieved the Supreme Court Justices from traveling on circuit, but it also gave President Adams, then a "lame-duck" President, the opportunity to appoint sixteen new judges. This he hurriedly accomplished on the eve of his departure from office.

JEFFERSON WAS SUSPICIOUS of the judiciary system established by the Federalists. He feared the tyrannical control it could establish over the national government and he particularly loathed all Federalist incumbents on the bench. He therefore carefully and systematically organized a scheme to destroy their power. The first obvious move was to repeal the act establishing the separate circuit courts and to remove from office the "midnight judges" of the outgoing administration by abolishing their positions. After a long and bitter debate in Congress, the Judiciary Act of 1801 was repealed on April 29, 1802. With the purpose of preventing the Supreme Court from attacking its effect, the repealing act provided in addition for the abolition of the August term of the Court. This drastic action resulted in the suspension of the sessions of the Supreme Court for almost fourteen months!

When the Supreme Court finally met again in the February Term of 1803, Marshall had his opportunity to strike back. Deciding the case of *Marbury v. Madison* in which Marbury, one of the "midnight judges" whose commission had been withheld by Secretary of State Madison, appealed to the Supreme Court for a mandamus, he established the power of the Supreme Court to invalidate laws repugnant to the Constitution.

Jefferson rebelled. In a letter to Mrs. Adams (Sept. 11, 1804), he asserted that "nothing in the Constitution has given the judges a right to decide for the Executive, more than to the Executive to decide for them. Both magistrates are equally independent in the sphere of action assigned to them." In essence, he later stated, the people were the final arbiters when such a conflict existed. They could decide at the next election which of the three branches of government was correct in its interpretation. If a conflict arose between the legislature and the judiciary, however, the legislature had the power to initiate impeachment proceedings and remove dissenting judges, and this process was sanctioned by the Constitution. The opinion in *Marbury v. Madison* was "an obiter dissertation of the Chief Justice and a perversion of the Law."

Jefferson was determined to secure the removal of Marshall and his Federalist colleagues from the bench. But how was this to be accomplished? Somehow, the principle had to be established that judges could be removed through impeachment for "high crimes and misdemeanors" as provided in Article II, section 4 of the Constitution. Once a series of precedents could be obtained in

this respect, the final assault could be made on the Chief Justice himself.

The position taken by the administration was expressed by Senator Giles of Virginia, a Republican Senate leader. John Quincy Adams reported Giles' view as follows:

"He treated with the utmost contempt the idea of an *independent* judiciary, said there was not a word about such an independence in the Constitution, and that their pretensions to it were nothing more or less than an attempt to establish an aristocratic despotism in themselves. The power of impeachment was given without limitation to the House of Representatives. The power of trying impeachments was given equally without limitation to the Senate; and if the judges of the Supreme Court should dare, *as they had done* to declare an act of Congress unconstitutional . . . it was the undoubted right of the House to impeach them, and of the Senate to remove them, for giving such opinions, however honest or sincere they may have been in entertaining them. Impeachment was not a criminal prosecution; it was no prosecution at all. The Senate sitting for the trial of impeachments was not a court, and ought to discard and reject all process of analogy to a court of justice. A trial and removal of a judge upon impeachment need not imply any criminality or corruption in him. Congress had no power over the person but only over the office. And a removal by impeachment was nothing more than a declaration by Congress to this effect: You hold dangerous opinions, and if you are suffered to carry them into effect you will work the destruction of the nation. *We want* your offices for the purpose of giving them to men who will fill them better."

CAREFULLY SELECTING THEIR VICTIMS the Republicans struck. First came the impeachment of Judge Alexander Addison by the Pennsylvania House of Representatives for high crimes and misdemeanors. The Republican Senate of Pennsylvania found him guilty and removed him from the bench in January, 1803. Shortly thereafter, with the purpose of testing their contention that impeachment was unrestricted and could be enforced against any officer of the government deemed undesirable by two-thirds of the Senate, Jefferson in February 1803 transmitted certain complaints against Judge John Pickering, the U. S. District Judge for New Hampshire, to the House, "to whom the Constitution has confided a power of instituting proceedings of redress if they shall be of opinion that the case calls for them."

The documents indicated that Judge Pickering had improperly released the ship *Eliza,* which had been libelled by the Surveyor of Customs and that he was also "a man of loose morals and intemperate habits," sitting on the bench "in a state of total intoxication, produced by the free and intemperate use of inebriating liquors, and did then and there frequently and in a most profane manner, invoke the name of the Supreme Being, to the evil example of all good citizens of the U. S." Although clearly insane, and not present during the trial, Judge Pickering was found guilty by the Senate in March, 1803 on a resolution of impeachment adopted by the House.

To establish their theory that impeachment was unrestricted and applicable to any officer deemed undesirable by two-thirds of the Senate, the House Managers refused to allow evidence of Pickering's insanity to be introduced at the trial, for if proved, he could not be convicted of high crimes and misdemeanors! When the Senate decided to allow evidence of insanity "in mitigation," the House Managers withdrew in disgust temporarily. The significance of Pickering's conviction was impaired, however, by reason of his obvious insanity.

Next on the list for impeachment was the aggressive and irritating Chase. Then, Marshall and the other Federalist members of the Supreme Court would follow. John Quincy Adams writing to his father on March 8, 1805, concluded that the Republican plan was to "have swept the Supreme Judicial bench clean at a stroke." Senator Pickering wrote, "the Judges of the Supreme Court are all Federalists . . . They stand in the way of the ruling power . . . The Judges therefore, are, if possible, to be removed by impeachment."

Chase was next on the list, for his conduct had been such that he was a "shining mark" for impeachment. "Of all the Judges," writes Warren, no one was more hated than Chase. His unnecessarily strenuous support of the Sedition Law, his prejudicial and passionate conduct of the trials of the two Republicans, Thomas Cooper and James T. Callender, under this law, his arbitrary and unusual rulings in the trial of John Fries [involved in the Whiskey Rebellion] for treason in resisting direct tax laws, and his personal traits had long subjected him to vicious and unmeasured attack." Finally, and as immediate ground for his impeachment, Chase in charging a Baltimore grand jury, delivered a political harangue in which he severely criticized the acts of the Republican Congress, concluding that they "will in my judgment, take away all security for property and personal liberty." Then "pointedly insulting" the President of the United States he continued, "the modern doctrines by our late reformers, that all men in a state of society are entitled to enjoy equal liberty and equal rights have brought this mighty mischief upon us, and I fear that it will rapidly progress until peace and order, freedom and property, shall be destroyed."

CHASE'S JUDICIAL INDISCRETION was just what Jefferson needed in order to promote his grand attack against the Judiciary. At this point he wrote the letter to Congressman Nicholson, suggesting that the time was ripe for Chase's impeachment. Nicholson, who was in line for Chase's position, was advised by Macon, the Speaker, not to take the initiative. John Randolph was requested to manage the impeachment, as he was not a lawyer and hence ineligible for Supreme Court appointment. The most capable administration men in the House were appointed to assist Randolph.

A commentator on the Chase impeachment has said that on the decision of the Senate hung not only the future of the Constitution but probably the fate of the Union. For

New England had already on several occasions threatened
secession. The North resented what was termed "Virginia
Tyranny" and it was feared that these feelings of dissatisfaction might be strengthened. Judge Tapping Reeve
wrote to Senator Tracy, "I have seen many of our friends;
and all that I have seen and most that I have heard from,
believe that we must separate, and that this is the most
favorable moment."

Samuel Chase was charged on February 12, 1804 by
the House of Representatives with being guilty in his judicial capacity of "high crimes and misdemeanors." A Committee was appointed with John Randolph as Chairman, to
appear at the bar of the Senate to impeach him of these
crimes. On Dec. 4, 1804, the Committee reported articles of
impeachment which were adopted and seven members of
the House were elected as managers to conduct the impeachment on behalf of the House. John Randolph, popularly known as "John Randolph of Roanoke," has been
described by Beveridge as " of medium stature, thin as a
sword, his straight black hair . . . his intense black eyes
flaming with the passion of combat, his high and shrilling
voice suggesting the scream of an eagle . . . that haughty,
passionate, eccentric genius — personified the aggressive
and ruthless Republicanism of the hour." He was the
Republican master of the House and of the Senate. According to Senator Plummer he sat in the House booted
and spurred, with his whip in his hand, in imitation of
members of the British Parliament. He was about thirty-
one years old at the time. The other members of the Committee were Joseph Hopper Nicholson, who later became
a Judge of the Maryland Court of Appeals, Caesar Rodney,
a signer of the Declaration of Independence, Peter Early,
later Governor of Georgia, George Washington Campbell,
later Judge of the Supreme Court of Errors and Appeals of
Tennessee and Christopher Clarke.

The articles of impeachment were eight in number.
The first set forth his arbitrary, oppressive and unjust
treatment of Fries on his trial for treason. The next five
charged him with having oppressed Callendar on his trial

for libel by forcing a prejudiced juror to serve, by ruling out evidence, and by acting so partially and intemperately, that counsel had been compelled to abandon their client and their case; in violating the laws of Virginia by issuing a *Capias* (bench warrant) against the body of Callendar instead of a summons, and by trying the prisoner at the same term at which he was indicted, though the law declared that he should not be tried till the term following. The seventh alleged that he had refused to dismiss a Grand Jury until it placed a printer on trial for sedition. The eighth was concerned with his conduct at Baltimore in 1803, charging him with seeking to stir up the anger of the jury against the Government of the U. S., and "with prostituting the high judicial character with which he was invested to the low purpose of an electioneering partisan."

THE TRIAL BEGAN IN JANUARY, 1805, and was presided over by Aaron Burr, then Vice-President of the United States. The city of Washington, indeed the whole nation was teeming with excitement over its implications. An effort was made, perhaps at the instigation of Burr, to dress the trial with dignity and solemnity. The arrangement of the Senate chamber was impressively spectacular. There was a conscious effort to imitate the pomp and circumstance of the Warren Hasting trial which was still fresh in the Senators' memories. On the right and left of the Presiding Officer's chair, two rows of benches, reserved for the Senators, were covered with crimson cloth. Before these rows, a semicircular raised gallery was erected for the spectators, mainly wives and friends of officers of the government. These were covered with green cloth. Under this gallery, covered likewise in green cloth, were three rows of benches, set aside for heads of departments, foreign ministers and the members of the House. Facing the Vice-President were two boxes covered with blue cloth — one for the use of the Managers, the other for the accused and his counsel.

There were several other interesting aspects to the trial. Although his impeachment was pending, Chase assumed his seat on the Supreme Court bench at the 1805 term! Great indignation was expressed over this boldness. The Richmond *Enquirer,* for example, stated: "by such conduct Mr. Chase manifested little respect to the Tribunal before whom he is impeached, to the grand inquest of the Nation, or to the sentiment of the American people." Oddly, too, Aaron Burr had recently slain Alexander Hamilton in a duel, and was under indictment for murder in New York and New Jersey. He was being condemned for this evil deed everywhere. Probably still ringing in his ears was the (factually inaccurate) doggerel lampoon left upon his doorstep by an inflamed New York populace:

"Oh Burr, oh Burr, what hast thou done,
Thou hast shooted dead great Hamilton!
You hid behind a bunch of thistle,
And shooted him dead with a great hoss pistol!"

When the Senate convened in January, 1805, Burr was there. Senator Plummer wrote: "This is the first time, I believe, that ever a Vice-President appeared in the Senate the first day of a session; certainly the first (God grant it may be the last) that ever a man indicted for murder presided in the American Senate. We are indeed fallen upon evil times . . . the high office of President is filled by an infidel; that of Vice-President by a murderer . . ." Yet despite all this, Burr made a striking impression as presiding officer. Senator Plummer later admitted that "Burr presides . . . with great ease and dignity. He always understands the subject before the Senate, states the question clearly and confines the speakers to the point." A contemporary newspaper stated, "He conducted the trial, with the dignity and impartiality of an angel, but with the rigor of a devil."

On the opening day Chase interposed a short answer in which he denied that he had committed any crime or misdemeanor or for that matter, with a few exceptions, any of the acts with which he was charged. Noting the importance of the impeachment, he asked for an adjournment of the trial until the next session of Congress so that he might retain counsel and prepare his answer. Instead he was given but a month's time.

The trial started in earnest on Feb. 4th. The Senate went into session at about one o'clock and the Managers appeared, as did Judge Chase with his Counsel. It has been said that prior to that time, there had never been such an array of legal talent assembled in Washington as Chase had retained for his defense. Leading the defense counsel was Luther Martin, the arch-enemy of Jefferson. The worst expression Martin could use to condemn anyone, and he was a master of invective, was to call him "as great a scoundrel as Tom Jefferson." Jefferson on the other hand, called Martin "The Federal Bull Dog."

MARTIN, WHO WAS BORN IN 1748, was an acknowledged leader of the American Bar for two generations. He was attorney general of Maryland for thirty years, a position he owed to Chase's influence. At the age of 43 he was Maryland's most influential member in the Constitutional Convention. Chief Justice Taney knew Martin and considered him a "profound lawyer who never missed the strong points of his case. . . . He had an iron memory, and forgot nothing he had read, and he had read a great deal on every branch of the law." He was also a lifetime friend of Chase.

Martin has been described by Henry Adams as "most formidable of American advocates, the rollicking, witty, audacious Attorney-General of Maryland; boon companion of Chase and the whole bar; drunken, generous, slovenly, grand; bulldog of Federalism as Mr. Jefferson called him; shouting with school-boy's fun at the idea of tearing Randolph's indictment to pieces and teaching the Virginian democrats some law."

Burr was so impressed by Martin's advocacy at the Chase trial that he later retained him in his own defense when indicted for treason. When later in his career, Martin suffered a paralytic stroke which incapacited him, he was so highly thought of, that the General Assembly of Maryland adopted a resolution directing every practicing lawyer in Maryland to pay an annual license fee of $5.00, the proceeds of which were put in trust for his use. Although the constitutionality of this act was doubtful, it was never questioned by the Maryland Bar!

Associated with Martin were Robert Goodloe Harper, formerly Federalist leader of the House during Adam's administration, Joseph Hopkinson author of "Hail Columbia," Philip Barton Key, related to the author of the "Star Spangled Banner" and Charles Lee, formerly Attorney-General under George Washington. They read Chase's answer, which took them about three hours and a half. Randolph requested a copy and time to consult the House of Representatives and to submit their replication.

Chase's defense was based on the theory that serious as his offenses were, they were not of the type indictable by a Grand Jury. He had not violated any principle of common law or any statutory enactment. True, his acts were in bad taste and not to be condoned. But could he be impeached when he had committed no high crime and had been guilty of no misdemeanor? The Managers replied that an impeachment was not a criminal prosecution but a mere inquest of office. Impeachment lies for abuse of power done by an officer in his official capacity. Indictment lies for acts done by men acting as men and not as officers. They are tried differently and punished differently. Criminals are indicted—officials impeached. Where an indictment lies an impeachment will not.

Mr. RANDOLPH MADE HIS OPENING speech for the Managers on February 9th. Randolph was a brilliant orator, but not a lawyer. He boasted that he had been solely responsible for the drafting of the eight articles of impeachment. But he considered the proceeding to be merely an inquest of office rather than a state trial. Adams, in his biography of Randolph, opined that considering Randolph's opponents, "the best lawyers in America," "his rashness becomes laughable." In all probability, Randolph and his supporters mis-managed the Chase impeachment. Randolph's arguments were poor. "The feeblest made in the course of the trial. He undertook to speak as an authority upon the law . . . Naturally given to make assertion stand for proof, he asserted legal principles calculated to make Luther Martin's eyes sparkle with delight."

Upon the conclusion of Randolph's speech, the Managers called eighteen witnesses who testified for four days. Six were cross-examined, occasionally by a senator. Their testimony, although damaging as far as Chase's conduct on the bench was concerned, did not establish the commission by Chase of any indictable offense. Thirty-one witnesses testified for the defense, and interestingly enough they included John Marshall and Luther Martin. Marshall made a poor witness, fearing to alienate the Managers and Chase. Senator Plummer wrote he showed "too much caution — too much fear. . . . He ought to have been more bold, frank and explicit than he was. . . . That dignified frankness which his high office required did not appear . . ."

JOSEPH HOPKINSON SPOKE FIRST in summation for the defense. His oratory made a deep impression, especially his appealing comment: "We appear for an ancient and infirm man, whose better days have been worn out in the service of that country which now degrades him. . . ." Hopkinson went on to argue "that no judge can be impeached and removed from office for any act or offense for which he could not be indicted. It must be by law an indictable offense. . . . The converse of the proposition however, is not true; that is that every act or offense is impeachable which is indictable — far from it: a man may be indictable for many violations of positive law, which evince no mala mens, no corrupt heart, or intention, but which could not be the ground of impeachment . . . 'high crimes and misdemeanors' meant 'high crimes' and 'high misdemeanors' . . . 'Misdemeanor' is a legal and technical term well understood and defined in law; used in the construction of a legal instrument, one must give to words their legal significance; a misdemeanor, or a crime, for in their just proper acceptation they are synonymous terms, is an act committed or omitted, in violation of a public law, either forbidding or commanding it."

Mr. Randolph began: "Mr. President. It becomes my duty to open the case on the part of the prosecution. . . .

The Managers are in this instance to establish the guilt of one of the judges of the Supreme Court. . . . The arraignment of a man of such talents before this tribunal, is one of the saddest spectacles ever presented to the view of any people. Base indeed must be his heart who could triumph over such a scene . . ."

Although legal issues were involved in the trial, every one recognized that much more than the removal of a judge was at stake. The trial represented an intense effort to assert the right of representatives of the citizens to control the judiciary. This the Republicans actually admitted. The Federalists were even more perturbed by the realization that John Marshall and his associates would ultimately be removed, too, if the Republicans were successful.

For the first time in his career, even the dauntless Marshall was frightened by the sweeping implications of the Chase impeachment. Weakening under the pressure of this fear, he considered abandoning the doctrine of judicial supremacy he had so strongly enunciated in *Marbury v. Madison* in order to secure the independence of the judiciary. Writing to Chase at the time, he suggested, what appeared to Justice Robert Jackson to be an "amazing" proposal "to scrap the whole pretension to judicial supremacy." His letter read:

> "I think the modern doctrine of impeachment should yield to an appellate jurisdiction in the legislature. A reversal of those legal opinions deemed unsound by the legislature would certainly better comport with the mildness of our character than (would) a removal of the Judge who has rendered them unknowing of his fault."

Luther Martin took the same position as Hopkinson. When he rose to speak on Feb. 23, "the senate chamber could not contain even a small part of the throng that sought the capitol to hear the celebrated lawyer," writes Beveridge. Martin's speech took almost two days to deliver and was one of the best of his notable career. Professor Adams wrote in regard to it: "Nothing can be finer in its way than Martin's famous speech. Its rugged and sustained force; its strong humor, audacity and dexterity; its even flow and simple choice of language, free from rhetoric and affectations, its close and compulsive grip of the law; its good natured contempt for the obstacles put in its way — all these signs of elemental vigor were like the forces of nature, simple, direct, fresh as winds and ocean."

Listening to Martin's speech must have been a harrowing experience for Randolph, for Martin ripped his legal arguments savagely. Martin read Randolph a lecture on the law and then added "if Sir, Judges are to be censured for possessing legal talents, for being correctly acquainted with the law in criminal cases and for not suffering themselves to be insulted, and the public time wasted, by being obliged to hear arguments of counsel upon questions which have been repeatedly decided and on which they have no doubt — I pray you let not our courts of justice be disgraced, nor gentlemen of legal talents be degraded by placing them on the bench under such humiliating circumstances; but let us go to the corn fields, to the tobacco plantations, and there take our judges from the plough and the hoe. We shall there find men enough possessed of what seems to be thought the first requisite of a Judge, a total ignorance of the law."

After Martin's associate counsel and the Managers had spoken, Randolph tried to answer Martin on Feb. 27. He was ill, exhausted, and unprepared. John Quincy Adams noted that his speech had "as little relation to the subject matter as possible, without order, connection, or argument; consisting altogether of the most hackneyed commonplaces of popular declamation, mingled up with panegyrics and invectives upon persons, with a few well-expressed ideas, a few striking figures, much distortion of face and contortion of body, tears, groans and sobs, with occasional pauses for recollection, and continual complaints of having lost his notes."

WHEN RANDOLPH FINISHED, the Court fixed March 1st as the day for pronouncing judgment. The Court met at 12:30 p.m. and the Senate chamber was crowded. Not a Senator was absent on that day. Senator Tracy of Connecticut was brought to the Capitol in a coach and carried to his seat so that he might vote. A tense air prevailed throughout the room. Burr banged his gavel and the Sergeant-at-Arms bellowed: "Oyez! Oyez! Oyez! All persons are commanded to keep silence on pain of imprisonment while the grand inquest of the nation is exhibiting to the Senate of the United States sitting as a Court of Impeachments, articles of Impeachment against Samuel Chase, Associate Justice of the Supreme Court of the United States." Burr then ordered the civil officers in the galleries to face the spectators and enforce this order. He then directed the Secretary to call the roll and record the vote on the First article of Impeachment.

Thirty-four Senators were present, of whom nine were Federalists and twenty-five Republicans. Twenty-three votes were required to convict Chase. As the vote on the first charge was recorded the suspense grew. It was obvious that the sense of the Senate on the entire impeachment would be revealed on this call as the Managers had practically based their case on Chase's behavior on the Bench.

"Senator Adams of Massachusetts! How say you? Is Samuel Chase, the respondent, guilty of high crimes and misdemeanors as charged in the article just read?"

"Not guilty!" responded John Quincy Adams.

As the roll call proceeded, it appeared that Jefferson had lost control over his party. Sixteen Senators voted "Guilty"—eighteen, "Not guilty." Nine Republicans had bolted!

Although the votes on the other charges varied, at no time could the Republicans muster the required two-thirds vote. As the votes were tallied and checked, Burr rose and dramatically announced: "It appears that there is not a constitutional majority of votes finding Samuel Chase, Esq. guilty of any one article. It therefore becomes my duty to declare that Samuel Chase, Esq. stands acquitted of all the Articles exhibited by the House of Representatives against him."

Randolph rushed out of the Senate Chamber in a rage. He submitted an amendment to the Constitution in the House: "The Judges of the Supreme Court and all other courts of the U.S. shall be removed by the President on the joint address of both Houses of Congress." He failed to obtain sufficient support, however, and the proposal died. Jefferson never forgot this defeat. Fifteen years later he stated that "impeachment is an impractical thing, a mere scarecrow. [The judges] consider themselves secure for life; they skulk from responsibility . . ." The Federalists were jubilant. Marshall's position became secure for the first time since he had been appointed.

SINCE THE CHASE TRIAL, THE SENATE has sat as a Court of Impeachment for seven other judges. Four of these were found guilty. Mr. Justice Burton has analyzed these cases and is of the opinion that a judge may now be impeached for an abuse of judicial authority within the special constitutional meaning of the words "high Crimes and Misdemeanors," although his offenses were not indictable. "The trial of Justice Chase did not involve the issue whether the authority of the Senate was broad enough to reach an abuse of judicial power involving corruption. It was whether the authority of the Senate could, and should, be used to remove a judge because of his procedural rulings, and his statements to a grand jury in criticism of the national administrators . . . Since the Archibald and Ritter convictions and removals, in 1913, and 1936, it is, however, now reasonable to assume that, the Senate recognizes, there are at least some non-indictable offenses that are impeachable and which, if proved, may lead to removal from office. At the same time, the Senate accquittal of Justice Chase and other judges has demonstrated that the Senate is reluctant to weaken the independence of the judiciary."

In a sense a similar confrontation, as between Jefferson and the Supreme Court, arose between a President of the United States and the Judiciary when Franklin D. Roosevelt was re-elected in November, 1936, by an overwhelming vote of the electorate and, in the flush of his great victory, decided to come to grips with a recalcitrant Supreme Court which had been frustrating his New Deal Program. His "famous" court packing plan would have allowed him to appoint a new judge to supplement any judge over seventy who failed to retire. This would have enabled him to appoint six new justices who obviously would have approved his proposed New Deal legislation. Just as Jefferson had in mind the removal of the Federalists from the Judiciary, so did Roosevelt plan to equalize the conservative "die-hards" on the Supreme Court bench. The battle that ensued was as acrimonious and political as during the Chase impeachment. Yet the tradition of judicial independence stemming from the statesmanlike action of the Senate in the Chase trial carried the day—despite the great political power wielded by Roosevelt at time. The controversial court-packing plan was fought to a standstill in Congress and as McCloskey expressed it, this "failure is a significant testimonial to the prestige that attached to the Court's Constitution in the American mind. Not all the influence of a master politican in the prime of his popularity was quite enough to carry a program that would impair judicial review."

It is not without interest to note that the political liberals of our day who identify themselves with the principles of Jeffersonian Democracy would be unalterably opposed to Jefferson's credo of states' rights and a judiciary subordinate to the Legislature and the Executive, whereas the Conservatives, who in a sense are directly descended from the Federalists, by a strange contraposition object to judicial supremacy and favor strong states' rights.

Bracton

Father of Modern Law

MORE THAN 700 YEARS HAVE elapsed since Bracton wrote his *De Legibus*, and to this day that ancient work is considered of primary authority in interpreting the common law. Only a few decades ago it was described by Pollock and Maitland as "the crown and flower of English medieval jurisprudence," and by Winfield as "The longest and most important institutional work that our law knew until Coke's Institutes." Holdsworth adds it "had no competitor either in literary style or in completeness of treatment till Blackstone composed his commentaries five centuries later."

De Legibus et consuetudinibus Angliae (Laws and customs of England) was written between 1250 and 1258 by Henry Bracton, also known as Henry of Bratton or Bretton. Bracton was a judge of the King's Bench from 1248 to 1257 and later in 1264 became Archdeacon of Barnstaple and Chancellor of Exeter Cathedral. He died about 1268.

Bracton was quite unhappy with the legal training of his contemporaries on the bench. He was concerned lest their ignorance of the law should corrupt the younger generation of lawyers. His purpose in writing the book therefore, was to lead the younger members of the bar to a more professional understanding of the law. He attempted to accomplish this by evaluating and restating the decisions of the more learned judges who had served shortly before his time. He particularly mentions Martin Patteshull and William Raleigh and refers to them as "his masters."

Bracton's book is unique in that it is the first attempt to arrange the English law of his day systematically. Prior to Bracton the only author of significance was Glanvil (Ranulfe de Glanville, *Laws and Customs of England,* c. 1187 – 1189), who dealt mainly with procedure and the enforcement of writs issued out of the King's Chancery. This work and the few minor tracts written in the period were more of the "how to do it" type – how to start an action – how to plead a proper defense. There was no realization or appreciation of the law as a system. Bracton's *De Legibus* evolved an entirely new concept of the law, the influence of which is felt to this day.

Bracton's work can best be appreciated by understanding the state of the common law in 13th century England. That was a period in which the common law was dynamically developing and expanding. Judicial decisions were multiplying so fast that the law profession could not keep track of them. The King's Chancellor was issuing writs freely, and the King's judges were deciding the controversies on which the writs were issued in a conflicting manner. Bracton's *De Legibus* gave the lawyer of England, for the first time, an evaluation of the many cases that had been decided in the half century before 1250. The courts had kept records of their activities on parchment, known as plea rolls. Bracton studied these plea rolls over the years and actually cited them as precedents for the general propositions of law he expounded. Of course, as heretofore indicated, he selected what he considered to be the better examples, following in the main the judgments of Patteshull and Raleigh. As a byproduct of his research, he compiled a rather large *Note Book* of cases which was discovered in the British Museum by Professor Vinogradoff in the late 19th century – a really remarkable achievement of scholarly detective work.

FROM THESE MANY CASES, almost two thousand of them, Bracton arranged a system of law, with general rules, subdivided into logical compartments. For the first time lawyers were able to see their legal system as a complete picture rather than as a melange of many unrelated cases. By so doing, according to Holdsworth he actually helped to create that system. He also thus influenced the development of the "common law" as "case law."

It is not clear today how Bracton planned to arrange his treatise. Legal historians conjecture that Bracton actually followed no preconceived arrangement, but simply worked on *De Legibus* for many years and was continually revising it. It is also to be noted that he never finished his work, and it is possible he felt the final arrangement could await the completion of his research and analysis.

Maitland astutely describes *De Legibus* as "Romanesque in form, English in substance." It is known that Bracton was familiar with many sources of Roman law. He had read the *Summa* of the famous Italian lawyer, Azo of Bologna, as well as the Canonist Tancred. Bracton also had studied parts of the *Corpus Juris Civilis*. This knowledge of Roman law and Canon law was used by Bracton with great effect in outlining the scope and method of the *De Legibus*. Writing in Latin, Bracton borrowed liberally from Roman legal sources in arranging his topical outline. This becomes particularly clear when we read the introduction, in which Bracton divides law into the classic Roman law divisions of persons, things and actions. Actually, however, Bracton could not develop his thesis under these subdivisions. The common law of England just did not fall into those categories. The result is a book divided into tracts which treat the various criminal and civil actions adjudicated at the time in the King's courts. As Bracton developed his treatise it emerged as a complete and orderly presentation of the law of thirteenth century England. Reflected throughout the work is Bracton's intimate knowledge of the plea rolls and his sound legal reasoning.

Unfortunately, there is no contemporary manuscript copy of Bracton's *De Legibus* available for study today. The oldest one extant, it is believed, was copied about 1350, almost a hundred years after it was written. Winfield states that there are approximately 49 MSS copies of *De*

Legibus known today, some being fragmentary, some incomplete, some abridged, and quite a few with variations and *addiciones.*

The first printed edition of Bracton was published in 1569 by Tottel. It was "sumptuous, but uncritical." An edition by Sir Travers Twiss in the Roll Series, published from 1878 to 1883 in six volumes was criticized by Beale as being "equally beautiful and at least equally uncritical." The most scholarly text of Bracton was prepared by Professor G. E. Woodbine in four volumes and was published by the Yale University Press from 1915 to 1942. It has received the highest praise.

IN THE PRINTED EDITIONS, *De Legibus* is presented in five books: Bk I—Persons; Bk II—Personal Property; Bk III —Actions and Criminal Law; Bk IV—Various Assizes (statutes, ordinances, etc.); Bk V—Real Actions based on title (writ of right and of warranty). Unfortunately, Bracton never completed his work. As he begins the discussion of procedure in personal actions, the text ends abruptly.

Plucknett brings out that one of Bracton's innovations was to set forth complete transcripts of the pleadings in certain cases, a practice which gave him an opportunity to comment critically on the judge's decisions. He also suggests that Bracton had no concept of the rule of *stare decisis.* The cases he selected were authoritative to him only because they had been decided by judges for whom he had great respect. By concentrating on the cases as he did, however, Bracton directed the attention of the law men of his day to a similar consideration of the cases that followed, thus eventually influencing our modern treatment of cases. It is also probable that Bracton's use of the cases was recognized by his contemporaries as so important that he thus encouraged and stimulated the writing of the *Year Books.*

It is known that Bracton's book became an immediate success. Shortly after publication it was epitomized and summarized by two successive Chief Justices of the King's Bench, Gilbert de Thornton and Hengham. *Britton* and *Fleta* (c. 1290) were epitomes of Bracton and very popular in their day. Printed versions were published in the 16th and 17th Centuries and then, of course, in our day. About 200 of Bracton's cases can be traced in *Fitzherbert's Abridgment* of the *Year Book* cases (1516). Coke in the preface to his *Reports* holds Bracton to be an authority and draws freely from him in the body of his *Reports*. Hale similarly considers Bracton of primary authority, and Blackstone praises his work, too.

It is interesting to note that Bracton's references to Roman law were not considered of importance by the judges who followed him. Probably, not being sophisticated in Roman law, they could not understand his references. The Roman law system was foreign to them, and yet in *Coggs v. Bernard,* Chief Justice Holt followed Bracton's interpretations of the Roman law in summarizing the principles of the law of bailment; and as Holdsworth states, "at a later date, [Bracton's] borrowings from the Roman rules as to servitudes helped to settle and to systematize our modern law of easements." *Cochrane v. Moore,* and *Brinckmann v. Matbey* are two modern cases which have looked to Bracton as authority.

COKE USED THE AUTHORITY of Bracton to sustain the supremacy of the common law courts in the 17th century; and Bracton's maxim, the King must acknowledge as his superior the "law that made him King" *(lex per quam factus est rex),* also translated as "the King is below no man, but he is below God and the law," was used to refute the King's absolutism in the struggle between King and Parliament in the 17th century. *De Legibus* was specially reprinted in 1640 to make Bracton's views on the limitation of the King's powers popularly known.

In the fields of private and public law, Bracton's influence still continues after seven hundred years wherever the principles of the common law are administered. Kent considered him "the father of the English law, and the great ornament of the age in which he lived."

Winfield aptly concludes that "for the student of legal history [*De Legibus*] is one of the starting points in any piece of research."

Sᴿ IOHN FORTESCU Kᵀ

Fortescue's De Laudibus

The First Popular English Law Book

FORTESCUE'S *De Laudibus Legum Angliae* has been described as "a very curious book." And so it is, for it is a treatise which has been considered an authoritative source of English medieval common law since its publication around 1470. Yet it was written by an exiled judge for a lay audience – and mainly from memory!

Sir John Fortescue's birth date has never been established exactly, although it was probably about 1390. It is recorded, however, that he was Governor of Lincoln's Inn in 1425, 1426, and 1429 and a Serjeant-at-law about 1429. Fortescue was Chief Justice of The King's Bench from 1442 to 1460 and during the War of Roses took up the Lancastrian cause. He fought in the battle of Towton in 1461, and his name is included in an act of attainder in the following year. He followed the Lancaster family into exile from 1461 to 1471, from Scotland to Flanders and finally to France, where he continued his studies of English legal institutions.

While in exile, Fortescue had few, if any, English legal sources to consult in writing his book. He lived with the other followers of Margaret and her son, Prince Edward, in the small French town of St. Mighel in Barrois away from the centers of European culture. Leaving England in exile and under emergency conditions, he could scarcely have taken with him any of the legal literature of the period. Yet from sheer memory he composed one of the most important law books in the history of English law — a real *tour de force* by a most remarkable scholar!

De Laudibus Legum Angliae has been described as "not so much a law treatise as a treatise about law." Written in Latin, Fortescue's thoughts are developed in the form of a dialogue between Prince Edward and him with the purpose of preparing the Prince for his royal duties. As the Prince is a youth and a neophyte in the law, Fortescue's style is intentionally elementary which eases its comprehension. This clarity of presentation plus the attractiveness of his logic and great learning aroused the interest of his contemporaries from the day of its publication. Winfield considers this aspect of the book "fascinating," giving "any researcher in the English law of that period and the era before it a blessed breathing space in the dense atmosphere of the procedural pall that enveloped nearly all our legal literature then . . ."

FORTESCUE IMPRESSES ON THE YOUNG prince that he should become familiar with the law of England as a prerequisite to royal leadership. For the prince's benefit, he compares the English legal and constitutional systems with those found on the continent of Europe (limited monarchy versus absolute monarchy), concluding that the former were far superior and more reasonable. He also comments on English social conditions, the law and the judiciary, and legal education in the Inns of Court.

In his attempt to eulogize the law of England, Fortescue at times went out of bounds. Winfield comments in this respect: ". . . some passages in it would have maddened any contemporary Bentham. This is notably so in Chapter LIII on the delays of the law. Fortescue can defend the practice of essoins in real actions on no better ground than that the French law was much worse in hanging up justice . . ."

James Kent was very much impressed by Fortescue's liberality. Writing in his *Commentaries* he stated, "[De Laudibus Legum Angliae] displays sentiments of liberality and a sense of limited monarchy, remarkable in the fierce and barbarous period of Lancastrian civil wars, and an air of probity and piety runs through the work." Characteristic of this "liberality" was Fortescue's praise of the English jury system in civil and criminal cases as contrasted to the use of turture prevalent in Europe at the time.

Although Fortescue wrote mainly from memory, his contribution to our knowledge of the substantive law of England and the development of the English legal profession as evidenced by its organization and training is now recognized as authoritative and original. Fortescue did more than present the English legal system. He actually analyzed the many facets of English substantive law and procedure, probing and expounding the reason and theory therefor. In so doing he formulated a system of constitutional law based on theory which inspired and stimulated other legal writers to theorize on the elements of the common law.

Fortescue also gave his contemporaries and ensuing generations an understanding of the development of English law and government which had not been realized until then. For the first time it was made clear that the common law had had an independent growth, separate and apart from the Roman law or civil law predominant on the continent of Europe; that it had an historical development which was characteristically and essentially English. This accounted for the differences between the common law and the civil law and also added to the dignity of the common law.

Hazelton writes on this point: "Littleton and Fortescue, who were the earliest of English writers on law in the age of the Renaissance represent a revival of legal scholarship in the spirit of Bracton. The historical significance of that revival of scholarly studies in law which they inaugurated lies in the fact that it was an English and not a Roman legal renaissance. By making the first of all the many contributions to the renaissance literature of English law, these two late fifteenth-century judges set in motion an insular juristic movement which resulted during the sixteenth and early sevententh centuries in the historical and scientific study of the laws of England as revealed by the sources and lawbooks of the middle ages." Brunner notes too, that Fortescue was important on the continent as "the precursor of those modern authors who by pointing out the advantages of English law prepared the way for the reception of English institutions by continental Europe." *De Laudibus*, for example, achieved great popularity with French scholars. Montesquieu quoted often from it with approval.

De Laudibus Legum Angliae was considered an important book as soon as manuscript copies of it became available. Rastell used excerpts from it as early as 1513 in his *Liber Assissariium*. St. Germain used it effectively in writing his own *Dialogue between a Doctor and a Student,* which was published in English in 1530. Sir Walter Raleigh considered Fortescue "that notable bulwark of our laws." Fortescue's work was referred to often as a book of authority during the constitutional debates of the 17th Century. Lord Coke's brief in the *Case of Proclamations* (1611) was founded on one of its chapters. Coke derived much help from it, too, in his *Institutes* and *Reports*, stating that because of its "weight and worthiness," it should be "written in letters of gold." John Selden, England's first great legal historian recognized its scholarly worth and edited it as a legal classic in 1616. An excellent translation of the text with explanatory notes and fine biographical information was published by S. B. Chrimes in 1942.

WHEN WE CONSIDER THE CONDITIONS under which this masterpiece was written, in exile, without original source material to draw upon, when the venerable writer was over seventy years old, and then note the originality and freshness of the author's approach and the vitality of his ideas, we can well understand the profound admiration and respect in which Fortescue has been held over the years.

It is good to know, too, that Fortescue eventually returned to England, was pardoned by the King after he was captured at the battle of Tewkesbury where Prince Edward was killed, and lived peacefully thereafter for many years with honor and distinction.

Cowell's
Interpreter

A Controversial
Legal Dictionary

THE CURRENT CONTROVERSY ON THE MERITS of Webster's Third New International Dictionary brings to mind a similar, albeit more dramatic clash that occurred three hundred fifty years ago in England. The political power struggle that ensued stirred the nation and threatened to shake its very foundations — and yet the cause of it all was only a law dictionary!

When Dr. John Cowell, Regius Professor of Civil Law at Cambridge, compiled and published a law dictionary in 1607, little did he realize how it would excite the English people — nor for that matter the many vicissitudes that lay ahead of him. Actually, his purpose was highly commendable and there is little doubt that he sought to help the English legal profession.

English lawyers and judges of Dr. Cowell's time depended for legal definitions on legal glossaries or vocabularies known as *Expositiones Vocabulorum*. Written in Latin or Anglo-Norman, they did not follow any alphabetical order, but merely explained the difficult words and terms in a twelfth century book purporting to be a collection of customs and usages in force during the reign of

Edward the Confessor which William the Conqueror guaranteed to the English people, known as the *Laws of Edmond the Confessor*. They could also refer to a publication compiled and printed by John Rastell in 1527, entitled *Expositones Terminorum Legum Anglorum*, more popularly known as *Termes de la Ley*. It is interesting to note that not only did the *Termes de la Ley* contain definitions of words arranged alphabetically in order, but it also preceded in time the first English general dictionary, *Elyot's Dictionarie*, which was published in 1538. Its value was rather limited for the 17th Century English lawyer, however, as it reflected the common law of the medieval period.

Doctor Cowell entitled his book *The Interpreter*, "or Booke containing the Signification of Words." Significantly, it was written entirely in English. Cowell borrowed a great deal from the *Termes de la Ley*, quoting, discussing and even plagiarizing from it. He did, however, add selections from the statutes and other authorities.

AS A CIVILIAN, COWELL WAS impressed with the superiority of the civil law over the common law and so indicated in his preface. This approach aroused the animosity of the common lawyers, especially Coke, who was then Chief Justice of the Common Pleas. Coke objected particularly to a quotation Cowell had taken from Hotoman's *De Verbis Feudalibus*, criticizing Littleton's scholarship as inaccurate, stupid and absurd. Coke had great respect for Littleton's *Book of Tenures*, considering it "a work of sound perfection in its kind . . . and exquisite learning, comprehending much of the marrow of the common law . . . a work of absolute perfection in its kind, and as free from error, as any book that I have known to be written of any human learning . . ." Even then he was contemplating the writing of *Coke on Littleton* which was to appear in 1628 as the first volume of his *Institutes*. Thus, from the very first day of its reception, *The Interpreter* was greeted with suspicion and resentment by the legal profession.

This was but the beginning of Cowell's difficulties. He had created even more problems for himself. Under the words "Parliament", "King", "prerogative" and "subsidy", he made assertions supporting the King's absolute power over Parliament. For example, under the definition of King, Cowell stated: ". . . He is supra legum by his absolute power. And though for the better and more equal course in making laws, he do admit three Estates, that is, Lords Spiritual, Lords Temporal, and the Commons into Council, yet this derogates not from his Power; for whatever they act, He by his negative voice may quash." This was a time when the Parliament was jealously protecting its own prerogatives, vis-a-vis the King, and the Commons stigmatized *The Interpreter* as scandalous and offensive. The Commons became even more incensed when it was learned that James I had actually praised the book and its leaders asked the Lords to arrange for a conference on it.

THE JOINT COMMITTEE APPOINTED to review Cowell's *Interpreter* in 1610, was indeed impressive. The Lords appointed approximately fifty members, including two archbishops, thirteen bishops, thirteen earls, a viscount, twenty one lords, the Lord Chancellor, Treasurer, Privy Seal, Admiral and Chamberlain. The Commons appointed a number of equally important members consisting of the whole Privy Council, the Attorney General, the Solicitor General (then Francis Bacon), the Recorder and eighteen others.

For more than a month the affairs of Parliament and James I practically stood still while the controversy raged over *The Interpreter*. Finally, James realized that the matter was getting out of hand and could possibly affect his fiscal demands then being considered by the Parliament. He therefore intervened, and on March 8, 1610, the Lord Chancellor reported to the Lords that: "His Majesty had taken notice of the matter, and had lately perused the places in the book whereunto exceptions were taken; and had called the said Cowell before him, and had heard his answer thereunto."

After the hearing, Cowell was committed to the custody of an alderman and his *Interpreter* was suppressed by proclamation. As an added indignity, it was ordered to be burnt by the public hangman on March 26, 1610. This was indeed a smashing victory for the Parliament "for which the Commons returned thanks with great joy at their victory." It is not certain whether the public burning actually took place, as there are still extant copies of the 1607 edition, but it is known that Cowell resigned his professorship. Poor Dr. Cowell died the following year, possibly of a broken heart.

Ill fortune pursued *The Interpreter* even in later years. It was reprinted in 1637, allegedly with the consent of Dr. William Laud, Archbishop of Canterbury, although he vehemently denied it. Later, this consent was brought up in Parliament as one of the charges against him in his trial for treason in 1640 — for it was a violation of the proclamation of suppression to have permitted its republication.

Finally, *The Interpreter* attained respectability! It was reprinted in 1648, 1672, 1684 and in 1701. The famous legal historian, John Selden and others, referred to it often. It continued as a popular and much used book until the publication of Jacob's *New Law Dictionary* in 1729.

Whether Cowell ever regretted publishing *The Interpreter* is not known. Certainly for a law dictionary, it had a most unusual reception!

The Year Books

Medieval Law Reporting

S IR WILLIAM DE BEREFORD, A STERN and just man, had an uncontrolled temper. Dignified of mien, he presided over the King's Common Bench in Westminister Hall with an iron hand. King Edward II, had expressed his pleasure with his Chief Justice's services by bestowing upon him honors and landed estates as had his father King Edward I some years before. Not that he needed them however, as he had amassed a considerable fortune as a Serjeant at Law. Sir William was quite content with his lot! He loved his work, and the bustling scene before him. But, it had been a trying day! The first case had been called at 8:00 in the morning, and here it was three hours thereafter and time for adjournment!

"By Saint Peter," he swore to himself, "when will those fools stop arguing and accept the Court's judgment on the pleading?" As he squirmed under the weight of his scarlet robes lined with white fur, and gently scratched his head under the close fitting coif he had worn since his creation as a Serjeant, he looked about him once again. From his vantage point, for he was seated on a raised dais by the wall, he noted immediately the exasperated appearance of his brother judges on the bench. As for his "brethren" the Serjeants standing before him in their multi-colored robes and coifed heads, plaguing him with their clever arguments, plausible at times, unsound at others, he would have to stop them soon! "Perhaps, another moment," he thought.

In the meantime, he could see the clerks of the Court carrying on their business at a table directly in front of the bench, referring on occasion to the long skins of parchment on which the pleas were being recorded. The Bishop's Ordinary was also present, ready to claim the benefit of clergy for all defendants entitled thereto. Then there were the patient townsfolk, standing in a corner, ready to be called for jury service when an issue of fact was to be determined. Near them were the various litigants and witnesses concerned with the cases argued that day. On the right he could see the apprentice students and "juniors", uncomfortably crammed together in their box stall, popularly called the "cribbe." They were observing the proceedings intently, occasionally scribbling on scraps of parchment. "There they go taking notes of the arguments, again," he mused, "I wonder what nonsense they will record this time!"

He was brought back to the contest before him by the resumption of the pleading by Serjeant Howard. Howard was a good lawyer, but he should really have known better than to make such an absurd plea! Chief Justice Bereford could contain himself no longer. "In God's name" he shouted at him with anger, "now this is good!" Quickly and with relish, all the students in the cribbe made notes of this insult.

QUITE UNABASHED, HOWARD CONTINUED, recalling as a precedent what had taken place in the same Court several years prior in a similar case. Judge Berewick, sitting on Bereford's right knew better however, for he had participated as a Serjeant in that case himself and it was not quite pertinent.

"If you wish to cite a case, cite one in point" he exclaimed. Once again, the students made quick note of this sarcastic comment.

Serjeant Toudeby interjected at this moment as did several of the other Serjeants, even though they were not the attorneys of record, — all talking against each other. Proverbs, sarcasms, repartées were bandied back and forth in the debate and as they argued the students in the cribbe hastily continued to take notes in their peculiar shorthand. Especially noted were the bitter and clever quips. Associate Judges Stonor and Mutford took up the argument with counsel. Judge Mutford finally found it necessary to exclaim: "Some of you have said a good deal that runs counter to what has hitherto been accepted as law." At this moment Bereford bellowed: "Yes, that is very true and I won't say who they are." A short silence accompanied almost immediately thereafter by a low undercurrent of comment followed this strong indictment. Listening eagerly to what the Serjeants were saying to each other, one student wrote in his report of the case "some thought he meant Stonor."

BEREFORD, HOWEVER, HAD REACHED the end of his patience. Addressing himself to all the Serjeants he spoke with great deliberation while his colleagues on the bench nodded in approval.

"We wish to know whether you have anything else to say, for as yet, you have done nothing but wrangle and chatter."

Unperturbed, Serjeant Westcote, started again on another tack. He was prepared to argue all day if necessary, as long as the Court would permit it. But Bereford had heard enough!

"This is an issue of fact to be determined by the jury," he said, "call the jurors." He could then leisurely have his long awaited dinner, he thought, while the jury decided the issue. Westcote, however, took issue with Bereford's judgment stating reasons for his disapproval. Bereford hit back hard: "Really" he replied with a tongue-in-cheek attitude, "I am much obliged to you for the challenge, not for the sake of us who sit on the bench, but for the sake of the young men who are here." As a loud, deep roar of laughter resounded throughout the courtroom, the students, although enjoying the by-play still did not fail to add this bit of local color to their report of the case.

Not particularly concerned with the jury's verdict or the outcome of the case, the apprentices scurried out of their cribbes and hurried to the nearest *scriptoria* or writing rooms where they were eagerly awaited by a group of copyists known also as scribes.

Reading aloud from their notes, the students described to the copyists what had transpired in the courtroom. Each copyist then put down his version of the case as he gathered it from the dictation. Some proceeded at a slower pace than their colleagues and concerned that they were falling behind them in committing the report to writing, left out portions of the recital to avoid censure of their speed. Then again, while they concentrated on what had been told them at the time, they lost the trend of the story and necessarily had to depend on their memory to recollect what the reporter had actually stated. Being ignorant of the law and not understanding what they were copying they thus left out important segments. At the same time, they spelled words differently or used them incorrectly. In order to conserve space on the valuable and scarce skins of parchment, these reports were made even more unintelligible by unexplained abbreviations to cut down on the length of the report. Compounding the confusion, these copies often were copied anew by other scribes who perpetrated their own errors, or negligently omitted further sections of the report. As a result, they finally ended up as a "hopeless mass of corruption". Yet unrevised and uncorrected, they were then sold to medieval English lawyers for their guidance and instruction.

WHILE THESE CASES WERE BEING thus reported at Westminister, reports were being similarly made available of cases decided in Yorkshire, in Kent, in Cornwall and in virtually every county in England. When the King's Justices went on their periodic Eyres (circuits), they were followed by an entourage of Serjeants, "juniors" and apprentices who not only reported the cases of almost every kind that were triable at a general Eyre, but also described in detail the pomp and ceremony of the occasion. And in the county towns and larger market towns, where the King's Justices held assizes twice a year to try issues of fact in civil and criminal cases, they, too, were similarly reported.

It is almost impossible to imagine a greater confusion than these medieval reports! What with their baffling abbreviations, obvious omissions, interesting interpolations by the Bench and Counsel, discursive and conversational asides, and the not infrequent failure to indicate the final decision in the case, one may well ask – what were these reports and why should we be interested in them today? The answer is quite clear. These are the celebrated and fabulous *Year Books* of medieval England. Without them it is probable that the common law would have developed so differently that it would be unrecognizable to the modern lawyer.

To the best of our knowledge the earliest *Year Book* was written in the eighteenth year of Edward I (1289–90). From then on, in an almost continuous flow of reports with but minor intermissions, we find them published anonymously until the twenty-seventh year of the reign of Henry VIII (1535). At that point, just as mysteriously as they were started, they abruptly ceased to appear!

To appreciate the significance of the *Year Books*, a knowledge of the court procedure of the period is essential. In the thirteenth century, pleadings were made orally in court under the supervision of the judges. The writ was returned, read in open Court and a *conte* or statement of the facts prepared. The Court then permitted oral argument to formulate the issues. These were then recorded in the plea rolls by the clerks. It was only by a slow and gradual process that oral pleadings gave way to written statements of the case. It is interesting to note that this finally occurred about the time of the invention of printing in the reign of Edward IV. Caxton, it will be recalled first established his printing press at Westminister in 1476.

"The spirit of the earliest *Year Books*," says Maitland, "will hardly be caught unless we perceive that instruction for pleaders rather than the authoritative fixation of points of substantive law was the primary objective of the reporters." For this reason the oral argument of the case is the very essence of the *Year Books*. Once the proper issue was resolved by the process of pleading, the bar had no other interest in the case. Thereafter, it became a mere mechanical matter to permit the judges to decide the issues of law and if the pleadings terminated in an issue of fact, to arrange for its solution by ordeal, trial by battle or a jury. The real importance of the case was not its final outcome, but how the issue was formed by means of pleading! In this respect, Winfield states that actually the *Year Books* were "hints on pleading collected from proceedings in the courts . . . When lawyers of the thirteenth and fourteenth centuries put down anything in writing, whatever it might be, it was almost always essentially practical. It was something that told their brethren how an action could be begun, delayed, carried on, defeated, or a record of what had been done in the past, if that were likely to be useful in the future. Scientific arrangement was a secondary affair, theoretical speculations hardly existed."

It is understandable, therefore, why the *Year Book Reports* take on the appearance of a dialogue between judge and counsel. As the object of the pleading was to arrive at an issue of fact or law, each side would suggest a pleading orally, which was then debated on fully by counsel and the judges. Based on this argument one or another pleading would be adopted to raise the issue upon which the case would be decided. These arguments concerned the medieval lawyer most—for arriving at the issue, questions of law either apposite or not were brought into play. What happened to the issue once joined was not important. The main problem was how to arrive at an issue of fact or law by means of pleading. In reporting these oral debates, no distinction was made between argument and decision. Anyone who ventured an opinion, which made sense — whether Judge, Serjeant or apprentice, — was reported. And thus we see the *Year Books* take on the form of a report of argument in which the discussion of the legal principles involved provided the lesson for future conduct in Court.

Holdsworth's comment on this situation is interesting: "It was not till the rules of process were simplified that the number of cases which turned on the intricacies of medieval procedure was diminshed. It was not till the growth of a law of evidence, and the beginnings of the modern system of written pleadings, that the style of the law report changes, and the *Year Books* give place to the modern reports."

BY GIVING A FIRST-HAND ACCOUNT of what actually transpired in the King's Courts, the *Year Books* intimately present to us the processes by which the Judges of the thirteenth, fourteenth and fifteenth centuries laid down the legal doctrines which developed into the principles of the common law. We can read the exact colloquial phrases and idioms used by literate Englishmen of the period. We can also note the manner in which French was spoken in England several hundred years after the Conquest. The *Year Books* are also a unique English source of medieval history. It has been said that no other nation has any historical material in any way like them.

Another feature of the *Year Books* is the wonderful picture they give us of the legal profession of Medieval England. The Serjeants, who are members of the Order of the Coif, are the leaders of the bar. Called "brother" by the Judges, they are next in line for promotion to the bench. We can see them practically monopolizing the practice of the Court of Common Pleas. They are first to be heard, and although other Counsel are noted at times, the right of audience in the Common Pleas was eventually to be reserved for the Serjeants only. The students of course, are there too, and the give and take of the daily battle in court is gloriously recorded. The reporter usually has great respect for the Serjeant's opinion. At times, he suggests that he prefers it to the Judge's decision.

In the *Year Books*, we can note the beginnings of the use of precedent and case law. In an anonymous case decided in 15 Edward III (1341) in the Common Pleas an action in dower was being argued: "*Thorpe* (Counsel for defendant, pleading). She was not when her husband died of such age as she could merit dower. *Hilary (J.):* State with certainty of what age she was. *Thorpe:* Not nine years old. *Gayneford* (Counsel for plaintiff): She was nine years old and more. Ready, etc. *Thorpe:* Show her age to have been such that she would have been dowable thereat, viz. ten years at least. *Hilary* (J.): In the case of John Benstede the widow was endowed at the age of nine years and a half." It should be observed that precedent was cited not so much as a decision but rather as a general restatement of a discussion in which the applicable principle had formerly been considered by the Court.

Note, too, the comment of Serjeant Herle in 1304 to the Bench that a good decision would be followed as a general rule by the Court. "The judgment to be given by you, will be hereafter an authority in every *quare non admisit* in England."

THE YEAR BOOKS ALSO GIVE US an unusual opportunity to observe how the jury was treated by the Judges . . . In the Year Books of Edward I an anonymous case in the Common Pleas is reported as follows:

"*Roubery* (J. to the Assise): How say you he is next heir?

"*The Assize:* Because he was born and begotten of the same father and the same mother, and his father on his death bed acknowledged that he was his son and heir.

Roubery (J.): You shall tell us in another way how he is next heir or be shut up without meat or drink till tomorrow morning. And then they said he was born before the ceremony, but after the betrothal."

It is almost startling to read the sophisticated comments of these medieval judges and lawyers. Many of them would fit neatly into the give and take of any modern trial. "Leave off your noise and deliver yourself from this account" must have been said by a long suffering judge to a nondiscerning counsel. "That is sophistry and this is a place designated for truth" says Hengham, J. "Shame to him who pleaded this plea," comments Malone, J. "I am annoyed," said Honore, C.J. "that Grene makes himself out to know everything in the world, and he is only a young man."

Serjeant Pultney complained to the Court, "We do not see what will become of the first plea if this issue be entered." Judge Honore brutally replies, "It will go to the winds as does the greater part of that which you say."

The Judges carefully observed the technicalities of the law. On one occasion a Serjeant admitted something in error. "You have admitted this, God help you," said the Court. Consider too, the unfortunate counsel who made a slip in vouching the wrong person: *Robert* (Counsel for other side): "We pray judgment of this bad voucher." *Warwick* (Counsel who had made the slip): "Leave to imparl *for God's sake, Sir*" The Reporter noted "He obtained it with difficulty." One other case will suffice for this purpose. Judge Berewick was questioning the sherrif. "How is it you have attached these people without warrant? For every suit is commenced by finding pledges, and you have attached though he did not find pledges." *The Sherrif:* "Sir, it was by your own orders." To which the Reporter added: "If it had not been, the sherrif would have been grievously amerced. Therefore take heed."

UNTIL THE LATE NINETEENTH CENTURY it was believed that the *Year Books* were compiled by official reporters. This theory has been completely shattered by remarkable scholarship and the accepted version today is that they were the by product of student attendance in Court. In a sense, they started off as "students' notebooks." Later, Holdsworth believes, the reporters attempted to meet the requirements of a system of justice dependent almost entirely upon the practice of the Courts. Just as books of precedents of writs and pleadings were necessary in order that the lawyer might present his case in proper form to the Court, so reports of decided cases were necessary to ascertain the principles which the Court would apply to decide the case.

As heretofore indicated, the last printed *Year Book* appeared during the Trinity Term of 27 Henry VIII. Written in the French language of Normandy, they began to be printed about eight years after the introduction of printing into England. The earliest printer of Year Books was William de Machlinia (circa 1481). The first systematic publisher of the Year Books was Pynson who from 1493 to 1528 published about fifty editions. During the sixteenth century we come across the names of Rastell, Redman, Thomas Berthelet, William Myddeton, Henry Smyth and William Powell as publishers of the Year Books. Beginning in 1553 and continuing on for another thirty-eight years, Richard Tottel published so many *Year Books* that he drove out almost all competition in the field. Hardly any *Year Books* were published between 1638 and 1679. It is reported that they became so scarce that in 1678, a complete collection sold for forty pounds, a handsome price for that period. A standard edition appeared in 1679, known as the Maynard edition, which merely reprinted the published editions of the 16th and early 17th centuries with all their errors and missions.

Why were they so popular during this period? The reason is that they were considered important to law students for an adequate understanding of the law. It must be understood too, that despite their faulty publication, students more or less became aware of the errors and omissions by experience and could therefore make some sense of the report. Then again, printed abridgments of the *Year Books* began to be published and these were used as indices to them.

Recognizing the importance of the *Year Books* and thoroughly dissatisfied with the printed versions made available in the "black letter books," some of the most brilliant legal scholars of the late nineteenth and early twentieth century decided to do something about it. Maitland, Horwood, Pike, Vinogradoff, Ballard and Turner collected all the manuscripts of the *Year Books* they could find in the libraries of the British Museum, Oxford, Cambridge, the Inns of Court and other private libraries and started to re-edit them with elaborate notes and scholarly introductions. They refused to accept the manuscript versions of the report. Instead, they collated each report of a case with the Plea Roll record filling in the gaps and correcting the original errors. The result has been a masterful tour de force. The Rolls Series, the Selden Society and Ames Foundation publications in which they have appeared now reflect "this important advance in the study of English History." It will take many more years and many great scholars to bring this work to complete fruition. When accomplished, the *Year Books* will truly reflect the glorious formative years of the English Common Law.

TABLE OF STATUTES

TABLE OF CASES

326

INDEX

332

333

336